The Great Barrier Reef

The Great

Barrier Reef

Isobel Bennett

Photography by the Author

LANSDOWNE
Sydney·Auckland·London·New York

DEDICATION
To the memory of Professor William John
Dakin (Challis Professor of Zoology,
University of Sydney, 1928-1948), who guided
my first footsteps as a marine biologist, and
introduced me to that fascinating realm of
life 'Twixt Tide and Tide's Returning'.

By the same author
Australian Seashores   with W. J. Dakin and E. C. Pope
The Great Barrier Reef   with W. J. Dakin
The Fringe of the Sea
On the Seashore
Shores of Macquarie Island
Discovering Lord Howe Island   with Jean Edgecombe
Discovering Norfolk Island   with Jean Edgecombe

WELDON-HARDIE
—GROUP OF COMPANIES—
Published by Lansdowne Press,
a division of RPLA Pty Limited,
176 South Creek Road, Dee Why West, NSW 2099
First published 1971
Reprinted 1984, 1986
© Isobel Bennett 1971
Printed and bound in Hong Kong
ISBN 0 7018 0358 4

Contents

Sunday 12th August, 1770: "I immediately went upon the highest hill on the Island where to my mortification I discovered a Reef of Rocks laying about 2 or 3 Leagues with out the Island, extending in a line NW and SE farther than I could see on which the Sea broke very high."
(Voyage of the *Endeavour*. James Cook)

The twelve years that have elapsed since this book was written have seen a considerable growth in interest in the Great Barrier Reef, with a far greater public awareness of its value as a National Heritage.

Numerous major scientific papers have been published, including a comprehensive monograph series on the reef-building corals of the Province. The hopes expressed on page 173 have been fulfilled, for on 20th June, 1975, the Great Barrier Reef Marine Park Act became law, with Proclamation on 21st October 1979, of the Capricornia Section of the Marine Park.

Since that date, three further proclamations have been made, thus adding three more important areas to the Marine Park. Also, in 1981, the Great Barrier Reef was recommended by the Commonwealth of Australia for inclusion on the World Heritage List — and it was inscribed on that list on 26th October, 1981.

Controversies such as the Crown-of-Thorns, mining and oil drilling, have been waged in the media, thus the whole region of the Great Barrier Reef has been brought to public notice as never before.

With the establishment of the Great Barrier Reef Marine Park Authority, there now exists a body responsible for the management of, and co-ordination of research within the Province. With the expertise available today, and given the chance to proceed with its plans, the Authority augers well for the future.

Preface

The Great Barrier Reef—for most Australians these words inspire wistful visions or vivid memories of sundrenched days on tropical islands, sparkling, blue-green seas lapping on coral sands; skin diving in a new and unreal world—an almost unbelievable realm of coral bastions, exquisite in design, colour and form, through which bizarre and highly coloured fish flash by in their myriad schools. Sunbaking, water skiing, fishing for hard fighting game fish or exotic reef species—this is the Great Barrier Reef holiday depicted, in glowing prose, but with a great deal of truth, by the tourist brochures.

But few know the fascinating reality of this tremendously complex maze of reefs and islands that lie scattered haphazardly along the continental shelf of Queensland's coastline. How much of the immensity and extent of this submarine mountain chain of limestone can be realised or appreciated during even a prolonged visit? Its extent can perhaps only be grasped by seeing it from the air. The airline pilots of the commercial jet routes along the coast see its ever changing forms and patterns at a sweep of a couple of hours—bluff, densely covered continental islands, flat coral cays seemingly afloat on the translucent water, tiny sandspits, ribbons of clear green running through the mottled dark blue water that is coloured by the reef it covers or surrounds.

The master mariners and the Torres Strait pilots have another picture as they guide the modern ships and giant tankers through the long stretch of water between Queensland's mainland and the outer reefs. The inner reefs remain a menace against which the seamen must be constantly on guard. They know that corals continue to grow, that ships are larger with deeper draught each year, and that deeper or uncharted outcrops of rock or coral will one day be at a level high enough to be dangerous.

The most modern aids to navigation are available to these seamen, but they also place great faith in the charted tracks they follow.

A long and fascinating story could be told of the making of the Australian and Admiralty Charts of today by the officers and men of H.M. Survey Ships of the last century, and their Australian counterparts of the twentieth. Over many long years these men sailed thousands of square miles painstakingly making sounding after sounding, gradually filling in the blanks of this vast Barrier Reef region.

Finally there are the few scientists scattered throughout the world, geologists, geographers and biologists, who have made it their special study—discovering the secrets of its formation and its hidden wealth, and of the intricately balanced, mutually sustaining life forms that make the reef one of the world's great faunal regions.

The traveller sailing through the Barrier Reef channel by ship, or visiting the island resorts, is as unaware of this enormous rampart of reefs as was Lieut. James Cook, R.N. two hundred years ago. Cook's magnificent achievements are apt to pale into insignificance in this modern age of astronauts, yet as the sole effort of one man and his crew in a small wooden ship, with only the crudest of navigational aids and no fore-knowledge of the vast oceans traversed, the *Endeavour's* voyage through these then unknown Barrier Reef waters must always remain one of man's most outstanding feats.

In Australia today, a great industrial expansion is taking place, matched by a growing population. In this era of new discoveries in oil and minerals, attention is being increasingly focussed on the coral reefs along her coasts, since the petroleum geologists are well aware of the link between oil reservoirs and fossil coral reefs. Applications for drilling, and mining rights for limestone and silica, have already been made—and contested. The demands of ever-increasing tourist traffic with its dollar-earning potential, are leading to the opening up of more and more resorts on what are, at present, unspoilt offshore islands. Food production and potential are being explored, fishing rights are keenly debated. Legal boundaries, at the international level, are being questioned. Pollution, one of the world's greatest and ugliest problems, is unhappily making its presence felt in the Barrier Reef's pellucid waters.

It may be argued that marine animals, their names and life histories, are of little consequence, that knowledge, or the beauty of a unique natural heritage, is unimportant, but that tourism, oil and minerals are extremely valuable commodities with vast commercial benefits. This depends again entirely on the personal interest, ambition and point of view. The State of Queensland, in proclaiming many of the islands within the Great Barrier Reef Province as National Parks, has endeavoured to ensure that their terrestrial fauna and flora will be preserved for posterity. The Commonwealth Government, in April 1970, brought into operation The Continental Shelf (Living Natural Resources) Act of 1968, thus giving it control over the living natural resources of the Continental Shelf in accordance with international law. This Act will apply to a wide range of invertebrate animals including the sponges, corals and other coelenterates, crustaceans, molluscs and echinoderms.

The protection and conservation of marine animals are, however, a vexed and extremely difficult problem. Policing the Act over such an enormous area of sea is virtually a physical impossibility.

From a practical viewpoint it is essential that the waters of a port—Townsville for example—should be deeply dredged to handle the larger draught ships. The question arises of depositing the quantities of superfluous silt. Should it be dumped far out to sea where the tides and currents may more readily disperse it—a costly procedure—or should the more economical method, of depositing it close inshore be adopted, where it will eventually smother and destroy the corals surrounding Magnetic Island?

At this moment in time our knowledge of the reef fauna is far too inadequate to legislate to the best advantage. Where should the line be drawn? What form of action is better than another? The questions must be answered, for the destiny of the reef and its fauna lie in the hands of the generation of today and tomorrow.

Before it is too late, it is imperative that all Australians should endeavour to understand and appreciate the immensity of one of their greatest natural assets—one of the world's truly magnificent reservoirs of tropical islands and coral reefs, with all their associated plants and animals. This book has been written in an attempt to convey something of its magnitude, its might and grandeur, the beauty, romance and terror, bound up in that huge series of marine structures, built up with infinite labour by the lowliest of animals and plants, and built so strongly that they have withstood the fiercest battering of the tempest-driven Pacific for untold aeons.

Part of the platform reefs on the western edge of the Marginal Shelf of the Central region—Hook and Hardy Reefs—which are visited by tourist vessels from the resort islands of the Cumberland Group.

8

Heron Island from Wistari Reef—as seen at sea level.

Black and gold feather star, *Comanthina*. Lagoon, Lizard Island.

Looking north along Hinchinbrook Channel. Lucinda Point in foreground.

The strikingly coloured nudibranch *Notodoris gardineri*, Heron Island.

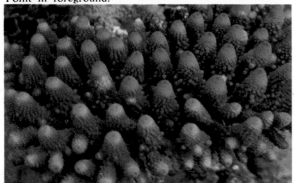
Mauve *Acropora*, Low Isles

The large Mud crab of the mangrove areas, *Scylla serrata*, is highly regarded for its edible qualities.

Goniopora is one of the few corals whose polyps are seen expanded in sunlight. The colour varies from brown, yellow and green to blue-grey. Heron Island.

Cyerce nigra on alga *Chlorodesmis*, Heron Island.

The stinging anemone, *Actinodendron plumosum*, lives on reef flats and can retract completely into the sand. The mouth surrounded by the multi-branched tentacles is visible in this animal which was slowly emerging with the rising tide.

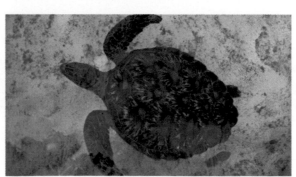
Juvenile Green turtle swimming.

An over-turned boulder on Watson Island revealed a Tiger cowrie laying its capsules of mauve-coloured eggs among encrusting sponges.

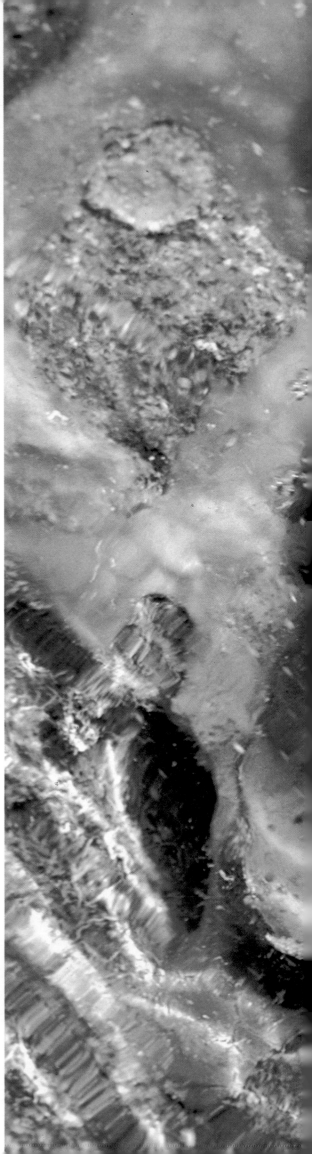

Acknowledgements

Soldier fish, *Holocentrus spinifer* in among coral boulders encrusted with brilliantly coloured encrusting sponges (c.f. Fig. 8 (3)).

I should like to express my indebtedness to the Commonwealth Department of Shipping and Transport for the privilege of travelling in the Lighthouse Service Ship, M.V. *Cape Moreton*, during one of her routine cruises in 1969, thus enabling me to work on a number of reefs and islands throughout the Barrier Reef Province which I should not otherwise have been able to visit. My work was very greatly assisted by the kindness and cooperation of Captain Harold Chesterman and the crew of the *Cape Moreton*, to all of whom my grateful thanks are given.

I am also indebted to the Queensland Department of Aboriginal and Island Affairs for permission to visit the Murray Islands in one of their patrol vessels, and my thanks are due to Captain Croppy Bowie and his crew of the P.V. *Tamwoy*, who looked after me so well on the voyage.

The facilities of the Great Barrier Reef Committee's Research Station at Heron Island have been at my disposal during many visits with groups of Sydney University students to the island. To the Committee and to the Poulson family of Heron Island for their many kindnesses, my sincere thanks are given.

Professor Charles Birch of the School of Biological Sciences of the University of Sydney granted me leave to do all the field work which has been necessary. For this, and his encouragement to me to write this book, I am deeply grateful.

I should very much like to thank Mr and Mrs Charles Britton of Alderney, Channel Islands, and Mr and Mrs Edward Archbald of Waterport, U.S.A., whose company made it possible for me to visit reefs which I should not otherwise have seen. To Mr and Mrs Lloyd Grigg of Yorkey's Knob, Queensland, I am particularly indebted for many kindnesses during several visits to the reefs.

Thanks to the courtesy of Mr Lloyd Grigg and Mr A. Miller of Green Island, and Mr Ian Croll of Marine Gardens, Magnetic Island, it has been possible to observe, both under natural and also extremely well-regulated artificial conditions, many of the reef animals and to note their differing reactions during the hours of night and day, and their various food preferences.

The Department of Illustration, University of Sydney, was most helpful in the preparation of black and white prints from my negatives, as was Mrs K. Maresso of the School of Biological Sciences in the preparation of the Text Figures.

I am indebted to the Great Barrier Reef Marine Park Authority, the Australian Institute of Marine Science, and to my friends Lloyd Grigg, Rob Littler and Bill Wood, for their kindness in permitting me to select from their very extensive photographic collections.

The various Curators of the Australian and Queensland Museums, and Phil Alderslade, Michael Borowitzka, Allan Cribb and Jiro Kikkawa, all assisted in checking the most recently accepted names for the marine plants and animals.

I am also particularly grateful to Peter Davies, Peter Flood, Richard Kenchington, Col Limpus, Michel Pichon, John Veron and Len Zell for their very helpful comments.

Finally, my sincerest thanks and gratitude go to my two sisters, Jean and Phyll, without whose help, both at home and in the field, this book could never have been finished.

Isobel Bennett

Chapter 1

The Great Barrier Reef Province

The Continental Shelf along the shores of north-eastern Australia, off the tropical coastline of the State of Queensland, differs from that of any other in the world in that, for over 1,200 miles of its length, there are scattered innumerable islands and coral reefs, all of which lie on this narrow shelf, or along its eastern margin, in waters which range from less than 20 fathoms in depth down to 80 fathoms. Some are lofty islands, a long series extending for several hundred miles, varying in distance from the nearby mainland from approximately three to over sixty miles. They are composed of rocks and other material of the same composition and geological ages as the continent itself, but cut off from it in past eras as the result of a series of events in the geological history of Queensland.

Others are solid structures, sometimes many hundreds of feet in thickness below the floor of the surrounding sea, built up by untold millions of minute organisms, and mainly composed today of their dead skeletons and the remains of many other animals and plants. These are the coral reefs, probably the most extensive series which has ever existed, and almost certainly the largest structure on the face of the earth today created by living organisms. They are structures too, which are far superior in their strength to any which man, with all his ingenuity, has been able to devise.

A glance at the map (Map I) shows that this region lies between the latitudes of 9° S. and 24° S., encompassing an area of approximately 100,000 square miles. Its width—from the coast of the mainland to the edge of the Continental Shelf (which is considered as lying along the 100 fathom line)—varies from approximately 10–15 miles at its narrowest point, near Cape Melville (14° 10′ S.), in the north, to nearly 200 miles in the southern part, about latitude 22° S., east of the city of Mackay (Maps I and II). Its western boundary is the

Eastern Highlands of Queensland, rising to heights of over 5,000 feet between Townsville and Cairns. To the north-east it is bordered by the deep Coral Sea Basin and the Queensland Trench, and in the central and southern regions by the shallower Coral Sea Platform and part of the Tasman Sea. (Map I and Figure 2)

Since the geographical distribution of reef-building corals is controlled to a large extent by the temperature of the sea water, with a minimal requirement of about 18°C., Lady Elliot Island (latitude 24° 07′ S. Map II), represents the southern-most reef within the province, and Anchor Cay (9° 22′ S. Map V), is usually quoted as the most northerly point of the Great Barrier Reef, although there is another outlier to the north-west, the tiny Bramble Cay and its reef, on which there is a light leading ships through the Great North-East Channel from the open waters of the Coral Sea westwards into Torres Strait. Off the adjacent coast of Papua-New Guinea, the heavily silt-laden waters of the Fly River preclude any further coral growth to the north.

The word Barrier as applied to these reefs along the north-eastern Australian coast was first used by Captain Matthew Flinders, at the beginning of the nineteenth century, when he made his voyage of exploration round the Continent. Since that time, many hundreds of papers, popular articles and books—historic, romantic, scientific, and otherwise—have referred to the general area as 'The Great Barrier Reef', even when only a small section of the reefs or a few islands have been described. As such, the name now appears on all atlases, maps, Admiralty and Australian charts, and the *Australia Pilot*.

Since, however, it is neither a single reef, nor even a series of reefs, and not a 'Barrier Reef' within the meaning of that term as it was first defined and used by Charles Darwin, leading

geologists of today have suggested the use of the term Great Barrier Reef Province, fitting it thereby into the overall picture of the various geographical and geological regions of the south-western Pacific Ocean. Within this province, as knowledge continues to accumulate over the years, especially with the increasing number of technological devices now being utilized by geologists to study its physical features, this vast complex of islands and reefs will become better known, and the reefs grouped according to their affinities with one another, and to their relationship to the area as a whole.

Vessels sailing from Moreton Bay in southern Queensland to Torres Strait have the choice of two routes to Asia and the Indian Ocean—they may take the Outer Route, travelling east of the reefs altogether, north through the Coral Sea, and enter Torres Strait through the Great North-East Channel. Alternatively they may take the Inner Route, marked on charts today and recommended as The Steamer Track (Maps I to V), and laid down for use by even the largest vessels visiting Australia.

The Steamer Track is one of the ocean highways of the world, closely surveyed and well-charted, with almost one hundred light-houses, light-ships, radio stations and beacons, as aids to navigation. Within its short-known history, there can be very few areas of the world which have packed more of tragedy, heroism, romance and adventure into each square mile of sea. Since the date of Captain Cook's voyage, there exists documented evidence of some 500 wrecks between Cape Moreton and Thursday Island, which occurred before the formation of The Queensland Coast and Torres Strait Pilot Service.

From the top of Good's Island, Torres Strait, one can look down the length of Normanby Sound to Thursday, Friday and Prince of Wales Islands.

Dauer Island, Murray Group. The black line along the shore of Mer Island is an immense shoal of small "sardines"

Guardian of the Barrier Reef waters, the Lighthouse Service vessel, CAPE MORETON, off Croquet Island, Howick Group.

The small group of master mariners constituting this body handles millions of tons of shipping annually, over the longest single stretch of pilotage in the world, where one pilot alone has full responsibility for the navigation of the ship throughout the whole voyage in Barrier Reef waters.

A long list of famous mariners painstakingly paved the way for these shipping lanes, following in the wake of Captain James Cook, R.N., after his momentous voyage—the first recorded—north along the Australian coast, in waters which he navigated unwitting of the dangers of the reefs surrounding him on every side.

In the early years of the 19th century, the whole region was considered to be one of the most dangerous waterways of the Southern Hemisphere traversed by ships, covering some 1,200 miles of tortuous channels amidst reefs and shoals, with strong tide-rips, and unseen and unsuspected dangers in the hidden depths. Slowly, year by year, a shipping lane was charted by the early pioneering Captains— Bligh, Flinders, Phillip Parker King, Stanley and Blackwood—in H.M. Survey Ships, with corrections and additions by the captains of schooners, barques and brigs, trading between Sydney and India and South East Asia. The early trading ships at first used the route beyond the reefs through the Coral Sea, entering protected waters again through one of the many channels, particularly to the far north, having negotiated what were then considered the more dangerous regions southward. The most significant of these northern passageways was perhaps the one known today as the Great North-East Channel (Map V). By the 1840's, however, many ships' captains were braving the shorter, more protected 'inner route' to the north. During these years there were discussions, wrangles with insurance companies, arguments and public protests about wrecks. All of these led not only to the beginnings of a pilot service, but to more and more comprehensive surveys by the various ships of the Royal Navy. It must be remembered, however, that these early explorers covered only a single line of soundings with lead-line as they sailed through uncharted waters, plotting the coastline as they sailed, but giving no indication of the underwater configuration of adjacent waters. If the ships were sailing at night, it would be quite possible to obtain soundings of clear, navigable water, very close to the margin of a reef. It was this very fact which caused the disaster to Captain Cook's ship when she struck Endeavour Reef.

Many of the Admiralty and Australian Charts of today still bear, in part, the original figures, and acknowledge these, as for example, Chart 2763—CORAL SEA AND GREAT BARRIER REEF: 'Compiled chiefly from the surveys of Captains Flinders, King, Blackwood, Stanley, Yule and Denham, R.N., 1802–60, with additions from Admiralty surveys in progress to 1888'.

There are still uncharted outcrops of potential danger to the ships of increased tonnage and draught which are now using the lanes. As recently as October, 1969, the Lighthouse Service vessel, M.V. *Cape Moreton* anchored the 'Iris Reef Buoy' near Iris Reef, between Cape Melville and Cape Direction, marking a previously unknown and uncharted submerged rocky outcrop reported by the *Darling River*, a large ore carrier, on one of her routine trips through Barrier Reef waters.

But, in terms of destructive power, shipping is more a threat to the reef than the reef is to shipping. *Oceanic Grandeur* gave warning of this menace. At 3 a.m. on the 3rd of March, 1970 this large oil tanker of 58,000 d.w.t. with a draught of 38 feet, struck an uncharted pinnacle of granite in the middle of the main shipping lane in Prince of Wales Channel in Torres Strait, east of Wednesday Island, and about five miles to the west of Twin and East Strait Islands (Map V). Holes between 200 and 250 feet in length were ripped in the port side of the ship, puncturing eight of its fifteen oil holds. No lives were lost but the tanker, bound for Brisbane, carried 55,000 tons of crude oil. Only

the most extraordinary good fortune—the coincidence of a week of perfect weather with calm, windless seas, together with the presence nearby of another oil tanker in ballast, saved a repetition of the Torrey Canyon disaster in the English Channel in March, 1967. (The disastrous sinking of the *Amoco Cadiz* in the English Channel in 1978 and the Gulf of Mexico oil spills of 1979 provide an even graver warning.)

Had the ship been more badly damaged, or had weather conditions in any way hampered the very delicate operation of transferring oil from one tanker to another in heavy seas, it is impossible to estimate the irreparable damage which might have been caused to islands and reefs of the Great Barrier, more especially as this was within the season when wind and surface currents could have carried the oil slick in the direction where it would have caused most damage. Most fortunately, the oil slick which did result, although costly, was small enough to be kept within bounds and dispersed by the few craft which were dispatched from Thursday Island. Adequate remedial facilities to cope with a major catastrophe were simply not available in the vicinity and time and distance alone would have prevented all efforts to avert disaster. This kind of incident could happen again, perhaps even in the more enclosed waters along the Steamer Track, with very different results.

Since 1950 Royal Australian Naval ships have been carrying out intensive work, their objective a detailed survey of a shipping route up to twenty miles wide around the entire continent, in an effort to provide safe passage for the deeper draught vessels. This is a gigantic task for the limited resources of the Navy Hydrographic Branch, even though its ships are equipped with modern electronic devices such as Echo-sounding machines for measuring vertical depths, and Sonar which sweeps in a horizontal plane directly ahead and on either bow of the ship, thus covering wide areas and eliminating the slow tedium of the lead-sounding days. Many other data are also collected during these surveys. Tidal observations are made, and sailing directions compiled to correct and supplement the volumes of the *Australia Pilot*. Magnetometers, instruments which measure variations in the earth's magnetic field, are towed astern in an effort to trace the presence of mineral deposits, and sea-bottom samples are collected—data necessary for the study of natural resources. Aerial photography, though costly, is a most valuable tool.

During this survey, H.M.A.S. *Paluma* (now replaced by H.M.A.S. *Flinders*) had been progressively re-surveying the Inner Route through Barrier Reef waters, for the all-important fact which must always be borne in mind is that, so long as conditions remain favourable for them, corals will continue to grow and flourish in these tropical waters, thus

demanding constant vigilance on the part of survey ships. The alternating wind and current systems cause movement of submerged sandbanks. Many blanks still remain on the northern Australian Charts, which today bear the words: ' Unexamined area ' across them, especially in the vicinity of the outer reefs well away from the shipping lanes. For economic reasons alone, these will probably remain thus for many years to come, since the emphasis must always remain along the inshore waters of the Steamer Track. To appreciate the immensity of the area as a whole, the numerous islands and countless reefs, large and small, with narrow winding passages and channels weaving between them, one would need to spend many hours poring over large-scale Admiralty Charts. A passenger travelling from southern ports to Torres Strait, is destined to disappointment if he anticipates sailing day after day through myriad-coloured, reef-strewn waters. It is extremely difficult to appreciate the fact that one *can* traverse the greater part of this long distance without even being aware of the existence of a coral reef. But it does enable one to understand the astonishing fact that Captain Cook, great seaman and navigator that he was, sailed for 800 miles through these same waters without realizing that he was among and almost completely enclosed by coral reefs.

The actual amount of island and reef area within the Great Barrier Reef Province is only about one-third the number of square miles of sea, and clear open water predominates for the greater part of the steamer voyage, especially in the south where proximity to land is the exception rather than the rule. From about 22° S. high islands and the mountain ranges of the mainland are constantly in sight, but coral reefs remain inconspicuous, though they may fringe many of the island shores.

To follow along the shipping lanes of the Inner Route of the Great Barrier (Maps II-V), is perhaps the clearest way to gain some comprehension of its magnitude, and of the number of groups of islands which impinge on it. The Steamer Track, for by far the greater part of its distance, lies in a narrow zone along the coastline which is comparatively free from coral. Thus, to the voyager, there is no indication that within the total area of the Great Barrier Reef Province through which he is travelling, there are scattered some 2,500 reefs with areas ranging from a few hundred acres to over twenty square miles, together with many more much smaller reefs.

Once the Inner Route is entered through the Capricorn Channel in the south, lying between the Capricorn Islands to the south west and the Swain Reefs away to the east (Map II), The Steamer Track lies in good clear water over 30 fathoms in depth. Beyond this point, however, a ship must sail over 400 miles north before reaching the latitude of Flinders Passage, 80 miles east of Townsville. This is the first

navigable passage for vessels of any size, wishing to penetrate the outer reefs to the Coral Sea and the Pacific Ocean. Some thirty or more openings between reefs through which some vessels could safely pass occur north of this point, but with the exception of one or two, such as Grafton Passage (Map III), and Trinity Opening (Map IV), just to the south and north of Cairns, advantage is rarely taken of these, since little is known of the waters lying between them and the Steamer Track.

The most important groups of 'high' islands along the seaway are the continental islands of the Northumberland and Cumberland Groups, approximately 120 islands and rocky outcrops, the exposed remnants of now submerged coastal ranges (Maps II and III). They vary greatly according to their geological structure and the degree of wave action to which each island is exposed. Bare rock, steep precipitous cliffs, grassy slopes, areas of stunted shrubs, and heavily timbered peaks, some of which rise to over 1,000 feet above sea level, all combine to give variety and attraction to surrounding scenery. Safe anchorages for small craft are to be found in sheltered coves and embayed areas among the islands, but swift tidal streams, offshore shoals and sandbanks call for caution and experienced navigators.

The northern Cumberlands—the Whitsunday and Lindeman Groups—are amongst the best known and scenically the most beautiful of the continental islands, and are one of Queensland's greatest tourist potentials. Here the Steamer Track passes through the famed Whitsunday Passage, named by Captain Cook who sailed through it on Whit Sunday, 1770. It is only a mile or so in width, hemmed in on either side by islands, tall and heavily wooded, bare or with pineclad slopes, a spectacular stretch of sparkling tropic sea, unmatched in beauty and with infinitely varied shades of colour in its blue-green waters. Out from the mainland ports of Mackay to the south, or from Shute Harbour, tucked away behind the shelter of neighbouring islands, small tourist vessels and chartered craft criss-cross the seaway daily, wending their ways among the islands, to open fishing grounds, to fringing reefs and, on calm days during periods of low spring tides, to the coral reefs away over the horizon.

Unless he studies the chart, the passenger on board an ocean liner cruising through the Whitsunday Passage, remains completely unaware of the presence of coral reefs in the surrounding waters. Yet, a few miles away to the east, covering a large area, the sea is literally strewn with a maze of reefs, varying in size, form and depth (Map III). Some are partially uncovered at low water, whilst others remain completely submerged, visible only from the air, or during periods of stormy weather when great ocean waves pound and break on their

Indian Head, the sheer perpendicular rocky cliff face at the north-eastern end of Pentecost Island, Lindeman Group.

ramparts. It is to the innermost of these particular reefs that the tourists to the Whitsunday region are taken, to reefs such as Hook and Hardy, reefs which, unfortunately, are too often referred to as 'The Outer Barrier', thus giving the visitor an erroneous impression, not only of the type of reefs but also their extent.

Beyond the Cumberlands, isolated islands and small groups such as the Palm Islands are visible along the seaway. North of these lies Hinchinbrook, second largest island off the Queensland coast, and separated from the mainland by the narrow Hinchinbrook Channel. Rugged mountain peaks on the island rise dramatically from sea level to heights of over 3,000 feet. A glance at Map III shows that The Steamer Track now lies very close inshore to the mainland, the Continental Shelf is continually narrowing and the reefs are beginning to close in. From Cairns northwards the shipping lane becomes beset with hazards, with the number of inner reefs increasing, whilst those along the margin of the shelf, instead of occurring as more or less scattered groups, gradually form into a long series of solid ramparts with only narrow passages or channels separating them, and facing the battering assault and immense pressures of the Pacific swell (Map IV).

The dangers to navigation in this region are well demonstrated by the matter-of-fact language of the sailing directions: 'A few feet of rise or fall of tide' they point out, 'will on a smooth day entirely alter the appearance of the reefs. At low water, their margins show distinctly, large masses of rock occasionally appearing. The interior, or lagoon parts, of the reefs are then of a light green colour, contrasting strongly with the dark blue of the channels between them. As the tide rises these features become less and less distinct and should there be passing clouds, or a bad light, the most vigilant navigator may be deceived'.

Shute Harbour, north of Mackay, protected by the Long and Molle Group of Islands, port of access to the tourist resorts of the Whitsunday and Lindeman Groups.

North of latitude 13° S., the coastline and the Steamer Track follow a north-westerly course, whilst the reefs of the Shelf Edge continue due north, gradually veering slightly to the east. Lying between these northern reefs and the large group of continental islands off Cape

A most conspicuous sight at certain times of the year in Barrier Reef waters is the presence of long streaks or large oily-looking patches of a rusty red colour. This is caused by a phenomenon referred to throughout the world as 'red tide'. The causal agents differ, both as to species and their effect on the populations of marine animals. In this instance, it is a *Trichodesmium erythraum*, which at certain times of the year multiplies at an enormous rate in the surface waters of the sea. Wind, currents and upwellings cause bundles of these very minute organisms to blow together in surface slicks or windrows. They are often locally but very misleadingly referred to as 'coral spawn'. The occurrence is widespread throughout the Indo-Pacific.
Off the Whitsunday Islands, May, 1969.

York, the most northerly point of the Queensland mainland, is the vast area of sea generally marked on the Charts as: 'Unexamined but considered dangerous navigation' (Map V).

Climatically the Great Barrier Reef Province is influenced both by the land mass of the continent to the west of it, and the South Pacific Ocean to the east. The broad sub-tropical belt of high pressure lying to the east of the continent, fluctuating approximately between latitudes 15° S. and 45° S. in summer, and between the equator and 40° S. in winter, gives rise to the South East Trade Winds which dominate the coast of Queensland for the greater part of the year—February to November (Figure 1). In the following late summer months the North-west Monsoon season occurs, bringing high rainfall to the northern part of the continent.

The area of highest rainfall, in excess of 100 inches per year, lies in the vicinity of the coastal towns of Ingham to Cooktown (18° 30′ S. and 16° S.). It will be appreciated, therefore, that run-off from the coastal drainage systems, as a result of this very high rainfall must, through geological time, have played an extremely important part in the deposition of silt and sediments over the Continental Shelf. It results at times in very turbid conditions in localized areas of the near-shore waters along the coastline. However, since the actual amount of land drainage from the Queensland coast into the Barrier Reef waters has been estimated at an annual figure of only 4·3 cubic miles of water, on the total figure this represents a very small percentage, so that its general effect on the reef province as a whole, taking into account the daily turn-over of water, is probably insignificant.

Cyclonic disturbances with high wind velocities are liable to occur, more consistently in the late summer and early autumn (January to March), though cyclone activity has also been recorded in December and April, and rarely in other months of the year. These cyclones usually originate in the Coral Sea, and although the course may be variable, the storms most frequently travel in a south-westerly direction. In the restricted waters within the province, they have a marked effect on the reefs and the mainland coast, since they are often accompanied by torrential rain, and the hurricane-force winds cause mountainous seas, and frequently considerable damage. This may occur along a very restricted path, such as that of cyclone Ada in January, 1970, which hit tourist resorts in the Whitsunday Passage and towns on the adjacent mainland. These cyclones may also be a cause of major damage on coral reefs. Huge waves break off large portions of branching coral colonies, and in some cases entirely

Some of the continental islands, such as Albino Rock, lying to the east of the Palm Island Group, are merely piles of rock projecting out from the sea.

Rocky island, Silversmith, in the Sir James Smith Group.

Lizard Island Group from the S.E.

Top
Little Fitzroy Island, south-east of Cairns, a rocky outcrop covered with low vegetation.

Purtaboi Island, a tumbled mass of rock and trees covered with epiphytic orchids, has a little sandy cove on its western shore. It lies just to the north of Dunk Island.

Right
Dunk Island, made famous by the stories of 'Beachcomber' (the late E. J. Banfield), as seen from Mission Beach on the Queensland coast.

22

remove whole blocks of coral. The purely mechanical effect of broken corals and boulders being tossed back and forth across a reef surface causes in its turn further abrading, resulting at times in serious damage to the fauna of the surrounding area. This is particularly noticeable in cases where a cyclone hits a reef from an unusual direction. The types of corals growing there are not usually the species which have evolved to withstand the greater pounding of high waves, and so are more vulnerable to destruction.

The enormous volume of water within the Barrier Reef Province has been estimated at 1,700 cubic miles. Twice daily over the greater part of this vast region, the rise and fall of the tide results in an interchange of oceanic water which is dominated by the currents of the Trade Wind Drift, flowing from the Coral Sea (Figure 1). As the Trade Wind Drift impinges on the reefs, it diverges into a northern stream which influences the greater part of the province for at least nine months of the year. Only in the south-eastern corner of the area is the effect felt of the southerly stream which flows south right down the coast as the East Australian Current. In the summer months (November to January), the North-West Monsoon reverses the current flow in the northern region.

The movement of water by these currents is of very great significance to the fauna of the reefs as a whole since it affects in general the surface waters and brings in warm, saline water from the huge body of water lying to the east and known as the Equatorial Water Mass, and from the north the warmer waters of the Torres Strait region known as the Gulf-Arafura and Coastal Water Mass (Figure 1). The physical qualities of this water bathing the reefs play an extremely important role in both the construction and maintenance of reefs, and the Great Barrier Reef Province is almost unique

Brampton and Carlysle Islands and fringing reef.

The light on Palfrey Island, Lizard Group, guides north-bound ships to their more westerly course along The Steamer Track.

Cape Flattery, just to the north of Cooktown, with a stock-pile of the dazzlingly white pure silicon sands which are being collected for export from the very extensive sand dunes along this coast.

Dawn at Heron Island

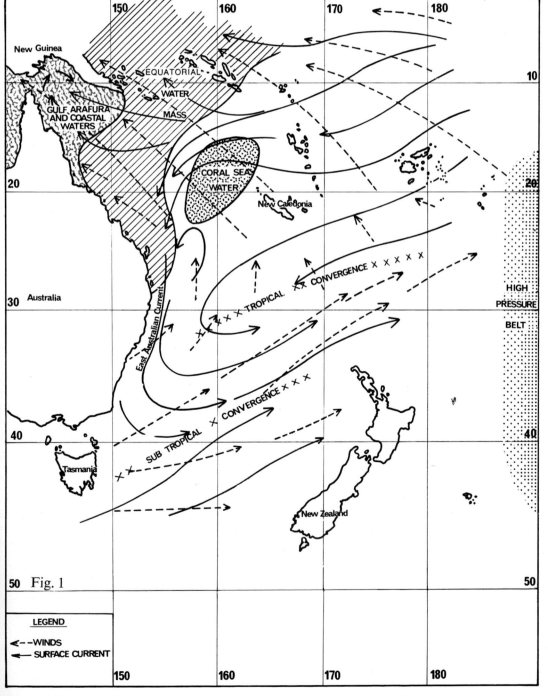

Fig. 1

LEGEND

← – WINDS
← SURFACE CURRENT

1. The winds, surface currents, and water masses which impinge on the Great Barrier Reef Province, affecting the climatic and hydrological conditions. (After Wyrtki and Maxwell).

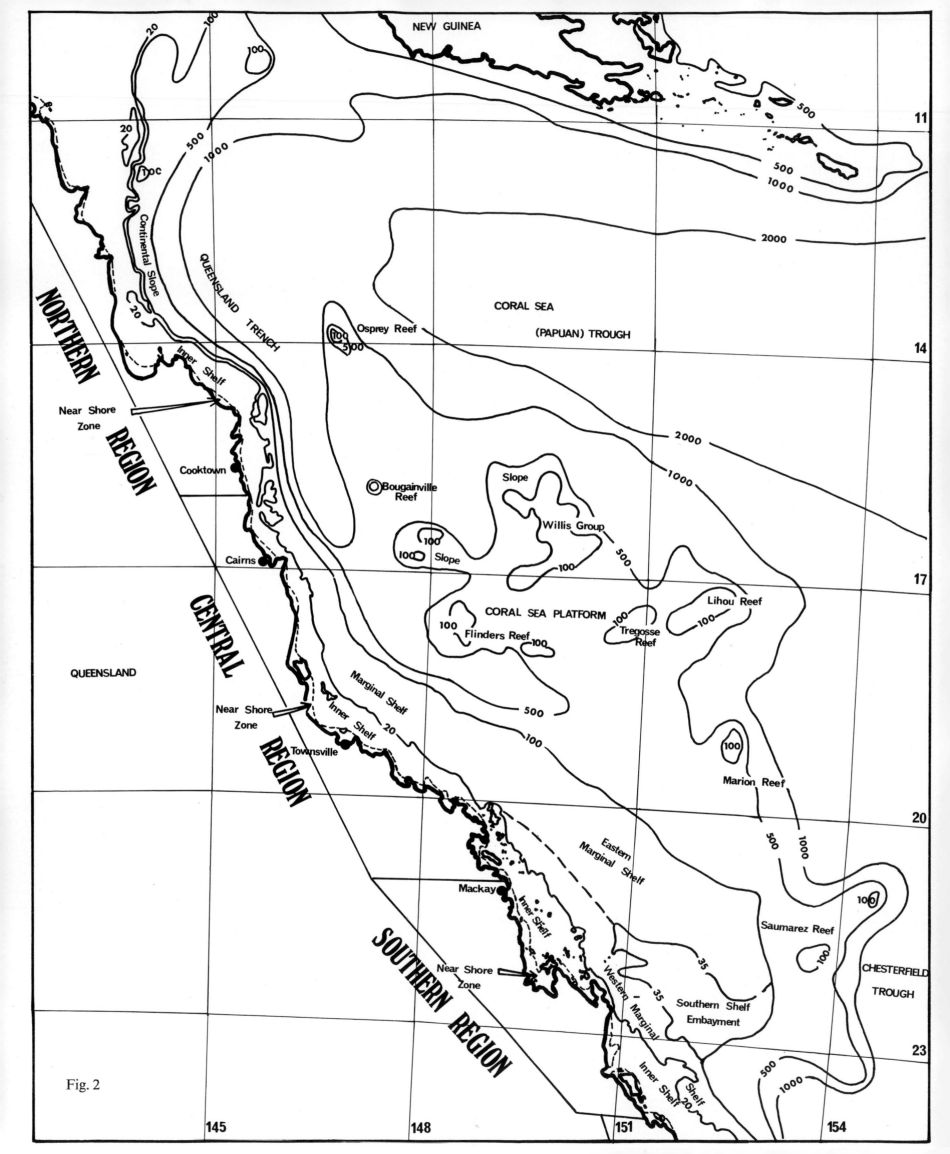

Fig. 2

among coral reef communities throughout the world in that it has an unusually high tidal range. Its minimum range of between seven and eight feet occurs in the southern-most region of the Province and this is at least four feet higher than that of any other reef area in the Pacific Ocean.

The general pattern of the tidal currents along the Queensland coast is controlled by the west-ward movement of tidal waves originating from the direction of New Zealand and New Guinea, parallel to the eastern coast of Australia. The shallow Coral Sea Platform (Map I and Figure 2), causes a break in this wave which converges again behind it. The reef development as a whole, its width north and south, and the presence of the land mass of the continent, combined with this convergence, result in a great build-up of water unable to escape easily, especially in the Gulf of Papua (Map V), and in the vicinity of Broad Sound, south of Mackay (Map II), the widest part of the Continental Shelf. In this latter area, where the highest tides of the province are encountered, there is a rise and fall of up to 35 feet during periods of extreme high water of spring tides. This great tidal range is also responsible for the very fast currents of up to 7 knots which are built up at this latitude, owing to the presence of the reefs and the numerous groups of large continental islands all interacting with the tidal waves.

It will be appreciated what this wide tidal fluctuation can mean to vessels of deep draught passing through these waters. And apart from the many factors involved in the turn-over of highly oxygenated, nutrient-rich waters neces-sary for reef development, it also means that there may be very extensive areas of reef, sand and mud flats, all exposed to atmospheric

conditions for periods up to 12 hours daily, at certain times throughout the year. This in turn necessitates a very considerable amount of adaptation to rigorous environmental changes on the part of large numbers of intertidal plants and animals living in these localities, particularly with the coincidence of low water and mid-day heat. Fortunately, over most of the province, the lowest spring tides of the year during day-light hours occur in the cooler months, May to August, whilst in the hot months, November to February, the lowest tides are at night.

Round the Northumberland and Cumberland Islands, the maximum rise and fall of the tide varies between 12 and 18 feet, whereas in the Capricorn and Bunker Groups at the southern extremity of the Province it is only between 8 and 10 feet. This latter range holds good for most of the northern regions between Cairns and Cape Melville, with a gradual increase to about 13 feet rise and fall in Torres Strait.

As previously mentioned, the temperature of the sea water is one of the major factors con-trolling growth of reef-building corals. (The optimal requirements for coral growth, and its limitations, are discussed in Chapter V). In Barrier Reef waters the sea temperatures increase gradually and fairly uniformly with latitude from south to north; the highest temperatures occurring during the summer months of Nov-ember, December and January, and the lowest temperatures in June, July and August. The mean maximum midsummer temperature over the length of the coastal region of the Province ranges from 29° C. to 32° C., whilst the mean minimum in midwinter ranges from 26° C. to 29° C., from Cairns north to Cape York, with 21° C. to 23° C. to the south.

Gelam—the ' Dugong's Back ', the high ridge of the large volcanic crater along the northern and western slopes of Mer, the largest of the Murray Islands. The white building in the centre of the village is a new Anglican chapel, completed in 1969. These islands are a conspicuous landmark along the northern edge of the Great Barrier (Map V).

The crew of the lighthouse service ship, M.V. CAPE MORETON, erect a concrete lighthouse on the edge of a coral reef—Watson Island, Howick Group. Dodging the high tides makes the pouring of concrete a difficult and irksome task.

2. The three Regions of the Province, with demarcation based on the bathymetric gradients of the Continental Shelf. (Depths in fathoms).

(After Maxwell, 1968).

Chapter 2

Coral Reefs and Atolls
The Reefs of the 'Outer Barrier'
The Shelf Edge Reefs—and the Inner Shelf Reefs

The earliest descriptions of coral reefs and atolls came from seamen—explorers, navigators, whalers and sealers—and in consequence they were, to a large extent, geographical in nature. At the beginning of the 19th century it had become standard practice for exploring expeditions to carry scientists on their voyages. And, since corals reefs and atolls of the world's tropical oceans had completely captured the imagination of those seafarers from cold northern climes, it is not surprising that the scientists, whenever possible, directed their attention to the investigation of these most fascinating structures.

The first theory put forward regarding the origin of reefs and atolls was that of a German naturalist, von Chamisso, after a voyage to the South Pacific during the years 1815–1818. Intrigued by the atolls he saw in passing, and pondering their origin, Chamisso conceived the idea that they were formed simply by the coral growing till it reached the surface of the ocean. Here, the corals on the outside, bathed by the ocean waves, continued to grow and flourish, whilst those in the centre eventually died and were eroded away, leaving a lagoon in the centre of a ring of coral. The depth of the sea bottom surrounding these oceanic atolls—a factor of the greatest importance for the presence or absence of reef-building corals—was unfathomable to the seamen of those days, but its significance even had it been known, would probably not have been realized at that time.

A year or so later a French ship, the *Uranie*, under de Freycinet, sailed from the Indian Ocean round the southern coast of Australia to the Pacific. On board she carried the scientists, Quoy and Gaimard, who were responsible for collecting and describing so many of the earliest-known marine animals from Australian seas. These two men were the first to suggest, in 1825, that reef-building corals flourished *only in shallow water*, and that corals growing round the rims of submerged volcanoes gradually formed atolls. This would certainly account for the ring-like or oval shapes of the atoll reefs. No volcanoes were known on land, however, with craters whose dimensions in any way approached those of the atoll lagoons. Therefore other forces would also have to be involved in order to give rise to lagoons of the great size of those of the large atoll groups of the Indian and Pacific Oceans.

Just at the time this theory for the formation of atolls was being given prominence in London by Sir Charles Lyell, a leading English geologist of the day, Charles Darwin was appointed as naturalist on the surveying ship, H.M.S. *Beagle*, which sailed round the world in the years 1831–36. During this voyage Darwin was to visit the magnificent atolls of the Cocos-Keeling Group in the Indian Ocean.

Although many years were to elapse before the publication of his epoch-making *Origin of Species*, written largely as the result of the data collected by him on that voyage, by 1837 Darwin felt sure enough of his facts to put forth a theory regarding the formation of coral reefs generally, including those of atolls.

Darwin accepted the premise that coral reefs flourished only in shallow seas. If this were the case, then it was axiomatic that there must be a shallow shelf or platform on which the corals were originally able to settle and grow. The great problem with which he was mainly concerned, therefore, was the origin of these platforms which supported the reefs. In the years following the publication of Darwin's book, *The Structure and Distribution of Coral Reefs*, controversy raged among the learned men of the day, some upholding his theory, others refuting it and putting forth their own in its place.

Darwin reviewed all that was known of coral reefs up to that period and presented evidence which pointed to the fact that in all areas where reefs were known to occur, subsidence—a sinking of the sea floor—either had, or could have taken place. If, therefore, the requisite conditions for the establishment and growth of corals were present in the sea water, they could settle and flourish on the shallow sloping shelf round an island. Thus a reef fringing its shore would be formed, with the coral eventually growing to the surface of the sea when the reef surface would in fact become a continuation of the shore.

With this as his starting point, Darwin postulated that if there were very, very slow and gradual subsidence of the land through geological ages, then upward growth of the coral on any reef fringing all or part of its shores could keep pace with this subsidence. Eventually the island would become smaller and smaller, surrounded by a great thickness of coral reef material, the outer edges of which would gradually have developed further and further from it, and separated by a wide channel of water. The end result, in the case of a single reef on part of a coast could be a 'barrier' reef parallel to the shore. With an encircling reef, when further subsidence had caused the disappearance altogether of the island, the place of the latter would be taken by a lagoon, thus producing a ring- or oval-shaped atoll.

Rival theorists, led by Sir John Murray, refused to accept that subsidence of the sea floor had taken place. An American scientist, Daly, produced a *Glacial Control Theory* postulating a fall in sea level in tropical seas, leaving them shallow as water was drawn from these regions with the great thickening of the polar ice cap during the last, most recent of the glacial periods.

Southern edge, Heron Reef, looking S.E.

Above
Carter and Yonge Reefs, separated by Half Mile Opening.
Yonge Reef was described and visited by members of the
British 1928-29 G.B.R. Expedition.

Shingle rampart on Low Isles encloses a "moat" area,
behind which are stunted mangroves, with a ground cover of
Sesuvium portulacastrum.

Below
High shingle rampart enclosing 'moat', Watson Island.

At the turn of the century, in 1899, The Royal Society of London, in an attempt to throw some light on the controversy, financed an expedition to the Atoll of Funafuti in the Ellice Group in the central Pacific Ocean. If Darwin's theory of subsidence were correct, then it followed that the original and ancient sea bottom, which was once shallow water, must now be at a very considerable depth, with a great thickness of coral overlying it. The late Sir Edgeworth David, then Professor of Geology at the University of Sydney, was in charge of the drilling operations. With great difficulty and cost, cores were taken which indicated depths of coral material of over 1,000 feet.

Again the theorists, led by Sir John Murray, claimed that these results were inconclusive, that coral fragments could easily have rolled or drifted down the side of a submarine mountain and piled up, and that the bores could have gone down through this material. In 1918, after World War I, the Japanese tried a different method on Jaluit Atoll in the Marshall Islands. Again very considerable thickness of calcareous material was found, but still the critics were sceptical, both of the methods and the results.

In Australia, the series of reefs along the Queensland coast was accepted as fitting into the category of a Barrier Reef. The historic first scientific description of the region was that of Professor Beete Jukes, who sailed through these waters in the years 1842–46, as naturalist on board the survey vessel, H.M.S. *Fly*. Later, in 1893, came the magnificently produced book, *The Great Barrier Reef of Australia*, by W. Saville Kent, at one time Commissioner of Fisheries in the State of Queensland.

During the following 30 years, small parts of the region were visited and described by geologists and by naturalists, one of the most prominent of the latter being Charles Hedley of the Australian Museum, and short articles appeared in various scientific journals. The year 1922 marked the beginning of a co-ordinated effort on the part of Australian scientists to gain a better understanding of this vast natural asset. In April of that year, the late Professor H. C. Richards of the Department of Geology of the University of Queensland gave an address in Brisbane to the Royal Geographical Society of Australasia on *Problems of the Great Barrier Reef*. It was as a direct result of this lecture that steps were taken by the President and Council of the Society to organize a full-scale investigation of the origin and potential of the Reef. Leading scientific societies and institutions in Australia, New Zealand and Great Britain appointed representatives to co-operate with the Queenslanders and as a result the Great Barrier Reef Committee, now in the Australian Coral Reef Society, was formed. This body, which today is working jointly with the University of Queensland, has been responsible ever since that date in trying to further research work in all the scientific disciplines

The southern end of Herald's Prong, a large reef of the Swains Group. It lies with a north-south axis along the western edge of these Eastern Marginal Shelf Reefs of the Southern Region.

which relate to the reefs and maintains with the university a Marine Biological Research Station on Heron Island.

This Committee, after its inauguration, immediately began a programme of physiographical and geological work, but it soon became apparent that there was a dearth of trained personnel in Australia able to carry out investigations of the many marine biological problems associated with the reefs, nor were there funds for such work. Through the efforts of the first patron of the committee, the then Governor of Queensland, Sir Matthew Nathan, who approached many leading scientists on his return to Britain, another committee was formed in England, with the specific task of raising funds and selecting biologists to come to Australia. The final result was the formation of a Great Barrier Reef Expedition, under the auspices of a British Association Committee, Leeds, 1927. Under the leadership of Dr. (now Sir Maurice) C. M. Yonge, a party of ten biologists sailed for Australia in May, 1928, being joined later by members of the geographical section of the expedition.

During their stay in Australia they were visited from time to time by members of the Queensland Great Barrier Reef Committee, and of the staffs of various of the Australian universities and museums. The latter, as specialists in certain groups of animals, were able to be of great assistance in the collection and identification of tropical species, most of which were new to the scientists from the Northern Hemisphere.

This first major attempt at a full-scale ecological survey of a coral reef in Australian waters was carried out at Low Isles north-east of the township of Port Douglas (Map IV)

(Figure 3), where the Expedition spent over a year, working mainly on Low Isles, but also making a few comparative surveys on other reefs as time and transport permitted. The results are to be found in a fine series of Zoological Reports—still being issued—published by the British Museum, some written by members of the Expedition, and others by experts on the various animal groups collected.

In 1926, just before this expedition came to Australia, the Queensland Great Barrier Reef Committee had raised enough money to make an attempt similar to that carried out on Funafuti, to help substantiate Darwin's subsidence theory, and at the same time learn something of the origin of the Queensland reefs. A bore was drilled on Michaelmas Cay on the Barrier Reef, about 22 miles north-east of Cairns (Map IV), in an attempt to discover the depths at which reef material might be found, and the nature of the underlying rock on which the reef had originated. At a depth of about 600 feet no such rock had been reached. (Reef-building corals, as will be described later, do not live in depths below 180 feet.) A further attempt was made by the Queenslanders in 1937, with borings at Heron Island in the Capricorn Group (Map II), down to approximately 700 feet, revealing again no basal rock platform. Taking into consideration the distance between the two cays, and their differing relationship both in distance from the mainland and position on the Continental Shelf, and the remarkable similarity of the bores, in thickness and in the physical composition of their contained coralline material, the geologists of the day considered this as convincing evidence of rising sea level or subsidence of the sea bottom.*

The formation of coral reefs, like that of most geological processes, is far too slow to be

*Cores from at least 16 bores have been studied by geologists within the past 10 years, and the picture is now much clearer.

directly observed, especially within one man's life span. Often conflicting and seemingly contradictory theories put forward by specialists, add, each in its own way, to the final sum of our knowledge. Only by comparing one reef with others in the same geographical area but in differing stages of development, by studying the geological structure and hydrological conditions of its surroundings, can any satisfactory conclusions be drawn regarding its history.

In over 40 years since the Queensland committee's tests man has accumulated a knowledge of the world's oceans possibly far greater than the sum total previously known. The combined efforts—with ships, subn.......nes, aircraft, and even satellites with photography, manpower and financial aid—by the larger maritime nations of the world have resulted in the production of an enormous amount of data and large collections of animals and plants from pole to pole and east and west across the oceans. And during many of the surveys, coral reefs, their origins, distribution and general ecology, have received and are still receiving very considerable attention. Two items in particular should be mentioned here as providing once again evidence of subsidence, as postulated by Charles Darwin.

The U.S. Atomic Energy Commission and its affiliated scientific institutions, using the most modern technological equipment, carried out a number of seismic and boring tests on atolls of the Marshall Islands in the north Pacific Ocean, where over 4,000 feet of reef deposits were penetrated before basal rock was found. Accurate isotope dating of the material has given figures which have indicated subsidence of a far greater amount than could be accounted for, in the change of sea level suggested by the Glacial Theory, for example, or in the other theories which had been put forward.

Scientific ships of several nations, traversing

the Pacific Ocean, have plotted great numbers of 'guyots' —flat-topped sea mounts—which must at one time have been above the surface of the ocean and planed off by surface waves. During one of the Mid-Pacific expeditions of a ship from Scripps Institution of Oceanography in California, shallow-water reef corals and molluscs were dredged from some of these flat-topped peaks, which are now down at depths of 5,000 to 6,000 feet, and it has been estimated that these animals lived during the Cretaceous Period, over 100 million years ago. On some of these sea mounts, where environmental conditions were more favourable for coral growth, the corals could have built upward at the same rate as the sea mounts were subsiding, and so eventually become atolls. On others, either conditions were not suitable for coral settlement, or growth failed to keep pace with subsidence, resulting in the flat-topped mounts of today.

The members of the British Museum's Barrier Reef Expedition, geographers, geologists and biologists, and other workers who have been interested in the region since that time, accepted Darwin's initial classification of reefs, and attempted to group the Queensland reefs according to their relationships with one another and with coral reefs elsewhere.

However in 1968 Maxwell, in a large geological monograph, pointed out that all the 19th century scientists were referring only to reefs occurring in the deep waters of the Pacific and Indian Oceans when they used the terms 'Barrier Reef' and 'Atoll'. Since these reefs must have arisen from a totally different set of conditions from the reefs along the shallow Continental Shelf of the Queensland coast, it is neither logical to make comparisons, nor to use definitions applicable to the deep ocean reefs, and Maxwell suggests that the use of these terms should be restricted to the latter.

As the result of almost 10 years of intensive surveys by a team headed by Professor Maxwell, using the more modern techniques available to the oceanographer and the geologist today, an attempt had been made to assess the Great Barrier Reef Province as a whole in terms of its geological history and relationship to the Australian Continent, and to divide the reefs and islands according to their origins and the geological structure of the shelf on which they have arisen.

The classical division of the reef province by previous workers had been the grouping together of the inner reefs lying within the confines of the Barrier Reef 'channel', as contrasted with those of the 'Outer Barrier', the reefs lying on or near the margin of the Continental Shelf. Few of these people had had the opportunity to visit more than an isolated reef or two in any given area and, to a certain extent, based their work and views on the knowledge which had gradually been accumulated. It had certainly been realized that there were a number of categories into which the reefs and their associated islands occurring within these two regions could be divided, and attempts had been made to group them according to their relationships along these lines.

Maxwell's approach had been to divide the Province into three separate regions (Figure 2), using the bathymetric gradients of the Shelf as the main basis for these divisions. The same measure allows further subdivision within each region. Since there is a gradual sloping of the sea bottom on the Shelf from north to south, this permits a reasonably clear-cut division into the three regions as follows:

1. THE NORTHERN REGION. This is considered as covering all the reefs to the north of latitude 16° S., and the area is characterized by the shallowness of the water covering the Shelf, the depth being generally less than 20 fathoms.

2. THE CENTRAL REGION. This covers the area from 16° S. to 21° S. on the mainland coast, and to about 20° S. on the Shelf Edge. Over the greater part of this region the depth of water ranges from 20 to 30 fathoms.

3. THE SOUTHERN REGION. From 21° S. to 24° S. This is the deepest part of the whole reef province, with depths ranging down to 80 fathoms. (Map I and Figure 2).

From the shoreline of the Queensland coast the Continental Shelf also slopes eastward to the outer reef zone and then drops down to the Continental Slope. And here again, within the above three regions, the Shelf can be divided into inner and outer areas (Figure 2), along the contours of the 20 and 50 fathom lines. In the dense reef area of the Northern Region, the Inner Shelf will be seen to extend eastward right to the reefs along the shelf margin, whereas there are two distinct shelves in the central region, and three in the much wider southern region. Since the main development of reefs occurs within about 40 miles of the Shelf Edge, the wide southern region is free of reefs for at least half of its area, whereas in the narrower parts of the northern region, reefs extend right across to the shore line.

The very extensive development of Shelf Edge reefs in the Northern Region, and the Marginal Shelf reefs in the Southern Region, is a reflection of the extremely important part played by the wind and current systems (Figure 1) which impinge on them, deflected north and south by the divergences and convergences caused by the deep Queensland Trench, and the Coral Sea (Papuan) and Chesterfield Troughs. Recent research seems to indicate that the principal cause of what was considered to be poorer reef development in the Central Region is structural rather than due to the presence to the east of the shallower Coral Sea platform.

This central area is underlain by a basin and the reefs there are growing from deeper subsiding substrate so that these reefs are immature, having only recently reached sea level.

Between the Inner Shelf and the coastline of the mainland, there is another narrow area varying from less than a mile to about 14 miles in width, and extending down to the five fathom contour in depth. This is the Near Shore Zone (Figure 2). Only in the Northern Region of the Province are reefs to be found in this zone, along the coastline. These Near Shore Reefs are the Fringing Reefs of Charles Darwin and the workers who have followed him. In the central and southern regions, the general hydrological and geophysical conditions prevailing preclude the growth of reefs along the mainland, but they are to be found round the coasts of the continental islands (Chapter IV), wherever conditions are favourable for coral growth.

There is tremendous diversity in the shape, size and overall pattern of the countless reefs within the province, all of which were originally determined by the place of settlement by the first coral polyps, and then fashioned by the hydrological conditions in the surrounding sea water. Superimposed on this has been the gradual developments of the reefs themselves, which in turn has modified the environment, altered current directions and led to further changes in shape and structure within this enormous and complicated maze of reefs and coral islands. Some of these facts were appreciated by the earlier workers but more recent studies making use of the accumulated data of the oceanographer and the geologist together with advanced technological aids and aerial surveys, have been able to add greatly to our knowledge, view the whole Province as an entity and present a more concise and clear-cut basis for future workers.

THE REEFS OF THE NORTHERN REGION

A glance at Maps IV and V will show the formidable chain of reefs stretching for nearly 500 miles, lying along the edge of the Continental Shelf, and separated from one another by narrow channels through which succeeding tides surge at a speed of several knots. Ranging in size from small patches to elongate ' ribbon ' reefs several miles in length, this outer series of linear reefs present a wall-like structure which takes the full battering force of the great rollers of the Pacific Ocean, generated by the South East Trades. Along their front, the shelf slopes precipitously to the deep waters of the Queensland Trench (Figure 2).

The greater number of these reefs are either submerged or at most only uncovered for very short periods during the lowest spring tides of the year, and then only on days of very calm seas. Islands are found only on one or two of

---

Endeavour Reef—on which Captain Cook's ship ran aground in 1770—and Rudder Reef lie across the Inner Shelf with an east-west axis.

Top
Reef of the Inner Shelf, lying just to the south west of Lizard Island—Eyrie Reef and its developing sand cay.

Reefs along the Shelf Edge, Northern Region—Looking south-west through the narrow opening, Cook's Passage, through which the *Endeavour* sailed from the enclosed waters of the Barrier Reef to the open ocean. Day Reef to the north and Carter Reef to the south.

Right
The 'algal-coral rubble' area of the reef flat—Inner Shelf Northern Region—Watson Island. showing sandy patches and Horse's foot clams scattered on the reef.

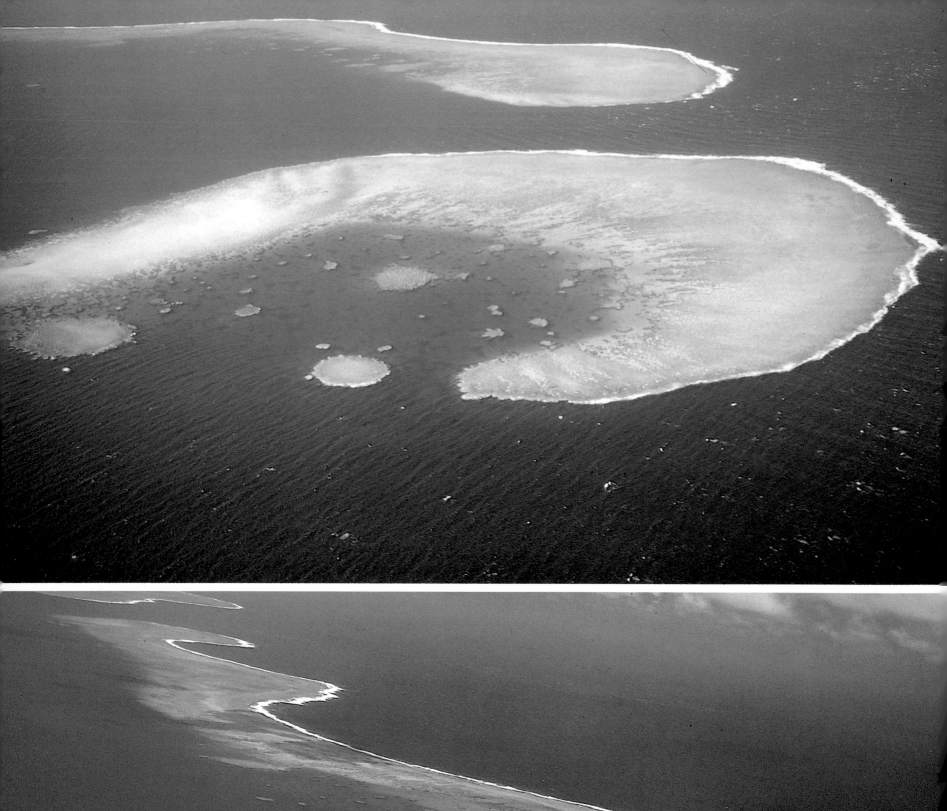

these outer reefs. Raine Island (11° 36' S. and 144° 01' E.) is one of these and it consists of older, solidified reef material formed at a period when the sea level was higher. It lies about 50 miles north-east of Cape Grenville and is almost unknown to most Australians, yet it marked an important stage in the maritime history of the Continent.

Raine Entrance (Map V), was used extensively in the 1840's and 1850's by ships intending to sail through Torres Strait from the east. The whole of this area was treacherous for shipping and the scene of several wrecks. In the year 1844 when the Macquarie Light on South Head, Sydney, was the only one in existence on the whole Australian mainland, Captain Blackwood, R.N., in H.M.S. *Fly* with an assistant cutter, transported a party of convict labourers, guards and supervisors to this remote spot. Here, to a plan designed by the ship's carpenter, a solid 5 feet thick circular tower, 64 feet high, was erected, its walls of ' stone ' being quarried out of the solid reef. Although its wooden dome, built from the timbers of ships wrecked in the vicinity, has long since fallen into decay, the tower remains today as an efficient beacon, marking the entrance channels leading from the Coral Sea to the Inner Route, navigable for small vessels with local knowledge.

Few of these outer northern reefs* had been investigated to any extent, both because of their inaccessibility and the general weather conditions prevailing along them for the greater part of the year. The most detailed published biological work had been the paper on the reefs of the Murray Islands (Chapter IV), and the series of Reports by the Great Barrier Reef Expedition of 1928–29, some of whose members were able to make short visits to reefs to the east of Lizard Island. From their observations, made chiefly on Yonge Reef (Map IV), with short visits to one or two reefs to the south, there does emerge a pattern of horizontal zonation across the reef which, with the variations which must always be expected in any marine environment, appears to be characteristic of these reefs along the Shelf edge.

From the air, the different zones can be quite clearly discerned on Yonge Reef which is about four miles long and up to a mile in width, separated from the reefs lying to the north and south of it by narrow channels, very conspicuous because of the dark blue of their deeper water. A marked feature of reef development, where a reef is subjected to winds and currents from the one direction for long periods, is well illustrated on this shelf edge reef. The force of the currents flowing through the channels separating the reefs eventually causes

the coral reef to grow in such a direction that it curves back on itself.

Only on a day of very calm weather with an extremely low tide is it advisable, or at all possible, to venture on to such a reef. Careful navigation with a small dinghy and outboard will enable one to negotiate the back region of the reef between the curved-back ends. Here the sandy bottom gradually shallows from the deeper waters of the sea between the mainland and the reefs, and in water sloping up from about 3 fathoms to knee height, masses of coral ' rock ', varied in size and form, some with curiously table-like structure, are to be seen, each with a rich covering of living corals on their sides and upper surfaces. As one goes closer towards the reef the coral growth becomes much denser.

This westward region of luxuriant coral flourishing within the slight protection of the lagoon-like region formed by the incurving ends of the reef gradually merges into a narrow belt composed mainly of boulders, fragments of dead coral skeletons and mollusc shells. Beyond this, either as pools or as a long, narrow and shallow 'moat', water separates this boulder region from the crest of the reef, a broad pavement of solid coral rock which runs for about 3 miles along the length of the reef, varying in width between 100 and 200 yards. This Reef Crest, a most conspicuous feature common to many different kinds of coral reefs, takes the full brunt of the waves that pound on it unceasingly, so that its surface is smooth, and clear of boulders and debris. Often referred to as the Algal Rim, this reef crest has been gradually built up until it is slightly higher than the remainder of the reef, and its smooth concrete-like surface has been created by massive encrustations of calcareous algae. These cementing red algae, referred to throughout coral reef literature generally as 'lithothamnia', nullipores or Melobesiaea, belong mainly to the genera *Porolithon*, *Neogoniolithon* and *Lithophyllum* of the family Corallinaceae. Only following the intensive studies of coral reefs during the past few decades has the extremely important role they play in the construction and maintenance of reefs been fully appreciated.

On Yonge Reef, as on many others, living corals and other animals which live among them, occur sporadically on the reef crest, but the corals are usually stunted and solid, and the greater part of the surface is a veneer of the encrusting coralline algae. The bright pinkish mauve colour of these algae in life adds greatly to the vividness of the scene as one looks back towards the mainland across the greenish yellow of the waters lying over the pure white coral sand of the back-reef area, studded as it is with colourful patches of flourishing coral colonies.

Seaward, beyond the reef crest, there is an outer 'moat' up to 100 yards in width, the floor of which slopes gradually downwards

Part of the jagged, pitted limestone platform along the edge of the algal reef flat, with the mangrove swamp behind it—characteristic of the Inner Shelf reefs, Northern Region. The sides of the rock are covered with a band of the oyster, *Crassostrea amasa*. Watson Island.

Aerial views showing the reef crest, lagoonal back-reef areas and narrow passages between the reefs.

Looking along the Algal Rim of a reef, consolidated by encrusting algae.

Looking directly down on Northern outer reefs which slope steeply down to the deep waters of the Queensland Trench, the various zones and curved-back end of the reef shaped by the force of the current, are clearly visible.

Below
Ribbon Reef No. 7 and Lark Pass.

*See Stoddart & Yonge (1978).

towards the ocean. Irregular masses and flat platforms of coral rock, heavily encrusted with coralline algae, or covered with densely growing corals, occur throughout the length of this moat which, even at low water remains covered, and the water is never still. Several species of the staghorn coral, *Acropora*, are to be found here, as well as other more massive genera of corals (Chapter V).

Along the seaward margin of this outer moat, on Yonge Reef, there is another much narrower solid ridge, at a lower level than the reef crest proper. Given perfect weather conditions, it is just possible to stand on this ridge and look down over the seaward slopes of the reef face where the grade is gentle for a few yards, until suddenly, the intense blueness of the water gives the feeling of a sharp descent to a fathomless chasm.

The seaward slopes on most reefs are the areas where the greatest and most virile coral growth takes place. Along this great series of reefs of the shelf edge of the northern region of the province, the clear highly oxygenated, nutrient-rich waters from the Pacific Ocean break unceasingly, bringing with them the optimal requirements for growth and survival of the reef-building corals and their associated algae.

This outer margin of the reef, with its tremendous development of species, is the most difficult to study since it is almost inaccessible, except to skin divers on days that are very calm with little or no wave action. On reefs where some fraction of this area may be uncovered during the fortnightly periods of the lower tides, it is sometimes possible to see the 'notched edge' of the reef, which is much more clearly visible from the air. The whole face along the windward edge of the reef may be 'toothed' with deep grooves separated from one another by wide buttresses. The sides of the grooves are covered with a wealth of encrusting species, and provide, with their depth and incision back into the face of the reef, a far greater amount of settling space for the various reef fauna than would be possible along a flat, unbroken area. As the tide ebbs water races off the reef surface, cascading down the grooves as a wave recedes in a swirl of foam.

Within the confines of this outer series of reefs along the shelf edge, lie the reefs of the Inner Shelf. Geological evidence indicates that there was a period when the level of the sea was up to 4 feet higher than it is today, thus enabling reefs to have become established at that level. With the gradual drop to present day level, the tops of these reefs died, and erosion processes began. On the outer Shelf Edge reefs, the heavy surf and swift currents removed all rubble and other detrital material, preventing the formation of cays and other superimposed structures which are to be seen on the more protected Inner Shelf reefs.

North of latitude 14° S. many reefs are visible,

Beach rock, dead coral-Alcyonarian zone, and lagoonal 'Anchorage' area, northern edge, Low Isles Reef.

As the tide ebbs, water races off the reef flat and cascades into the deep grooves along the edge of the reef. Heron Island.

Three Isles Reef with its sand and mangrove cays—looking west.

under the right conditions of light and tide, from the deck of a ship sailing along the Steamer Track in this narrow northern region. They may be almost entirely submerged, but their presence is clearly indicated by the paler yellow-greens of the shallower water overlying them. One of the largest of these is Corbett Reef, just to the north-east of Princess Charlotte Bay (Map IV). It is over 8 miles in length, covering an area of about 25 square miles, and it extends right across the Inner Shelf almost to its outer margin. Very little living coral is to be found on the sandy reef flat and shallow lagoon, and it has been estimated that, to a depth of about 30 feet, there could be 100 million tons of calcareous material.

Between latitudes 14° S. and 16° S., several of the reefs are capped with islands which range from mere sand spits emergent only at low water, to wooded cays, with or without high ramparts of coral shingle, boulder tracts and mangrove swamps, relics of older reefs formed when sea level was higher. Referred to in the literature as 'low wooded islands', and restricted generally to fairly small reef platforms in these more protected areas of the Northern egion, these particular island reefs have few counterparts anywhere else in the world.

Only two of the islands of this type have been studied in any detail by biologists—Three Isles and Low Isles. However, in making comparisons of other islands with the very detailed studies carried out by the Great Barrier Reef Expedition in 1928-29 at Low Isles (Figure 3), a remarkable similarity of the various physical structures and of the associated fauna and flora of the reefs is at once apparent. Low Isles (16° 23′ S. and 145° 34′ E.) lies just to the south of the boundary line and is, therefore, more correctly included in the Central Region.

Small sand cays (Chapter III) occur on both Three Isles and Low Isles, but on most of the 'island reefs' found on the Inner Shelf of this Northern Region, small shifting sandbanks are a feature, as are shingle beaches, boulder tracts and shingle ramparts, and mangrove swamps. These have all been formed as superficial structures on the reef platforms. The size and the shape of the original platform, its tidal level and orientation relative to prevailing weather conditions and to other reefs, have all played a part in the formation of these superimposed cays and ramparts. But the development of the mangrove swamp could only follow after the formation of the shingle ramparts or other coral rock provided the conditions necessary for its establishment.

On these inner shelf reefs, as compared with those of the Shelf Edge, apart from the shallower water in which they have developed, there are two other particular differences in the physical conditions prevailing—those of tidal level, and the composition and movement of the waters surrounding them. The reefs themselves are at a higher level than the shelf edge reefs, and both their closer proximity to the mainland, and the presence of the outer reefs, have a profound influence on the quality and movement of the sea water.

The Shingle Ramparts, a conspicuous feature of these reefs, are high elongated mounds of fragments of corals, mainly the branching staghorn species, all interlocking with one another. These are generally considered to have formed as the result of wave action breaking portions from actively growing coral colonies from the seaward slopes, rolling them upwards and eventually tossing them, under the influence of the ever-blowing South East Trades, into the long rampart structures of today. Since these shingle ramparts are not always found on the windward sides of reefs, it has also been suggested that their origin could more probably be related to the fall in sea level which left the older, higher reef exposed and the coral to die. Subsequent exposure and erosion over the years would remove the softer and less resistant components of the reef, leaving the ridges of much harder coral fragments.

The rampart on the windward side of Watson Island in the Howick Group (Map IV), resembles those on Low Isles, which are also on the windward side of the reef, and the same species of massive corals are to be found growing in the 'moat' inside the rampart. Lying scattered about on the reef flat of Watson Island one finds the large Horse's Foot Clam, *Hippopus hippopus*, exactly as it occurs on the reef flats of Low Isles, though at neither reef does it any longer 'occur in thousands' as recorded by Professor Yonge in 1930.

Mangrove flats are one of the striking features of these inner shelf reefs. Mangrove swamps are characteristic of the mainland shores in these northern latitudes, and the proximity of the inner shelf reefs to the coast makes them accessible to colonization by the mangrove seedlings.

The mangrove swamp or forest is one of the most distinctive of all plant communities, and of great interest to the biologist, although regarded with feelings of repulsion by the average person —a place of slimy black mud, impenetrable tangles of roots, and teeming with sand flies and other biting insects. The great variety of aerial roots, pneumatophores, of the mangroves are highly characteristic, and vary considerably with the different species. It is the extraordinary development of these root systems in the thick layers of mud which accumulate amongst them, which makes working in a mangrove swamp so difficult and unpleasant.

Mangroves do not belong in one plant family as might be expected. Instead the term is applied to many trees of various families which are found growing in muddy intertidal areas. The mangrove occupies a most exacting littoral habitat, almost invariably in salt or brackish water, in coastal silt, clay, sand in varying proportions, and, in very exceptional cases,

Ridges of shingle 'beach' made up of fragments of coral, with stunted *Casuarina* trees in the background, Coquet Island, Howick Group.

Shingle bank and coral rubble. Wilson Island. Capricorn Group.

Sandy flat and Boulder zone along the western margin of Low Isles.

Coarse sand and boulder area of Watson Island at low water. Horse's Foot and Giant clams in foreground.

sand only. This type of vegetation is normally found, therefore, mainly in bays, estuaries and coastal lagoons, almost always in shallow seas. A few individual trees occur sporadically far inland along the shores of large rivers, but only so far as there is tidal influence.

Mangrove formations follow the silting of coasts, largely from the heavily silt-laden rivers of wet regions, so the greatest development of the mangroves is in the everwet regions of the tropics. The very characteristic mangrove forests or swamps may consist of a mere fringe of trees along a coastline or, where wide mud flats occur in sheltered bays and estuaries which are covered by water at high tide, they may be a mile or more in width. For the mangroves, as with many other plants and animals of the seashore, the tide is a most important ecological factor, since it is the agent which affects the exchange of water, and its vertical range determines the extent of tidal flats which may be exposed and submerged with each tidal cycle.

The mangrove forest's component species of vegetation have been developed and adapted to conditions totally at variance with the general concept of what is necessary for plant growth. Removal of a mangrove from its special habitat results in its death since its physiological requirements bind it to the intertidal regions. The dispersal of fruits and seeds of mangroves is exclusively bound to drift by sea water. The seeds are one of the most striking adaptations of the mangrove to its environment. To meet the peculiar conditions of settling and up-growth on tidal mud flats, the seeds of almost all species show a remarkable early development of the plant embryo which, in various ways, pierces the seed coat and becomes viviparous.

In the species of *Rhizophora*, and allied genera, so easily distinguished by their extensive array of tangled prop roots, the solitary seeds in the small fruits germinate whilst the fruit is still attached to the tree, and produce a long, thick and pendant radicle, which in some species may reach a length of several feet. The heavy thickened radicle will, by its weight, eventually cause the whole seedling to break off—the radicle plunges vertically into the soft mud where the young seedling is able to start growing immediately, having been planted in an upright position. Relatively quiet waters are needed for the establishment of mangrove seedlings.

More frequently, and especially if the seeds fall during periods of high water or ebbing tides, they will be floated away, sometimes for relatively long distances. Since they are very resistant to salt water and may remain afloat for long periods before being deposited, young mangroves may commence their growth far distant from their places of origin. Because of their viviparity—the extensive development of

The mangrove, *Rhizophora stylosa*, with its characteristic prop roots, forms a fringe along the edge of the algal-covered reef flat, Watson Is.

The scene from the sand cay across the sandy reef flat with the mangrove cay to the east, Low Isles.

Far left:
Looking from the mangroves across the reef to the sand cay of Low Isles.

Left:
Watson Island—looking towards the mangrove cay from the small sandspit which is only visible at low water.

Below:
Sand cover of creepers, and *Pandanus* trees looking south-east over the reef, Heron Island.

the seedlings whilst still attached to the parent tree—they are able to pioneer and establish themselves on shallow shoals and reefs off the coast, provided a set of ecological conditions necessary for their settlement and growth has already been made available. Such would be the case along the western boundaries of the Inner Shelf, where they would come under the influence of more turbid waters resulting from mainland drainage. Along the inner scarp of a shingle rampart, and on the reef flat within its lee, the mangrove seedlings can settle and develop. With time they will form a swamp on top of the sand of the reef, creating their own mud as they spread.

Aerial photograph of Low Isles, July 1974, taken at period of low water.

Coral limestone on south-western shore of Watson Island. The low bank of shingle partially encloses a "moat" region in which a number of colonies of several different species of staghorn corals flourished.

Low Isles, showing the different structures superimposed on the reef.

(After Spender, Stephenson *et al.*)

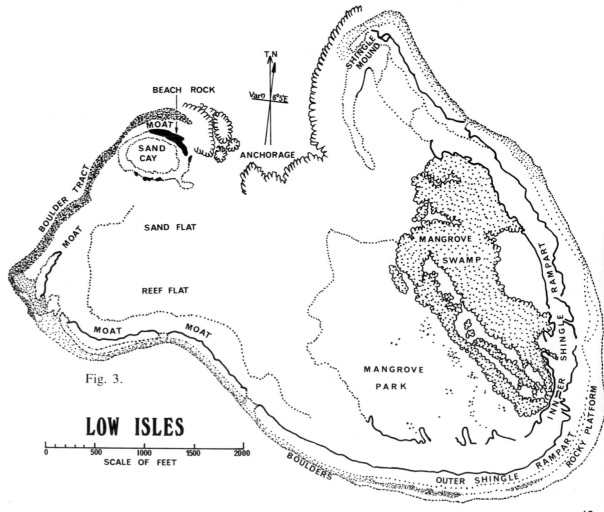

Fig. 3.

LOW ISLES

SCALE OF FEET

42

There is a pattern of horizontal zonation to be found across these reefs of the inner shelf, just as described for Yonge Reef as one of the reefs of the shelf edge but, because of the superimposed structures on their reef flats, strict comparisons cannot be made. And since there is so much greater variation among these Inner Shelf reefs than in the more uniform outer series, the zonation picture may change from reef to reef, depending to a certain degree on its geological age and the factors mentioned above, together with the presence or absence of cays, shingle ramparts and mangrove swamps.

If one were to traverse one of the ' low wooded island ' reefs from the leeward N.W. side to the exposed windward S.E. side, one might expect to cross growing corals along the reef edge, followed by a narrow reef flat leading to a vegetated cay, then a wider expanse of sandy or rubble reef flat merging into a mangrove swamp backed by a shingle rampart. This may be followed by a 'moat' enclosed within an outer rampart as at Low Isles (Figure 3), or there may be a single rampart sloping to a flat 'rocky' area of semi-consolidated coral rubble covered by encrusting and epiphytic algae, to the seaward of which actively growing coral may be seen down over the windward, seaward slopes of the reef.

The islands of the Howick Group (Map IV), with their surrounding reefs, illustrate very well a number of features characteristic of these northern inner shelf reefs. Beyond the Howick Islands, the outer Shelf Edge reefs are closer to the mainland than anywhere else within the Province. Typically, on the islands of this particular group, there is no sand cay as such. The islands may, instead, consist of an exposed platform of older consolidated reef material with shingle beach ridges instead of a sandy beach, such as those found on Coquet Island. Another variation within this same Group is to be seen on Watson Island. At high water only the mangrove-dominated cay with its eroded limestone platform and shingle rampart are uncovered. At low water a sand spit, a small area of coarse sand, shingle and boulders, and a much larger algal-dominated region, form the bulk of the reef flat. The larger area consists of dead coral boulders completely overgrown with algae, so that the term 'algal flat' very adequately describes it. Apart from very small isolated colonies, the only living corals are found growing on the outer seaward slopes of the reef. There is one area where the 'Blue Coral', *Heliopora coerulea*, dominates the reef, although the greater bulk of this species is also dead and overgrown today with brown algae. The algal flat has, however, a wealth of animals living on it, and the underside of almost every boulder reveals a fascinating array of multi-coloured, encrusting colonies of animals as well as shade-seeking species which only emerge at night or during very dull weather. Molluscs and echinoderms burrow in the sandy areas of the

Looking down on the mangrove cay. Low Isles, high water. August 1977.

Megaera reef, Howick, has a very small sandspit emergent only at low water.

Under side of boulder along northern edge. Heron Reef.

flat. Crabs and mantis shrimps dart for cover under rubble and seaweeds. Cone shells, spider shells and ring cowries, holothurians and brittle stars, may all be found lying in the open or half concealed among the semi-consolidated rubble of the outer flat. There are small fish, so perfectly matching the mottling of their algal background, that only movement reveals their presence. Everywhere, as one walks across the shallows, rays which have been lying partially buried in the sand, or the small beautifully marked reef sharks, shoot away from underfoot.

Along the landward margin of the reef flat the prop roots of the mangrove, *Rhizophora stylosa*, prevent further growth of the typical reef-dwelling algae, and the various species of mud-dwelling crabs and molluscs may be found. A very distinctive feature of Watson Island in particular, and this may well be characteristic of other reef islands in these latitudes, is that its mangrove swamp is surrounded on the weather side, by a protective wall of limestone. From its position relative to the shingle rampart and the rest of the reef on Watson Island, this platform of ancient reef material appears to correspond to the position of the inner rampart present on Low Isles (Figure 3), but it has undergone further transformation into a rocky substance forming an extremely solid platform, about 6 feet in height and several yards in width, its jagged, pitted surface being razor-edged in places and very difficult to walk on. The outer face of this limestone rock is now partially protected from further erosion since it is solidly encrusted with a band of the oyster, *Crassostrea amasa*, at about mid-tide level. Stunted mangroves and the small halophytic succulent, *Sesuvium portulàcastrum* have managed to obtain a foothold, precarious in the extreme, with their roots penetrating into minute fractures in the solid substrate, and they occur sporadically across the platform. The only other obvious inhabitants of this sun-baked inhospitable region are the bright green, fleet-footed rock crabs, *Grapsus albolineatus*, which disappear rapidly over the edge at the slightest movement.

The ten years since the publication of Maxwell's *Atlas of the Great Barrier Reef* have seen a considerable increase in our knowledge of reef structure, largely through the efforts of scientists from James Cook University (David Hopley and others), the Bureau of Mineral Resources, and the Royal Society 1973 Expedition team. As a result if their work and the Workshop run by the Great Barrier Reef Marine Park Authority in 1978, a number of important papers have been published, some referring in particular to this Northern Region where previously little or no information on the reefs had been available.

THE REEFS OF THE CENTRAL REGION

In this region (Maps III and IV), as one proceeds southwards, there is a difference both in the width of the Continental Shelf and in the depth of the ocean fronting it, by comparison with the northern region. As will be seen in Figure 2, there is a much more clear-cut division of reefs into those of the inner shelf and an outer marginal shelf. However, the outer reefs are no longer to be found as a linear series facing east along the very edge of the Shelf, lying more or less parallel to the mainland. In fact, Arlington Reef (Map IV), lies almost obliquely across the Shelf, with its seaward slopes facing south rather than east. And to the south of this the reefs of the Marginal Shelf arise some distance in from the Shelf Edge, and are widely scattered. Some are always completely submerged, others have small sandbanks visible at low water. Others again dry out several feet on the ebbing tide, revealing long stretches of boulder zone and reef flat. Patch reefs and larger platform reefs, with and without lagoons and exhibiting all the variations shown in the photographs, are included in these marginal shelf reefs of this central region.

Another marked difference from the northern region, where the continental islands (Chapter IV) are mainly grouped round the Cape York Peninsula, the northern-most point of the Queensland mainland (Map V) is the presence of a long series of continental islands, either isolated or in small and large groups, throughout the length of the central region, where they rise abruptly on the inner shelf.

Although Professor Maxwell's division of the province places the Low Isles reef in this central region, its affinities are with the Inner Shelf reefs of the northern region. Until the recent work by the Americans on the Atolls of the Marshall Islands, and some of the reefs of the West Indies, probably no other coral reef in the world had been more thoroughly and continuously studied than Low Isles. Several members of the Yonge Expedition spent periods up to a year at Low Isles, where they studied not only its physical features, the physics and chemistry of its surrounding waters, but also the physiology and growth of corals and other reef animals, their ecology and life history. Large collections were made for future identification and study of all the major representatives of the various groups of reef organisms.

In the year 1954, a further expedition was organized by the Queensland Great Barrier Reef Committee to visit Low Isles, to re-survey the reef as a comparative study 25 years later, in order to assess, not only changes in the environment resulting from cyclone damage during that period of time, but also the nature and extent of any changes in the reef flora and fauna.* This was the first occasion in all the years during which man has been interested in

Footnote: see also: Stoddart and Yonge, (1978).

Beaver Reef—a Marginal Shelf reef of the Central Region has a small developing sand cay.

Arlington Reef, Marginal Shelf reef, Central Region, also lies obliquely across the Continental Shelf with its seaward margin facing south rather than east.

A patch reef on the outer shelf of the Central region. Hook and Hardy Reefs.

Platform Reefs of the Marginal Shelf, Central Region, showing deep channel separating reefs, Algal Rim and Resorbed reef in lagoonal area. Hook and Hardy Reefs. (Map 3).

Mangroves and the succulent plant, *Sesuvium*, on the solid limestone platform, Watson Island.

Sesuvium portulacastrum in flower, Wyburn reef.

Reef flat—coral pools and algal-covered rubble—northern side Heron Island, looking south.

Sand bank, East Strait Island, Torres Strait, uncovered only at low tide.

The clear, sandy glade among the mangroves, Low Isles. Corals were growing on the prop roots of the *Rhizophora* and fishes and cowries were found there. A large colony of the needle-spined urchin, *Diadema*, was living in the nearby sandy area.

coral reefs, that such a comparative survey has been possible.

Many of the reefs of the central region, especially those of its Inner Shelf, are today much closer to centres of rapidly expanding human populations. New tourist resorts are continually being established on offshore islands, most of which are within easy reach by small, fast power boats. These reefs are all being subjected to change and modification of their flora and fauna at a far greater rate than at any previous period since man's occupation of this continent. This applies also to the closer inshore reefs of the marginal shelf in the southern-most part of the Region, where proximity of the reefs to the tourist resorts of the Cumberland Islands, permits easy access during periods of low spring tides (Map III).

Masthead Island, Capricorn Group, showing zonation from the densely wooded cay, beach, reef flat, coral growths, algal rim, to the grooves and buttresses of the sloping reef front.

Reef along inner edge of Eastern Marginal Shelf of Southern Region—Swain Reefs.

Back-reef area of western-most reef of the Swains.

THE REEFS OF THE SOUTHERN REGION

Not only is the Continental Shelf much wider in this Region than in the two to the north of it, but it is the area in which the greatest tidal range occurs, and the waters covering it reach a greater depth than in any other part of the Province (Map II and Figure 2). As will be seen from Figure 2, not only is the Inner Shelf wider here, but the marginal shelf is divisible into an eastern and a western part, based on bathymetric contours.

In this southern region The Steamer Track follows along the deep clear waterway of the Capricorn Channel, clear of reefs (Map II). North of latitude 22° S. the groups of continental islands lying on the inner shelf, are to be seen away to the west, the most important being the Duke and Percy Isles and the various isolated islands which together make up the Northumberland Group. The largest and most north-westerly of the Northumberlands, Prudhoe Island, to the south east of the city of Mackay, forms perhaps the most obvious

North Reef, Capricorn Group, and its lighthouse—leading light into the Capricorn Channel and to The Steamer Track north through Barrier Reef waters.

landmark in the vicinity, its prominent peak rising to over 1,000 feet above sea level.

The only important reefs of the western marginal shelf (Figure 2), are in the southernmost part, those of the Capricorn and Bunker Groups, with their associated coral cays (Chapter III). The eastern marginal shelf, however, presents a very different picture with an infinite variety of reefs of all shapes and sizes, elongate wall reefs, some just emergent at low water, others always completely submerged. Others again with superimposed small sand cays sparsely covered with vegetation. These are the reefs of the Pompey Complex and the Swains Group. They cover an area varying in width from a few miles to a maximum of 80 miles, in waters to a depth of 80 fathoms, and further from the mainland than the other reefs throughout the Province (Map II).

Since these distant southern reefs come under the influence of westerly and south-westerly winds for certain periods of the year, unlike those north of latitude 19° S., where the westerly effect is much less marked, a number of the reefs of the eastern marginal shelf in this far south-eastern corner of the province have formed as long narrow reefs with an east-west axis, and their algal rims face south west rather than east.

Chapter 3

Coral Cays and their Associated Features

Within the Great Barrier Reef Province, the term *Cay*, which is comparable with the word *Key* as used in Florida and the West Indies, is applied to all small islands which have arisen on coral reefs, as opposed to continental islands with their relationship to the geological structure of the adjacent mainland.

These cays, which have been briefly mentioned in the previous chapter, are a product of the reefs, and they vary in their size, shape and position relative to the reef on which they have arisen, in their height above sea level, and in the degree of stability which they have achieved today. They are usually found on platform reefs of different types. When the reef-building corals have grown to a sea level height at which they are exposed to atmospheric conditions, they die off on their upper surfaces, continuing their growth horizontally only. Over geological time these dead corals have been broken off by wave action and pounded into fragments of rubble. To this has been added the calcareous remains of the coralline algae, molluscs and other reef animals. Further pounding and abrading reduces this rubble to sediments which are carried across the reef flat to its more protected areas, and gradually accumulated into ridges and banks by the interaction of prevailing winds, tidal currents and wave refraction round the reef. Gravel banks and boulder tracts formed of much larger, coarser coral fragments are usually found on the windward side where wave action causes a certain amount of destruction of coral colonies, and these heavier fragments, too large for transport by currents across the reef flat, have gradually accumulated.

There are many reefs throughout the Barrier Reef Province today, partially exposed at low water, on which it is possible to see the beginnings of islands of the future—small sandspits on part of the reef. These sandbanks are extremely unstable and may alter their size and position on the reef very considerably whilst in this unstable state, especially under adverse weather conditions during cyclones. Also, keeping pace with the sand or shingle cays, during their development, the reefs themselves are slowly growing outwards. These reefs range in size from a few hundreds yards, as on Bramble Cay to several miles. The larger, well-developed reefs will have algal-encrusted crests along their outer seaward slopes, and this slightly higher crest and the reef flat which has been formed behind it both serve to break the force of the waves and so help in the stabilization of the developing cay.

Once the pulverized rubble and sand have been built up by these various interacting factors of wind, tidal currents, and wave action to a level where they remain exposed at extreme high water of spring tides, various species of sea birds take advantage of these emerging sandbanks as resting areas. With time, the resulting guano forms a thin layer of organic humus. And thus there gradually accumulates land space available for plant colonization by any saltwater resistant seeds which may be blown or drifted there, or have been carried by birds. The instability of the substrate, its highly saline and calcareous nature, would at first prevent all but halophytic plants from surviving. These plants, highly specialized and adapted for living in this wind-blown strand region, are subjected to continuous salt spray with little or no fresh water for considerable periods of the year. Once a sufficient area has been established to prevent the dissipation of all fresh water into the open sea, a certain amount of fresh water will remain in the sand at sea level, floating on top of the salt water below it, and thus aiding the propagation of the seeds. The density of the vegetation on the various cays today depends almost entirely on their position relative to the high

A submerged reef as seen from the deck of a passing steamer, visible only by reason of the colour of the sea over it.

Small sandspit, emergent only at very low water—Megaera Reef, Howick Group.

Aerial view of Upolu Cay, with Oyster Reef in the background.

Michaelmas Cay and Reef. N.E. of Cairns.

Heron Island, from the S.W. with its man-made boat harbour.

Strewn along the tidelines of sandy shores of coral cays and other islands, seed pods of many kinds show the means of dispersal utilized by some of the tropical species of plants. The very large elongated radicle of a mangrove seedling is seen in the foreground.

Typical beach rock formation on the windward shore of a coral cay—Heron Island.

Beach rock may also occur on a lee shore. The long dark patch in the water stretching all along the beach is an enormous shoal of small Antherine fish. 'sardines'.

rainfall areas of the province.

Since the prevailing winds for the greater part of the year are the South East Trades, the tendency is for the coral sediments to accumulate on the lee side of the reef, that is towards its north-western corner. With only a few exceptions, the cays throughout the province are found in this general position relative to the reef on which they have developed. One notable exception is the cay on One Tree Reef, one of the eastern-most of the Capricorn Group. Here the cay stands on the windward S.E. corner of the reef where a shingle bank built up above high water mark has become stabilized with a cover of vegetation. In this exposed region a sand bank could not have remained long enough to become stable.

Thus today, within the Great Barrier Reef Province, one can find a whole series of cays, showing a gradation through all stages of development from the bare, unstable sand spits to small and large cays with differing physical features, and with vegetation cover ranging from sparse, coarse grasses, creepers and stunted shrubs to a climax state where a dense forest of trees covers the island. There are the cays on which the beach is composed entirely of fragments of coral shingle, and there may be little or no vegetation. Other reefs, such as those of Three Isles and Low Isles, have vegetated sand cays, shingle ramparts, and mangrove-dominated cays. These latter are found almost exclusively in the Northern Region, on the inner shelf. And there are cays which are composed entirely of sparkling white coral sand, often with protective banks of beach rock, usually on the weather side, and with their tree cover in varying stages of development. In the far north-eastern corner of the northern region there are also a number of fully developed coral cays which form part of the Eastern Torres Strait group of islands. Since several of them have been inhabited by Torres Strait Islanders, possibly for many centuries, their vegetation differs considerably from that of more southern islands, most notably in the groves of coconut palms.

In the central region there are both vegetated and unvegetated cays, the best known perhaps, apart from Low Isles, being Green Island and Michaelmas Cay. Not only was Michaelmas Cay the site of the historic first drilling carried out by the Great Barrier Reef Committee geologists in their endeavour to understand something of the origin of the reefs, but it is the nesting ground in the spring and summer months of thousands upon thousands of sea birds. Green Island, which was named by Captain Cook, is one of the well-known tourist resorts, and it has an extremely interesting underwater observatory where it is possible to see large numbers of colourful reef animals in their natural state. Its reef was the first, within Barrier Reef waters, on which damage was reported, caused by extensive predation of the reef-building corals by the Crown of Thorns starfish (Chapter VII). The best development of sand cays, however, is on the reefs within the southern region of the province. There are a number on the reefs of the eastern marginal shelf (Figure 2), especially in the Swain Reefs, in areas where there is slight protection by outer reefs. Their vegetation, where present, is mostly coarse grasses, and the cay is composed of a mixture of sand and rubble. The greatest development of vegetated sand and shingle cays is to be found at the southern extremity of the western marginal shelf, on the reefs of the Capricorn and Bunker Groups.

These islands (Map II), lie in an area where the qualities of the surrounding sea water have permitted extensive development of reefs. With no reef formations to the east of them, as on the islands and reefs on the Inner Shelves to the north, there are many areas where reef-building corals are as luxuriant in their growth as any within the Province.

The Capricorn Islands as a group provide a classical text-book illustration of the development of a sand cay, with every gradation from the almost submerged Polmaise Reef, the bare sandbank of Broomfield Reef, the small Erskine Cay, the sparsely vegetated Wilson Island, to the densely covered cays of Heron and North West Islands with their jungles of *Pisonia grandis*.

Masthead Island shows very clearly the characteristic sequence of species found on an island which has been more or less undisturbed by man, and without the introduction of his various exotic and domestic plants. The first arrivals are usually creepers and coarse grasses such as *Thuarea involuta*, and there are numbers of sand cays throughout the Province where the vegetation consists almost entirely of sparse clumps of such grasses and creepers. Where cays of this type are utilized as nesting sites by thousands of sea birds, even the grasses have difficulty in maintaining a foothold.

Around the periphery of the island the primary colonizer among the trees is the graceful *Casuarina equisetifolia*, usually to be found on the outer seaward fringe. The delicate tracery of its branches adds greatly to the enchantment of the surrounding scene with its indescribable colours of sandy beach, reef, sea and sky, a haunting imprint on one's memory that instantly recalls all the intangible magic of a coral island.

Under the slight protection of the Casuarinas, the shapely spreading Tournefortia *Argusia argentea* with its distinctive silvery-grey leaves, and the shiny green leafed *Scaevola taccada*, are to be found. These trees, once well established, stabilize the environment still further and help to augment the organic content of the soil by the decomposition of their fallen leaves and fruits, and also provide slight protection from wind-blown salt spray, thus permitting the development of other species.

Green Island, a coral cay of the Central Region, from the S.W. with Arlington Reef in the background.

The shingle cay on One Tree Reef from the S.E., June 1978. This reef is now one of the most studied areas within the Province.

Patch reefs within the lagoon, One Tree Reef, June 1978.

Reticulate coral patches at the western end of the lagoon on Wistari Reef.

To the zonation picture on Heron Island there is added the long stretch of beach rock along the southern shore of the cay.

Sparse grasses struggle for existence on Bramble Cay where thousands of sea birds nest in the summer months.

54

Pandanus tectorius, with its large bright orange fruits and the fascinating prop roots which characterize this tree, occurs in ones and twos or in quite thick groves. Although the Pandanus is a halophytic species, surviving in exposed places from which other vegetation has been removed by erosion, its seeds seem only to develop under shaded conditions, so that it is a secondary rather than a primary colonizer and needs the protection of the Casuarinas to become established.

These are often followed by another tree, *Cordia subcordata*, with bright orange-coloured flowers, which sometimes. forms quite dense thickets. Other trees occasionally found in this community are the fig, *Ficus opposita, Celtis paniculata* and *Pipturus argenteus*. Further undercover growth of herbs, creepers and grasses, the rotting leaves and the droppings from the many roosting sea birds result in the production of a much more favourable soil, providing conditions suitable for the establishment of the large *Pisonia* trees. Although the seeds of many of the plants have been brought to the islands by the action of either wind or water, there is no doubt that birds, often to their ultimate cost, have been responsible for the wide-spread distribution of the *Pisonia* trees among these islands. Its fruit is extremely sticky and attaches to the legs and feathers of the birds which alight on its branches, sometimes so thickly as to result in the death of the bird.

The *Pisonia* trees are magnificent in their height and their great butress roots, and through their large pale green leaves the brilliant light of the tropical sun filters in a dazzling mosaic of yellow-green tones. Although initially introduced to the islands by means of seeds, its further propogation is facilitated by its enormous powers of vegetative reproduction which have led to the dense jungle formation with a canopy of shade resembling that of a tropical rain forest. The ground beneath the *Pisonia* trees, as many visitors have found to their discomfort, is almost completely undermined by the activities of the shearwaters, the burrowing ' mutton birds ', and this would certainly be a deterrent to seed germination. The trunks of these huge trees are extremely brittle and during periods of heavy cyclones, they may be split asunder or have large branches stripped off. It is not an uncommon sight to see great trunks without any branches, but with a thick covering of the large, beautiful green leaves.

So there is a zonation pattern on these island cays as on their reefs, a zonation of vegetation shown by a succession of plant communities which has been made possible by the modifications the plants themselves have made to the environment, and their reaction to them.

In among the tall *Pisonia* trees—the ground here is riddled with the burrows of mutton birds.

A typical cluster of *Pandanus* palms showing the prop roots, so necessary to support the top-heavy crown structure so often seen on these trees. The large seed pod is golden orange when ripe.

The silvery leaves and creamy flowers of the Tournefortia tree, *Argusia argentea*. The flowers of this tree attract large numbers of nectar-feeding insects to isolated coral cays.

The shapely spreading *Argusia* tree.

Large numbers of vertebrate animals are dependent upon these coral cays as land mass, in contradistinction to the surrounding reefs with their populations of marine animals.

In the Great Barrier Reef Province where land space is at a premium in this vast region of sea, it is understandable that animals bound to land for breeding purposes, would seek out all available places suitably isolated and free from disturbance by man and other predators. Today their isolation is by no means assured, but man is slowly beginning to appreciate the necessity of preserving some space for the wild life of these islands. Numbers have already been declared faunal reserves, and most species are legally protected.

Mammals such as seals, and reptiles such as the sea turtles, are recognized by everyone as being aquatic animals. It is not generally appreciated that the sea birds are in this same category, since their relationship to sea and land, as concerned with feeding and breeding respectively, is precisely the same. None of these groups of animals have escaped the necessity of using the land as a breeding ground, but the whole source of their being is, nevertheless, the sea. Even the most beautifully air-borne of all birds, the Wandering Albatross of the icy wastes of Antarctica, or the Frigate Birds of the tropical oceans, must obtain their food from the sea to sustain that aerial supremacy, and seek the remote Antarctic and tropical islands as their breeding grounds.

The sea birds are by far the most obvious and numerous inhabitants of the Barrier Reef islands, be they bare shingle ridges or densely wooded cays.

On the continental islands nearer the mainland, several species of land birds are commonly found, and in the northern region of the province many of the cays are the roosting grounds during the spring and summer months, of the Torres Strait or Nutmeg Pigeon, *Myristicivora spilorrhoa*. This handsome black and white bird, a migrant from lands further north, arrives in northern Australia in the spring, feeding during the day on native fruits on the mainland, but returning at night to the safety of the offshore islands, where it has no enemies. One ornithologist is stated to have recorded as many as 48,000 birds crossing from the mainland during the hours of 4.30 to 6 p.m. (An estimate of this type would be made by taking up a station in the main flight path of the birds, and counting the number flying over within a given period of so many minutes.)

From the point of view of their phylogenetic relationships, marine birds fall into four main Orders of the Class Aves, but from an ecological point of view they can also be divided into four different groups according to their preferred habitat:

1 LITTORAL   birds characteristic of beaches and rocky shores—such as herons, turnstones, sand pipers, dotterel, curlews, godwits and oyster catchers.

2 INSHORE   birds confined mostly to waters within sight of land, and in some instances partly inhabiting fresh waters—such as cormorants, pelicans, gulls and terns.

3 OFFSHORE   birds ranging far out to sea, to the edge of the Continental Shelf and beyond—gannets, terns and petrels.

4 PELAGIC   birds of the high seas. Many of these only come within sight of land during the breeding season —tropic birds, petrels, shear-waters and penguins.

Whilst most of the smaller shore birds seen on the beaches of the cays and islands are seasonal migrants from the north, a bird well-known to all visitors to the various resorts is the Reef Heron, *Egretta sacra*. The two colour phases of the reef herons may be seen out on the reef flats at low tide, stealthily stalking their prey of small fish, crustaceans and molluscs. Although the white-plumaged birds appear to predominate in tropic seas, they mate indiscriminately with the dark, slate-grey birds, building a nest of a platform of small sticks high up in the trees.

The Silver Gulls, *Larus novaehollandiae*, with the slender, bright red legs and red bill, are scavengers along the beaches, as well-known on the mainland coast as on the inshore islands.

The Terns are perhaps the most numerous of the sea birds of the Barrier Reef Islands, at least six or seven species being commonly found. The largest are the Caspian Tern, *Hydroprogne caspia*, which usually breeds only in isolated pairs, and the Crested Tern, *Sterna bergii*, which breeds right down to more southern waters and is one of the commonest species seen on the islands and eastern coastline of Australia.

Like the Bridled Tern, *Sterna anaetheta*, it nests in depressions in the sand or among the coarse tussocks of grass, and both these species may be found congregating in their thousands. However, the Bridled Tern is not commonly seen south of the islands of the Capricorn and Bunker Groups.

Black-naped Terns, *Sterna sumatrana*, Little Terns, *Sterna albifrons*, and Roseate Terns, *Sterna dougallii*, are sometimes seen on some of the cays and islands. Michaelmas Cay, east of Cairns, is a near-shore breeding ground of the Sooty Tern, *Sterna fuscata*, and it is to be found there in enormous aggregations, often with two or three nesting pairs on each square yard of sand among the sparse tussock grass. This species is also found on the remote cays of the Swain Reefs and out in the Coral Sea, where colonies in excess of 100,000 birds have been reported.

Whilst the Sooty Tern nests on the bare open sandy areas of remote cays, the Common Noddy, *Anous stolidus*, often found nesting in association with it, is not at all restricted in its choice of a nesting site, and its single egg may be found anywhere from bare shingle to quite elaborate nests in trees.

The beautiful and dainty White-Capped Noddy, *Anous minutus*, in the absence of vegetation, will nest on the ground, but it normally breeds in the trees, especially amongst the dense *Pisonia* forests of the coral cays, where its untidy nests are to be seen in thousands. The nest is usually made of the dead leaves of the *Pisonia*, glued together with excreta into a flat sort of platform on which the single egg is precariously laid.

The sight, sound and smell as one approaches a breeding colony of any of these birds on a small island are breathtaking, a most unbelievable cacophony of sounds, with excited birds screaming in protest at the intrusion, yet gamely holding their ground when young chicks are present.

To watch the graceful terns among a shoal of fish is sheer delight, as they dive swiftly and neatly into the water. The White-capped Noddies are surface feeders unlike many of the terns, and at sea they fly about in small flocks skimming just above the waves.

Another summer visitor to many of the vegetated cays is the Mutton Bird—the Wedge-tailed Shearwater, *Puffinus pacifus*. Beginning in the month of October, as dusk falls, the birds come in from the sea in their thousands, making their way into the centre of the island, where they have their burrows among the *Pisonia* trees. These tunnels may be anything up to 6 feet in length and here, at the end of the burrow, the bird lays a snow-white egg, rather the shape and size of a small hen's egg. Because of the intensive undermining, walking among the *Pisonia* trees is a hazardous procedure.

As darkness falls, it is suddenly as though the demons of hell were let loose! The courting of these birds, the ghostly, weird and most deafening caterwauling which begins and continues interminably throughout the night, can only be appreciated by those who have experienced it. Standing among the trees one is likely to be bombarded on all sides as small black objects come hurtling in. Without a torch, there is every possibility that something soft and living may be crushed underfoot. But with the first light of dawn, the foraging partners silently set out to sea. Peace reigns for another day. On land this bird appears clumsy and apparently stupid. On the wing the shearwater is one of the most graceful of all sea birds, effortlessly gliding over the tops of the waves in its search for the small planktonic creatures on which it feeds.

Two larger species of sea birds which nest on the more remote islands thoughout the province are the Brown Gannet, *Sula leucogaster*, and the white Masked Gannet, *Sula dactylatra*. The Brown Gannet, often referred to as the Brown Booby, is the more commonly seen as it also

The Golden Orchid of north Queensland is found on trees and rocky slopes of many of the Barrier Reef islands—*Dendrobium discolor* growing on the top of Lizard Island.

The colourful Convolvulus is one of the most characteristic creepers found on islands and cays throughout the Barrier Reef, (*Ipomoea brasiliensis* (pes-caprae)).

Reef Herons returned from fishing, Green Island.

The Reef Heron, *Egretta sacra*, white phase.

Zonation of vegetation as seen on a coral cay — coarse grasses *Casuarina equistifolia*, *Argusia* and large *Pisonia* (background).

Several species of terns frequent the shores of the isolated Bramble cay in the far northern region of the reef.

Brown Gannets, *Sula leucogaster*. Fairfax Island, Bunker Group.

White-capped Noddy, *Anous minutus*, on its nest of dead *Pisonia* leaves. Heron Island.

Masked Gannet, *Sula dactylatra*, with newly hatched chick.

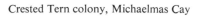

Crested Tern colony, Michaelmas Cay

frequents the inshore waters and islands in the non-breeding season. Booby Island, to the west of the Prince of Wales Channel in Torres Strait, was so named by both Captains Cook and Bligh, independently and unknown to the other. The number of boobies found there today has greatly diminished.

These large birds with their long wings and powerful bills are amongst the most magnificent divers of all birds. From heights of 60 to 100 feet, they plummet down with folded wings, hitting the water with great force, seldom missing their prey. A gannet is recorded as having been caught in a fish trap set at a depth of 80 feet of water at Norfolk Island.

These gannets breed on remote cays of the Swain Reefs, on Raine Island (Map V), which is a bird sanctuary, on Bramble Cay, and on the cays out in the Coral Sea, where a third species, the colourful Red-footed Gannet, *Sula sula*, is also found nesting.

Another sea bird, which normally breeds on isolated islands far out in the ocean, has been discovered, within the last 10 years, breeding on cays of the Swain Reefs. This is the Lesser Frigate-bird, *Fregata ariel*. The Frigate-birds —or Man of War Birds—are a pan-tropical family of about five species of different size and colour pattern, but with very similar habits and habitats. Despite their extraordinary powers of flight frigate-birds have been described as being of a sedentary nature, since they are normally never seen far from their island homes. These birds, pirates of the Pacific skies, as they have been called, are legendary among the islanders of the Central Pacific. On the Gilbert and Ellice Islands, in particular, they have been kept as captive pets by island chieftans.

The Frigate-bird is the most buoyant flying machine among the birds, having the greatest wing area in relation to its body weight. Its long, narrow, pointed wings, up to seven feet in the largest species, and long tail, are perfect instruments for high speed manoeuvres, as well as for the effortless soaring of its incomparably graceful and elegant flight. The Frigate-bird apparently never deliberately enters the water. Its preen gland is very small, quite insufficient to yield enough oil for water-proofing its feathers, and its plumage quickly becomes water-logged. In nature these birds inhabit windy situations for if grounded in a sheltered position, they seem helpless and unable to rise, quite off-balance with their huge wings and short legs and light body.

Flying fish and other small fish, jelly fishes and molluscs are picked up from the surface waters with a swift movement of the sharp hooked bill whilst the birds are in flight. But, as one of their common names implies, they also have hawk-like tendencies. It is a dramatic sight to watch these birds on the hunt. Fiercely they swoop on

Frigate bird colony, Gillett Cay, Swain Reefs.

Young Ospreys on nest, North Barrow Island.

terns and gannets, literally forcing the smaller birds to disgorge food they have just caught, then diving on it before it hits the water.

Because of the difficulty in taking-off, the Frigate-birds, especially the larger species, usually nest in trees, but the large colony found on Gillett Cay in the Swain Reefs, is on the sand among the low bush and tussock grass. Only during cyclonic weather are these birds seen nearer the mainland and inshore islands, wheeling in circles high in the sky.

In the Northern Region in places where there is little or no permanent habitation, the large nests of the Osprey, *Pandion haliaetus*, may be found, some up to 6 feet in height, composed mainly of sticks with a layer of seaweed on the top. The same nest is apparently used year after year. Some birds choose fallen trees on isolated islands, the forks of mangrove trees, or even the platform of an automatic lighthouse. They breed during the winter months and by October the young are almost ready to leave the nest.

Young Silver Gull, *Larus novaehollandiae*. Its bill and legs will turn red in the adult stage.

The Wedge-tailed Shearwater, *Puffinus pacificus*. Its burrow entrance is among the roots of the *Pisonia* tree.

Over thirty nests in this photograph give an indication of the density of the White-capped Noddies breeding on a coral cay in the summer months.

The sea birds frequent many of the cays and shingle banks of the reefs throughout the year, as roosting places at night, and during the breeding season one or other parent remains with the chick until it is able to fend for itself. But with the sea turtle, the story is very different. Only the female comes ashore, and she stays only long enough to lay her eggs. Thus only a few hours may be involved before she returns to sea, leaving her eggs dependent on the forces of nature for their development.

Three species of marine turtles which occur throughout the world's tropical seas are common in Barrier Reef waters. The small omnivorous *Eretmochelys imbricata* is more plentiful in the north and breeds on the inner shelf cays. The beautiful 'shell' (carapace), is usually less than three feet with a mottling of olive, dark brown and black and the plates of which it is constructed were once the 'tortoise-shell' of commerce.

The much larger Loggerhead turtle, *Caretta caretta*, which may weigh up to 328 lbs, is carnivorous and more abundant in southern reef waters and breeds each summer in large numbers on some of the Capricorn cays.

But the species most often seen, both ashore and at sea, is the Green Turtle, *Chelonia mydas*. This herbivorous animal is the most widely distributed of the marine turtles, being found in the tropical waters of the Atlantic as well as in the Indian and Pacific Oceans Owing to the delicacy of its flesh, it has suffered very severe predation by man, and there were once turtle canneries on Barrier Reef islands such as Heron and North West in the Capricorn Group.

The female turtle comes ashore at night, and laboriously heaves her huge body up the sandy beach, leaving behind a tell-tale track by which she is easily located. It is painful to watch her struggles, her ungainly movements in the soft and shifting sand of the sloping beach, especially if one is familiar with the speed and grace with which she swims in her natural element. Provided she is undisturbed—she should only be watched from a distance until after egg-laying—she will proceed to make a shallow depression large enough to hold her body, by flailing her front flippers, flinging sand in all directions. Then, using her hind flippers, one after the other, she proceeds to dig a hole about a foot deep, lifting out the sand meticulously with the cupped flipper. When it is deep enough she inserts her tail into the hole and proceeds to drop her eggs, about the size of a ping pong ball, with a flexible but tough 'shell', anything from 50 up to 200 at a time. The eggs are then carefully covered over with sand swept into the hole by the hind flippers. After this the turtle twists her body around, heaping up the sand to camouflage the presence of the nest still further before making her way down the shore again to the sea. With perfect timing she may come ashore on a very high tide, and reach her

Young Loggerhead turtle, *Caretta caretta*, aged 16 months. Heron Island, August 1971.

Hawksbill turtle, *Eretmochelys imbricata*. Heron Island.

Green turtles, *Chelonia mydas*, mating. Wistari Reef.

Green Turtle hatchlings, Heron Island, May 1969.

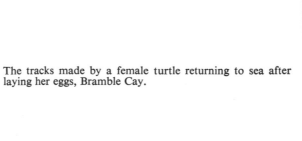

The tracks made by a female turtle returning to sea after laying her eggs, Bramble Cay.

nesting site on top of the bank with little trouble. She is then faced with a long trek back on a low tide, sometimes across wide areas of beach rock where she may get caught tight among jagged crevices.

Depending upon whether the eggs have been laid in a sunny or shaded spot, incubation takes between two and three months, after which the young turtles emerge from the sand and make their way to the sea. Experiments carried out with newly hatching turtles in the Caribbean indicated that they invariably turned towards the area of brightest light, which would naturally be the open sky above the sea—at least on all islands where vegetation backs the nests. This was demonstrated on Heron Island in May, 1969, when a batch of turtle hatchlings emerged from a nest which had unfortunately been made in an area of thick vegetation cover with no clear patches. The tiny turtles scattered in all directions, lost in their attempt to reach the sea. They were even found flapping their way into a number of the tourist cabins from which they were rescued and put in the water.

Predation at this stage in the life of the turtle is very high. Should they emerge during daylight hours, which they occasionally do, they fall prey to the ever-watchfull seagull scavengers.

At night, the hordes of Ghost Crabs attack them, and for those which do reach the sea, the reef sharks and other enemies are always on the lookout. It has been estimated that probably very few out of every thousand turtles hatched survived to breed. It is believed that the female turtle will return to the beach of her birth when it is her time to lay.

The Great Barrier Reef green turtle populations may be the last of the world's great green turtle herds, most of the others having been grossly over-exploited as they were hunted for their meat, oil, skin and shell.

At the present time the Queensland National Parks and Wildlife Service is conducting a large scale ecological study throughout the Barrier Reef Province, with principal study sites at Mon Repos, near Bundaberg on the Queensland coast, Heron and Raine Islands. Tagging programmes commenced in the summer of 1964-65 have shown that sea turtles are slow growing animals, taking many decades to reach maturity. Their feeding grounds are widely dispersed from nesting beaches to which they migrate with great accuracy. Most turtles may only breed for one season in their lives but in that one season each will lay many hundreds of eggs.

Green turtles coming ashore to lay. Raine Island, December 1974.

Female turtle returning to sea after laying—5.30 a.m. Heron Island, December, 1962.

The few females that do return to breed in later seasons return after a two to five year absence, each returning usually to the same beach or small island where she last nested.

In contrast, very little is known of the underwater life of the turtles, and the Great Barrier Reef Province is proving to be an ideal place for such a study.

So, as data accumulates with this long-term programme, more and more facts will emerge which will help in elucidating the life history of these fascinating animals.

Other reptiles such as small lizards and monitors are found on some of the continental islands and near-shore islands in the Northern Region. On occasion a sea snake may be washed ashore after cyclonic weather otherwise they are very rarely seen on land. They are quite common in the more northern waters, and round the far-out reefs, either lying or swimming in the surface waters or among the reefs. The sea snake is easily distinguished from other snakes by its flattened tail.

Sea snakes are often seen swimming on the surface waters in the more northern parts of the Reef Province and among the far offshore reefs. This grey species, *Aipysurus laevis*, was washed ashore on a coral cay after a storm. The flattened tail characteristic of all sea snakes is easily seen. There are several small clusters of stalked barnacles, *Lepas anserifera*, along the body and round the head.

Horizontal zonation across the reef flat has been described in connection with the shelf edge reefs, and those of low wooded isles on the inner shelf of the northern and central regions. As would be expected, it is also to be seen on the various reefs on which the sand cays are found and, especially on the marginal shelf reefs of the southern region, the basic picture differs from the two above.

It is more appropriate to describe this zonation starting from the inner rather than the outer edge of the reef since beach rock is as much a feature of the coral cay itself as of its reef. Bands of beach rock are characteristic of many of the present-day more stabilized vegetated cays, and are found along the shore line at about high neap tide level, between the sand beach and the lower level reef flat. Although more usually to be found on the windward side of the cay, beach rock may also be present on the lee as on Low Isles, and also at Heron Island where large, very distinctive bands are to be seen on both northern and southern shores.

Beach rock is a feature of the intertidal zone of the world's warmer seas and was first noted off the Brazilian coast by Charles Darwin during his voyage in H.M.S. *Beagle*. The first description of its occurrence within the Great Barrier Reef Province was given by Professor Beete Jukes, the naturalist on board the surveying vessel, H.M.S. *Fly*, who paid particular attention to this structure and speculated as to its origin.

Beach rock is formed by the cementing together of the calcareous sand and accumulated debris of the reef under certain physical conditions. The actual process of lithification varies, but the height of the water table on the cay and its temperature appear to be important factors necessary for the formation of beach rock by the binding of the particles by calcite. Typically beach rock forms as bands of horizontal slabs which vary in their size and the degree of consolidation. At the upper level, the band is very friable, and the consistency is such that the 'rock' can almost be broken off by hand. It is composed mainly of coarse sand grains with fragments of shells and small pieces of coral skeleton. Below this level, the band is a very much harder and more durable limestone formation, with jagged projections, and often very much pitted and difficult to walk on. At its lowest levels where it merges into the reef flat, the rock tends to be smoother and softer, often very slippery with an algal covering.

Cyclonic activity and general erosion may remove considerable amounts of sand from a beach, exposing layers of beach rock which have formed beneath it, or they may obliterate an existing band, blotting it from sight with a cover of encroaching sand. Once established, the surface of the beach rock becomes coated with small microscopic algae and marine lichens. Sometimes quite distinctive bands can be discerned from upper to lower levels, the colour-

Beach rock formation, S.E. shore of Heron Island, showing the horizontal bedding, the pitted and eroded central band, sloping down to almost horizontal rock at its lowest level adjacent to the reef flat.

The green alga, *Caulerpa racemosa*, Heron Island. Resembling clusters of small grapes, it is one of the most conspicuous seaweeds on many flat reefs.

Encrusting coralline algae, pinkish-mauve in colour, form a cement-like cover on the coral rubble of the reef—in many cases far stronger and much more solid than the living colonies of corals which surround it. The most commonly occurring species is *Porolithon onkodes*.

The brown alga, *Turbinaria ornata*, a common species on coral-rubble boulders on the reef flat. Here it is surrounded by species of green algae.

ation being in part due to the constitution of the algal cover. The uppermost band consists mainly of blue-green algae such as *Entophysalis deusta* and *Calothrix crustacea*, and the dark lichens, *Verrucaria* and *Arthopyrenia*, and the general appearance of the rock is usually a dark grey-black.

Below this there is a narrower band, whitish to pale pink in colour which is also dominated by a microscopic blue-green algal mat made up of several different species, together with small patches of red and green algae. At the lowest levels of the beach rock, the larger red alga, *Gelidiella*, and the green algae, *Enteromorpha* and *Cladophora* may predominate. This is a generalized picture as seen on beach rock on Heron Island in the Capricorn Group, but although it may vary, even along a band on a single shore, this type of zonation is to be expected on most beach rock areas.

Since this region is liable to much sand abrasion caused by wind and wave action, its associated animal species are not numerous, especially when measured against comparable rocky intertidal areas on the mainland, or on continental islands, and during daylight hours they may be quite inconspicuous. They are, however, quite distinctive, and though population numbers may vary considerably in different localities, the species remain fairly constant throughout the Province. The most important are the herbivorous molluscs, with the tiny purple-grey snails of the Family Littorinidae at the highest tidal levels, followed by *Planaxis*, two or three species of *Nerita*, small whelks,

and the large chiton or coat-of-mail shell, *Acanthopleura* (Chapter VII), and small crabs. The two latter kinds of animals are much more obvious by torchlight at night, owing to their cryptic habits. Careful observation in the lower bands will also reveal that the surface may be covered with numerous fine scratches which have apparently been caused by the teeth of the herbivorous fish as they graze on the minute algae coating the beach rock. In experiments conducted at the Marine Station at Heron Island, trapping was carried out to determine the types and numbers of fish feeding in this area when the beach rock was covered at high water, and it was found that the greater number of fish present were all algal feeders.

Areas of beach rock and reef platform were protected from browsing fish as controls during the experiments. Over a period of two years intensive trapping not only led to smaller catches, but there was a noticeable improvement in algal growth near traps, indicating that the removal of fish was effective in this regard.

Although the beach rock may occur as an isolated strip higher up on the sandy beach, in general the lowest level merges into the reef flat. The differences between the cays of the Northern and Central Region reefs and those of the Capricorn and Bunker Groups out in the open ocean at the southern extremity of the Province, have already been stressed, and this difference is even more marked on the reefs themselves. On the Northern Region reefs, there are extensive areas of sand flat and algal-

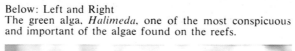

One of the more conspicuous and most easily identified of the seaweeds on many reef flats, is the brown alga, *Padina gymnospora,* with its fan-shaped thalli.

Below: Left and Right
The green alga, *Halimeda,* one of the most conspicuous and important of the algae found on the reefs.

The green alga, *Codium spongiosum,* is found growing beside coral rubble on the reef flat and on the sides of deeper pools along the reef edge.

The brilliant green of the alga, *Chlorodesmis fastigata,* commonly known as 'Turtle weed', makes it easily recognizable on the reef flat.

Above
Found attached to the undersides of large boulders, the shining green vesicles of the alga, *Valonia ventricosa,* make it easily recognizable.

The sea grass, *Thalassia hemprichii*, sometimes referred to as 'Dugong weed', covers large areas of the sandy flat on some reefs. Large numbers of *beche de mer*, (species of the black *Holothuria*), some covered with sand grains, may be seen lying on the flat, feeding on the organic detritus in the sand.

'Micro-atolls' of the coral, *Porites lutea*, on the fringing reef which connects Lupton and Haslewood Islands.

covered rubble areas, with little or no living coral growth on the reef surface. And this applies equally on the established cays of the Central Region (Figure 3). These are all Inner Shelf reefs. But on the western marginal shelf of the southern region (Figure 2), the zonation is very clearly discerned, especially in aerial view. Between the algal rim of the reef crest and the sand cay, there are typically three fairly clear-cut and distinctive zones of the reef flat, and these are easily recognized even from the shore. The size of the reef, its height above sea level, its relation to wave action, and the presence or absence of a lagoon within its borders, will of course, mean that the zones will vary from reef to reef which may be visited. The region nearest the sand cay is usually a flat with patches of dead coral boulders, thickly covered with various species of brown and green algae, under which

many sand-dwelling species of animals seek shelter.

On some reefs, sea grasses of various species, such as *Thalassia*, a marine plant widely distributed on coral reefs throughout the world, play an extremely important role on the flats, for not only do their leaves and stems slow down water movement but their roots aid in the deposition of sediments and the whole weed mat acts as an effective agent in preventing erosion. It also forms an ideal habitat for many of the reef animals especially the holothurians (Ch. VIII) and certain species of molluscs.

Where water remains over the reef flat at times of lowest tides, colonies of living corals are often found, more especially those species which have become adapted to withstand a certain amount of silt in the water, and also the much higher and more variable temperatures which are to be found there. 'Micro-atolls' of the massive species of *Porites*, which grow as a flat-topped mass which dies as it reaches the level of low water, but continues its horizontal growth, are very conspicuous on the sandy flats of many of the reefs, their colours varying from yellow and brown to mauve. Other corals which survive as small or sometimes quite large colonies here are species of *Goniopora* (very easily identified, since it is one of the few species of corals in which the polyps are expanded during daylight hours), *Goniastrea*, *Pocillopora*, and the massive, blunt-tipped *Acropora palifera* (Chapter V). The other more obvious animals seen here are the stromb shells which are often mistaken for cone shells, and various species of holothurians (*Bêche-de-mer*), more especially the black *Holothuria*, which has a habit of partially covering itself with sand.

Seaward, this sand flat merges into a zone of boulders and dead corals. Though this may appear as a very barren region with little or no animal life, the undersides of large boulders will be found with enormous populations of minute animals, either as single individuals or small colonies. Large boulders, two or three feet high, will be seen to be covered with oysters and barnacles, and often the large chiton of the beach rock zone. These boulders provide the only available rocky substrate at the right tidal level for these particular animals and they are not found elsewhere on the reef flat.

Beyond the dead coral region the rich zone of living corals and deep coral pools are to be found flourishing in the slight protection of the reef crest. The slender branching *Seriatopora*, *Pocillopora*, the foliose and encrusting species of *Montipora*, and several species of the staghorn coral, *Acropora*, are amongst those most commonly found.

Only visible when skin-diving, or from glass-bottomed boats on days of good visibility, the reef face sloping down to the sea floor surrounding the reef, appears as a series of terraces, with coral colonies and coral debris in varying proportions, but the uppermost few yards of the slope—the reef edge—are visible and even approachable on foot on many of the reefs on days of low spring tides and calm weather. Here one is able to see the very characteristic spur and groove system typically developed on the windward side of these reefs. These are the regions of vigorous coral growth in nutrient-rich, highly oxygenated water, and here in these surf-dominated zones of the reef, the many species of staghorn coral, *Acropora* are to be found in a magnificent array of form and colour.

Chapter 4

Continental Islands and Near-Shore (fringing) Reefs

The high, continental or mainland islands which are found in the greatest numbers in the Central and Southern Regions of the Great Barrier Reef Province, on its Inner Shelf, present a varied picture along their coastlines, of rocky shores, sandy beaches, mangrove glades, off-shore shoals and Near-shore or fringing coral reefs.

As in the case of the geological structure and vegetation of these islands, the animals found in the intertidal zones of these different ecological habitats, except for those on the reefs, are similar to the species on the adjacent mainland, more especially where the islands are situated close to the coast. The distance offshore varies from approximately three to sixty miles in the different island groups. The Percy Islands of the Northumberlands are the greatest distance away from the mainland, but High Peak Island, rising vertically to 700 feet above sea level, is the most easterly (Map II).

Some of these islands, such as Magnetic just offshore from Townsville, have a number of permanent residents. Some, especially in the far north, serve as temporary abodes for fishermen. A few such as Middle Percy, are leased for farming. Well-known tourist resorts are found on perhaps a dozen or so more. Several are lighthouse stations, some with unattended automatic lights, serviced by the Lighthouse vessel and others are permanently manned.

On most coral reefs, the division of the reef flat into *zones* is a horizontal zonation from reef edge to back-reef, or reef edge to coral cay, the zones being characterized by the varying physical and biological features typical of each. On sloping rocky shores, however, in the region covered and uncovered each day by the tide, the zonation is of a vertical nature, with certain kinds of animals living at or near high water mark, and capable of withstanding long periods of exposure to atmospheric conditions and fluctuations in temperature, and adapted thereby to cope with the problems of moisture conservation against desiccation. Other animals, less well adapted for such conditions, are found lower down the shore and so are uncovered twice daily for much shorter periods. Those animals which require constantly moist conditions are found only at the lowest tidal levels. The resulting picture shows a quite distinct pattern of zonation or banding of animals on these rocky shores.

Ecological surveys along the Australian coasts have shown that certain species of animals and plants are characteristic of these various vertical tidal bands, remaining more or less constant along many miles of coastline, where hydrological conditions of the sea water are similar, changing mainly with the factor of temperature (Figure 4). On the offshore islands within the Great Barrier Reef Province which have been examined, some differences both in species present and the size of the populations have been found, which appear to bear a relationship between the position of the island to the mainland, or to other islands, and exposure to wave action is considered to play an important part in this variation.

The most obvious animals visible on these sloping rocky shores at low tide, taking one of the Whitsunday Islands as an example, are a large grey barnacle, *Tetraclita squamosa*, and the oyster, *Crassostrea amasa*, both of which are encrusting species which may form distinctive bands at their preferred tidal levels.

When Charles Darwin presented his theory for the formation of coral reefs, he described the precursors of other reefs, those which fringe a coastline where conditions are suitable for coral growth. The essential requirements, as already mentioned, are tropical seas where temperature, depth and quality of the sea water are such that reef-building corals can become established, and continue to flourish.

On the more southerly continental islands, the Pine tree, *Araucaria cunninghamii*, covers many of the hilly slopes.

Steep, horizontally bedded rocky shore, Hook Island.

Continental Islands:
North Keppel Island, east of Rockhampton.

Large fringing reef, Double Island, north of Cairns.

Dunk Island and its fringing reef.

The reef which fringes the northern shore of Mer, Murray Islands. Looking down from the top of the crater rim over the recently burnt-off slopes and the Village below.

Extensive sand flats behind the near-shore Alexandra Reefs on the mainland coast between Cairns and Port Douglas.

Fringing reef along the eastern shore of the lagoon. South Island in the background, Lizard Group.

Fringing Reef, southern shore. Brampton-Carlysle Islands.

The shores along the coast of northern Australia, and the continental islands throughout the province have, in a number of cases, the potential requirements for the formation of such fringing reefs. South of the latitude of Cairns, however, these near shore reefs are not found along the mainland coast of Queensland. Here the marginal shelf reefs are widely dispersed across the Continental Shelf and this, in the first place, causes a completely different set of hydrological conditions from those surrounding the great linear formations along the shelf edge in the narrow northern region. The whole topography of the near shore zone of the central and southern regions (Figure 2), is both varied and complex owing to its shallowness, the high tidal rise and fall, the ocean swell caused by the South East Trades, and summer cyclones. Erosion, movement of sand and sediments, and the general instability of the sea floor are not conducive to successful settlement of corals.

In the northern region, however, north of Cairns, near shore reefs are to be found fringing much of the coastline, more especially in areas adjacent to deeper water. Proximity to river estuaries and mangrove swamps with their associated muddy substrate does not appear to have been a deterrent to the growth of reefs. There are flourishing corals in the vicinity of Darwin and other parts of the north coast where muddy shores and mangrove swamps are characteristic features of the coastline.

Although the fringing reefs along the mainland shores of the northern region of the province are closer to oceanic water, owing to the narrowness of the Shelf and the proximity of the outer reefs to the coast, the coral growth there today is poorly developed except on the outer margins of the reefs. The greater part of the reef surface is composed of dead coral-rubble, the coral presumably having been killed as a result of the last fall in sea level. Superimposed on this rubble are dense growths of various species of brown and coralline algae. Re-establishment of these reefs, with their closer proximity to the more turbid coastal waters, and more unstable conditions generally, has not been possible to the extent of that on the seaward reefs.

One of the most extensive and easily accessible of these near shore reefs fringing the mainland is that which extends off the coast near the mouth of the Mowbray River, between Cairns and Port Douglas—the Alexandra Reefs. Any silting or other deleterious effects from the run-off of river water in the area was obviously offset by the availability of oceanic waters when the reef was forming. There are very few reef areas to the east at this latitude which would have acted as any kind of barrier.

Along the upper shoreline behind the Alexandra Reefs, there is a fringing area of mangroves, mainly *Rhizophora stylosa*, followed seawards by extensive sand flats which merge into the rubble-covered reef proper. In pools

and drainage channels across the reef surface small colonies of living corals such as species of *Goniastrea*, *Galaxea* and *Turbinaria* (Chapter V) occur sporadically, with a greater number of small Faviids occurring as the outer edge of the reef is reached.

Among the mangroves, crabs of the genus *Sesarma*, are the dominant animals and occur in large numbers, making their burrows among the prop roots of the *Rhizophora*, and, on the trunks of the trees, often right up among the branches above high water mark, the littorinid snails, *Littorina scabra*, are found. When the tide is out and large stretches of sandy flat are uncovered, the whole area may be dotted with small mounds—worm-like piles of sand—the result of feeding activities by a species of holothurian (sea-cucumber, or *beche-de-mer*), which burrows down to a depth of about 10 inches. Starfishes, *Archaster typicus*, lie partially buried in the sand. Often it is only the star-like shape of the covering sand which indicates their presence, and the attractive small blue Soldier crabs, *Mictyris*, scuttle about on the surface. Radiating pellets of sand indicate the feeding activities of the Sand Bubbler crab, *Scopimera inflata*.

On the reef flat itself, although at first glance a place barren of all animal life, one may find innumerable crustaceans and molluscs—in the pools, among weed and under dead coral boulders. The most obvious and aggressive inhabitants are the swift-footed swimming crabs of the genus, *Thalamita*, whose bright blue claws, held high in a defensive manner, readily distinguish them. They are extremely common all over the reef flat as are the equally fast-moving mantis shrimps, *Gonodactylus chiragra*. Cone shells and other molluscs are to be found but because of the easy accessibility of these reefs to the main coastal road, their numbers are rapidly diminishing.

In the central region of the province, near shore reefs, although absent from the mainland coasts, are to be found round a number of the islands such as those of the Cumberland Group. Exposed coastal situations on the windward side of these islands would normally be the place to look for such reefs. In the vicinity of the Whitsunday Islands, however, reefs are prevalent on the western leeward sides of several of the islands. This region is in the vicinity of the highest tidal range of the Province, and added to this, there are deep channels with swift currents flowing through them, and the combination of these factors result in a great interchange daily of well-oxygenated ocean water.

Living corals are found, often as extensive and flourishing colonies on reefs which are just offshore and still submerged during periods of low water, round many of the continental islands. On others, however, living coral is restricted to the outer edges only of these near shore reefs, the greater area of most being

Looking down over South Molle and Daydream Islands. Whitsunday Group.

The Alexandra Reefs, just to the south of Port Douglas, are typical of the near-shore reefs which fringe the mainland coast of the Northern Region of the Province. Small colonies of corals are found among the coral rubble which has a dense cover of various species of brown algae.

The rock oyster, *Crassostrea amasa*, covers the rock surface where there is suitable substrate at its preferred tidal level. That it can only survive a certain amount of exposure to air is indicated by the sharp 'cut-off' at the top of the band.

The Brachiopod, *Lingula*, at the top of its burrow in the sandy mud at Yule Point, behind the Alexandra Reefs.

The large grey barnacle, *Tetraclita squamosa*, occurs on the more sheltered sides of continental islands.
The rock oyster, *Crassostrea amasa*, massed on the top of a large coral boulder. Low Isles.

On the sand flats backing Alexandra Reef worm-like castings covering extensive areas, are made by a curious holothurian, *Paracaudina chilensis*. These animals, found in similar localities round the northern coastline, are typical of soft sandy-mud flats where they lie buried below the surface, but with their oral and anal apertures level with it. Sand is ingested, the organic material removed as food, and the remainder discarded and passed out as the worm-like coils.

Typical rainforest vegetation of Northern Queensland. Similar vegetation is found in small pockets on some of the continental islands offshore, as in the deep ravines on Lizard Island. Russell Island, south of Cairns, is densely wooded with such trees and vines.

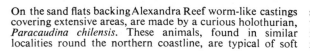

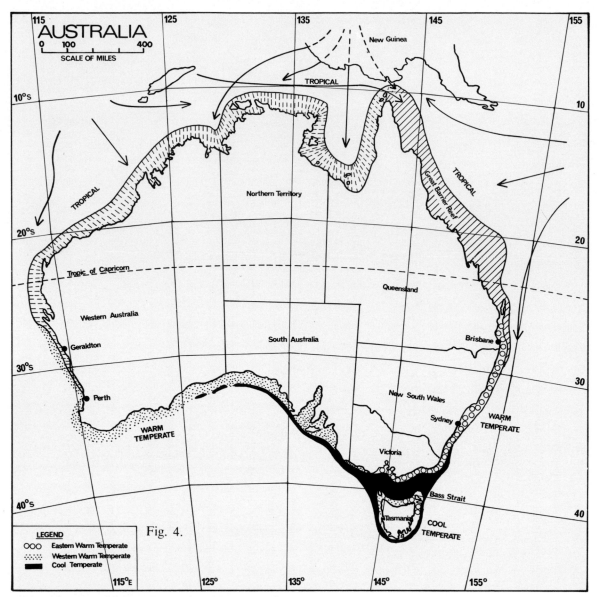

115 AUSTRALIA 125   135   145   155

0   100   400
SCALE OF MILES

10°S   10

New Guinea

TROPICAL

20°S   20

TROPICAL   TROPICAL

Northern Territory

Tropic of Capricorn

30°S   30

Western Australia

Geraldton   Queensland

Great Barrier Reef

Brisbane

Perth   South Australia

WARM
TEMPERATE   New South Wales

Sydney   WARM
TEMPERATE

Victoria

40°S   40

Bass Strait

Tasmania   COOL
                         TEMPERATE

LEGEND
ooo Eastern Warm Temperate
     Western Warm Temperate
     Cool Temperate

Fig. 4.

115°E   125°   135°   145°   155°

4. The Biogeographical regions round the Australian coast line, based on the distribution of the marine invertebrate animals of the Intertidal Zone. The arrows indicate the affinities of tropical species with the adjacent Indo-Pacific Region.

exposed at low tide. Where there are pools and channels, such as found on the small reef which joins Arkhurst and Hayman Islands, living corals may be seen. Otherwise the exposed reef flat will resemble that described for the Alexandra Reefs. The fringing reef which connects Haslewood and Lupton Islands to the east of Hook Island (Map III), has a few large micro-atolls of *Porites*, in slightly deeper parts of the flat, otherwise scattered Horse's Foot Clams, and crabs are the only obvious animals to be found, nor are the undersides of boulders very rich with an attached fauna. There are also reefs on Border Island, just to the north. Here again there is evidence of a once flourishing coral fauna, but today the reef is mainly dead boulders. On this reef, however, each boulder carries its population of burrowing clams, *Tridacna crocea*, and with the rising tide, this rather drab-looking reef magically becomes a riot of brilliant colour as the clams expand their large frilly mantles and begin feeding.

Extensive sand flats back many of these island

reefs. In areas near groves of mangroves, the fauna is more typically that of muddy situations, but in the sandy areas, different species of crabs such as those found at Alexandra Reefs, usually dominate the scene, with the Ghost Crab, *Ocypode ceratophthalma*, at the top of the tide line and often above it. During daylight hours, the large open burrow only is obvious. The crab is rarely seen and is difficult to dig out. But with the aid of a torch at night, many will be seen scavenging along the shore. Small creeping molluscs, tiny hermit crabs in borrowed shells, and the various sand-plough snails may be seen, the latter with the large muscular foot fully extended and pushing the animal along just under the surface of the sand. The 'egg collars' of these sand snails are familiar objects of the sandy shore. Most of these animals live on the sandy reef flats adjoining the sloping beach. And here the small burrowing bivalve, *Atactodia striata*, often occurs in great numbers. Its dead shells are strewn along the shore, but just shuffling the sand with one's foot will disclose numbers of living shells. Small pink holothurians occur in this vicinity, members of the Family Chirodotidae. The minute calcareous spicules in the body tissues of these little creatures are in the form of a perfect wheel,

designed long before man's arrival on this planet.

Further seaward in slightly moist areas of the sand flat one may be lucky enough to find a colony of Tongue shells, *Lingula*. These small animals are not molluscs, despite their common name, and are related to some of the most ancient animal forms best known from their fossil remains—the Brachiopoda. Unlike most of this group, *Lingula* lives with its stalk buried in the sandy flat instead of attached to some solid substrate, and the only indication of its presence is a number of small circular holes in the sand, in groups of three, surrounded by little piles of silt. The bivalve 'shells' are not calcareous but consist mainly of chitin, a substance more normally found in the bodies of insects and crustaceans. When undisturbed, *Lingula* lives within its burrow, the bristle-tipped tops of its valves just projecting above the surface of the sand. Food-bearing water is drawn in through the two outside holes, the organic particles filtered out, and the water expelled through the central hole.

In slightly deeper water again, the multi-branched tentacles of the anemone, *Actinodendron plumosum* may be seen, a dense mass of tiny branches, gently swaying in the current of water. This is one of the few animals on the reef flat which should not on any account be handled, since the stinging cells with which its tentacles are armed, are extremely toxic to man, and may cause a very long and painful reaction. The colour of this anemone varies through brown and greyish-blue tones, and although it looks rather flattened when seen contracted at low water, when fully covered as the tide rises it takes on the appearance of a miniature pine tree for its lower tentacles branch more widely and taper towards the centre.

Before 1918 many of the near shore reefs between the latitudes of Bowen and Mackay had rich coral faunas, together with all the species normally associated with them. Two very severe cyclones in January of that year were considered to have been the cause of great destruction. In 1925, a special examination was made of reefs in the area. Stone and Middle Islands in Port Denison (Map III), the localities where several of the photographs in Saville Kent's monograph were taken to illustrate luxuriant coral growth, were found to be completely barren. Surface destruction of corals on these near shore reefs down to a depth of 8 to 10 feet was seen in many areas, and only along some of the more favourably situated shores was there any significant sign of coral regrowth on the reef.

Since these near shore reefs exist in fairly unstable equilibrium in an ever-changing environment, it seems apparent that recurring cyclonic activity could create much localized damage, and perhaps play as important a part in preventing re-establishment of fringing reefs as a fall in sea level of a previous era.

74

But there are other damages apart from those caused by storm action. There are flourishing colonies of corals on the reefs lying just offshore at Magnetic Island, off Nelly Bay for example, and at Double Island to the north of Cairns. Today there is clear evidence of corals dying here. Over the past few years the turbidity of the surrounding waters has greatly increased, due almost certainly to the dumping of silt from dredging operations in the nearby mainland harbour. Although corals *can* cope with a certain amount of siltation, they cannot do so when it is dropped in massive quantities at one time, and layers of silt are accumulating within the lower branches of the big coral colonies. They will certainly die in a few years if this is continued.

In the northern region of the province, fringing reefs are to be seen round most of the group of continental islands lying offshore from the Cape York Peninsula (Map V). The complexity of the environmental conditions applying to southern near shore reefs is added to in this region because of the annual North-west Monsoon season with its attendant heavy rains and winds from a different direction.

In a very different situation, however, are the Near Shore reefs fringing the Lizard Island Group (Map V). Lizard Island, 14° 40′ S. and 145° 28′ E., lies only 15 miles from the mainland, but it is also only 10 miles at most from the edge of the Continental Shelf. From the 1179 foot summit of this granite island, the great wall of Shelf Edge reefs may be seen stretching as far as the eye can see to the north and south. The racing currents and tidal rips between these reefs counteract any deleterious effects from the mainland. From the top of the island the narrow band of reef fringing its eastern shore is very clearly discerned, its abrupt seaward edges outlined against the white sandy sea bottom. Looking south to the two smaller islands of the group, South to the east, and Palfrey to the west one can see the connecting reef between them, well defined with its deeper sandy lagoon in the centre.

Within this fringing reef there are several patches of corals, some of which are just exposed at low water of spring tides. The main reef-building genera of corals typical of virile reefs are to be found at Lizard Island, ranging from the delicately branching species like *Seriatopora*, to the massive species such as *Symphyllia* and *Porites*. At least 35 species of the staghorn coral, *Acropora*, have been recorded from this reef.

The most interesting of all the Near Shore reefs to be found within the whole Barrier Reef Province are, however, those which fringe the shores of the Murray Islands (Map V). These reefs are unique because, although they surround the shores of a high island, their distance from the land masses of Australia and New Guinea, and their position with regard to the

Mainland islands along the Steamer Track. Sir James Smith Group.

Algal-covered boulders on the fringing reef, Border Island.

Hayman Island, northern-most of the Whitsunday Group, as seen from the small fringing reef which connects Langford and Bird Islands.

The reef which connects Haslewood and Lupton Islands, Whitsunday Group.

Deep sandy lagoon on Fringing Reef, Lizard Island.

pure oceanic waters of the Coral Sea, place them within the same hydrological conditions as the surrounding reefs of the Shelf Edge. They lie within six miles of the seaward edge of the Shelf, surrounding the three volcanic islands of Mer (or Maer), Dauer and Waier. Mer, the largest of the group, is more or less oval-shaped, almost two miles long and a mile wide. Most of the island consists of a large crater with a smaller crater within it, the highest point being about 750 feet, on the western edge of the crater rim. Looking down from this height, the whole length of the northern coast with its fringing reef is clearly visible. Today, the greater bulk of living animals on this area of reef are Soft Corals (Alcyonarians—Chapter VI), with a narrow outer fringe of corals, mainly the staghorn, *Acropora*, along the seaward edge of the reef flat. Looking west and south from the top of the crater, the reef is seen to connect the two smaller islands.

There are deep ravines on Mer, cut by three streams which run into the sea from the N.E., E. and S.E. sides. These streams only flow during the wet monsoonal season, but since they cut through the cones of volcanic ash, the development of the reef must obviously have been influenced to a certain extent by the deposit of silt, volcanic larva and sand brought down by them.

The most luxuriant coral growth at Mer is found, as would be expected, off the S.E. corner of the Island. The distribution of coral species on the reef very clearly reflects the differing conditions of the reef environment. In the shallower, near-shore regions, affected by sand and silting and the greater fluctuations in temperature, the species occurring are those which are more temperature-resistant, and capable of removing silt.

These islands are in a region where cyclonic activity is apparently extremely rare. There are no native traditions relating to them, and no geological evidence that such occur. The result is that the corals growing on the outer windward areas of the reef flat have been considered by more than one coral reef specialist as being amongst the most luxuriant to be seen in the Pacific Ocean. In 1918, it was estimated that within an area of two miles of reef flat there were 3,600,000 coral heads.

The complete absence of huge boulders on these reefs, contrasted with the numbers to be seen on many of the reefs to the south where cyclonic activity of varying degrees may be expected annually, has been considered to support the theory that these large coral fragments *have* been tossed up on the reefs, rather than that they are the vestigial remnants of reefs formed during periods of higher sea level.

An interesting survival of by-gone days are the remains of a series of fish traps. Almost reminiscent of the fields of Cornwall in Britain, they consist of areas a hundred or so feet square,

walled in to a height of two to three feet with blocks of volcanic larva. The history of their building lies buried in the myths and legends of the islanders. The fish trap areas of the reef today support populations of molluscs such as cones and other shells similar to those found on more southern reefs, together with starfish and holothurians.

The islanders still harpoon an occasional turtle from a small craft as their ancestors did before them, diving overboard and attaching a rope to the flippers after the turtle has been harpooned, and then dragging it on board. And enormous shoals of small sardines are still to be seen along the shoreline as they were reported 50 years ago.

Native fish trap, built of small granite boulders from the near-by shore, North Barrow Island.

Friday and Prince of Wales Islands—looking S-W. from Good's Island, Torres Strait. The fish trap built of stones may be clearly seen in the foreground.

From the top of Lizard Island, north-east of Cooktown, looking south-west towards the mainland over Linnet and Martin Reefs.

Chapter 5

The Reef-Building Corals

The architects and designers, the construction engineers and builders of a coral reef are classified, zoologically, in the phylum Coelenterata or Cnidaria. This phylum comprises a large and heterogeneous group of lowly, soft-bodied animals of very simple organization which are, at the same time, amongst the most beautiful and elegant in the animal kingdom. It includes such well-known creatures as jelly-fishes and sea anemones, but it also covers very many animals which, at first sight, could well be mistaken for plants, or at least animals far removed from the delicate and colourful jelly-fishes and anemones. Amongst them are the fragile, plant-like hydroids, the sea pens, sea whips, 'soft' corals, and the stony corals.

These animals may appear, superficially, to be very different from one another but they all have a basic similarity which, in its simplest body form, is called a polyp or zooid. This has no differentiated head region, no respiratory, excretory or circulatory systems and, in transverse section through any animal within the group, there is a distinct radial symmetry in the arrangement of its various parts about a central mouth region which is the only opening (Figure 5).

Although there is great diversity in size and form to be seen among them, with an ability to adapt to very different environments in the sea, all these animals exhibit another feature in common, apart from their basic structure. This is the possession of batteries of stinging cells, cnidoblasts, in which there are capsules called nematocysts with ejectile stinging threads. With these nematocysts, of which 24 different types have been described, even the smallest, most delicate coelenterate can paralyse and so capture its prey, which ranges, among the group, from minute animals floating or drifting about in the sea water to fast swimming fish.

It was this ability to sting which led Aristotle, the Greek philosopher of the 4th Century B.C., to call the group the *Acalephe* or *Cnidae* (from the Greek: akalephe, cnidos—nettle). Aristotle considered them to be something between plants and animals, and he was aware that they could sting. Unfortunately, to the majority of the people today these animals are known only because of their reputation as stingers. Since the nematocysts, which occur mainly in the tentacles, are the animal's only means of food capture and defence, stings are inflicted by it quite unwittingly, and man, having invaded its realm, must be prepared to pay the penalty. Most stings are quite harmless, or very transitory in their effect on human beings. A few out of the great number of animals classified in the phylum are extremely painful, and two or three, including the so-called sea-wasp or box jelly-fish, *Chironex fleckeri*, can be lethal to man.

The phylum is divided into three main *Classes*, the first of which, the Hydrozoa, contains all the fragile plant-like hydroids, which are always attached to some object, as well as the solid hydro-coralline, *Millepora*, and free-floating forms such as the widespread Portuguese Man-of-War, *Physalia*, which is a creature of the surface waters of the world's oceans. This animal, so exquisite in life, is mostly known only by its stinging powers and the large floats washed up and stranded after strong winds have blown them ashore.

A second Class, the Scyphozoa, includes the different kinds of jelly-fishes, and the third Class, the Anthozoa, includes the sea anemones, the reef-building corals and their allies.

As a unified phylum within the animal kingdom, the Coelenterata has had a very chequered career in regard to the kinds of animals which have been considered as being related and therefore belonging to it. Because of the flower-like appearance of the delicate polyps found in so many of these animals they were regarded as plants by the early naturalists, and it was not until the 18th century that corals were proved to be animals, although stony corals had been described as early as 1576. It was a French surgeon, Andre de Peysonnel of Marseilles, who kept living corals in his aquaria and, basing his conclusions on direct observations, first stated that they were definitely animal in nature and not plant. Although his findings were communicated to the French Academy in 1727, and the Royal Society of London in 1753, little attention was paid to them and it was to be some years before they were finally accepted.

About a century later, the two first important works on corals were published, almost simultaneously. The enormous report on the corals collected by the United States Exploring Expedition of 1838–42 was published in 1846–49 by J. D. Dana. Dana was able to study both the hard and soft parts of a large number of corals from the Pacific Ocean, and his work was a great step forward in clarifying the relationship of many of the coelenterates.

This was followed by a number of publications, and finally a three-volume work on the Natural History of Corals by H. Milne Edwards and J. Haime. This latter work was not only a new classification of the group but it included descriptions of all the known fossil and living species of corals. Although a very considerable amount of work has been carried out on corals since that time by a small number of people, with detailed microscope studies of the structure of both skeleton and polyps, there is still a very great deal to be learnt about these tiny, fragile animals with their amazing powers of reproduction and skeleton formation.

Today, the stony corals are divided into two

The golden polyps of the little solitary coral *Tubastrea aurea*. Lady Musgrave Reef at night.

quite distinct groups, simply and easily by the important ecological difference between them. The first comprises the reef-building, or *hermatypic*, corals—which are found only in shallow, warm tropical waters. They are distinguished by the presence, within their tissues, of symbiotic algae—microscopic dinoflagellates known as *zooxanthellae*—and within their calcareous skeletons, there are microscopic, filamentous green algae, recently identified as belonging to the genus *Ostreobium*. Both these minute plants require sunlight for the processes of photosynthesis, and thus for their survival. The second group are the deep-sea, or *ahermatypic*, corals which do not possess any zooxanthellae and thus are not restricted by the necessity for light penetration. They are found over a much wider range of habitats, being known from depths down to over 17,000 feet. The reef-building corals, with very few minor exceptions, are restricted to shallow tropical waters, and flourishing growths are not found below a depth of 180 feet. Maximum reef-building takes place in depths between 15 and 90 feet. The water temperature requirement ranges between 20° C. and 30° C., with optimal growth occurring between 25° and 29° C. Within this depth and temperature range, in saline ocean waters, reef-building corals may settle and flourish wherever conditions are such that the temperature remains relatively constant, and plentiful supplies of nutrient substances are constantly replenished by highly oxygenated waters rich in calcium content. The temperature in the Caribbean Sea, and in the waters round the Hawaiian Islands is, on the average, less than that of the tropical Pacific Ocean, and this is regarded as the reason why the growth rate of reef corals in those areas is slower.

The minute, free-swimming coral larva, the planula, must find some solid substrate on which to settle, in order to grow and flourish to form reefs. The shallow, sloping shore round an island, or a submerged platform of any sort at a suitable depth on a Continental Shelf, is admirably suited for this, provided the necessary requirements are present in the sea water.

Since the word 'Coral' has been used, and misused, in so many different ways, it is perhaps necessary to define its meaning in its accepted zoological sense today. To many people, the white, bleached skeletons, too often painted in gaudy tints supposedly representing the true colour of the living colony, are *coral*. The colour, which is contained in the *living* tissues is lost when the coral is taken from the water. Once a colony dies in the sea, it soon becomes covered with a growth of various kinds of algae, or with a layer of silt, and assumes a drab brown, or greyish colour as a result. If a living colony is broken off and put into a bleaching agent which dissolves the animal tissue, and then placed in the sun to dry, one is left with a white, calcareous skeleton, sculptured in an infinite variety of forms, solid and massive, fragile and

branching, foliacious or encrusting, rivalling in their precise patterns and exquisite designs any work from the hand of man.

These skeleton-secreting coelenterates are, zoologically, the only *true* corals, and are classified in the Order Scleractinia of the Class Anthozoa. There are, however, a number of other animals which, with a prefix of some description, are commonly referred to as corals, and some of these play a part in reef-building. They have a hard or horny skeleton, but this is of quite a different composition altogether from that of the true corals. For example, the Stinging Coral, *Millepora* belongs to the Hydrozoa. The Organ Pipe Coral, *Tubipora musica*, the Blue Coral, *Heliopora coeurela*, the Red Coral, *Corallium rubrum*, which was the Precious Coral of Mediterranean Seas, the Black or Thorny Corals, the Antipatharia, all not only belong to different Orders, but in each case the skeleton retains its colour after the colony is dead. Together with the 'soft' corals, they do, however, all belong in the Anthozoa, the same Class as the true corals.

Since the earliest systematists studying corals had only dead materials, mainly dried skeletons, to work with, which were brought back to the museums and scientific institutions of Europe by various exploring expeditions, these skeletons were used as the main basis for the classification of corals. Today this situation still holds good, and it is almost impossible to be certain of the correct identification of a species without reference to its skeletal characters. If the colony is taken directly from the sea water and placed in a preserving medium, its living polyps will have almost completely retracted within the skeletal framework. It is extremely difficult, unless one has seen corals alive with their polyps fully expanded, to appreciate to the full their delicate beauty and their flower-like appearance. The colour of the polyps varies considerably with the different species, as do the shape and size, but the two latter also vary according to the state of expansion or contraction. Only in a few species are the coral polyps seen completely expanded in full sunlight.

In its structure, a single coral polyp resembles the well-known sea anemone—with one important difference—for as it grows the polyp secretes a protective skeleton of calcium carbonate in the form of aragonite, obtaining the basic salts from the sea water. The skeleton is secreted by special cells at the base of the polyp and, when deposited by a solitary polyp or a colony of polyps, is called a corallum (Figure 5). In colonial forms, the structures formed by each polyp are referred to as corallites. Each corallite usually consists of a circular wall, the theca, from which vertical partitions in the form of thin plates or sclerosepta, radiate inwards towards the centre of the corallite cavity. In some corals the sclerosepta are fused together at their inner ends and form a central

Two large colonies, yellow and pink, of the fragile branching *Seriatopora hystrix* are bordered by two colonies of the pink *Pocillopora damicornis*. Lagoon margin, Hardy Reef.

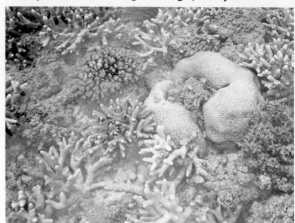

In a 'run-off' channel from a moat on Watson Island, flourishing coral colonies grow among the algal-covered rubble. Green and pink-tipped fawn *Acropora*, and two colonies of the pink *Pocillopora damicornis* surround a large Faviid coral.

Pocillopora verrucosa, Michaelmas Reef.

Three colour varieties of the foliose species of *Montipora*, together with species of Staghorn *Acropora* line the side of a deep sandy pool on the southern edge of Heron Island Reef.

These four unique photographs of stinging cells from the septal filament of the coral, *Plesiastrea urvillei*, show: 1. the threads completely coiled within the capsule; 2. at the time of discharge; 3. partially discharged; and 4. one capsule empty. The spiral barbing on the threads is clearly seen. (Magnified ×1,000).
(Photograph Dr R. B. McMillan from a preparation by the author).

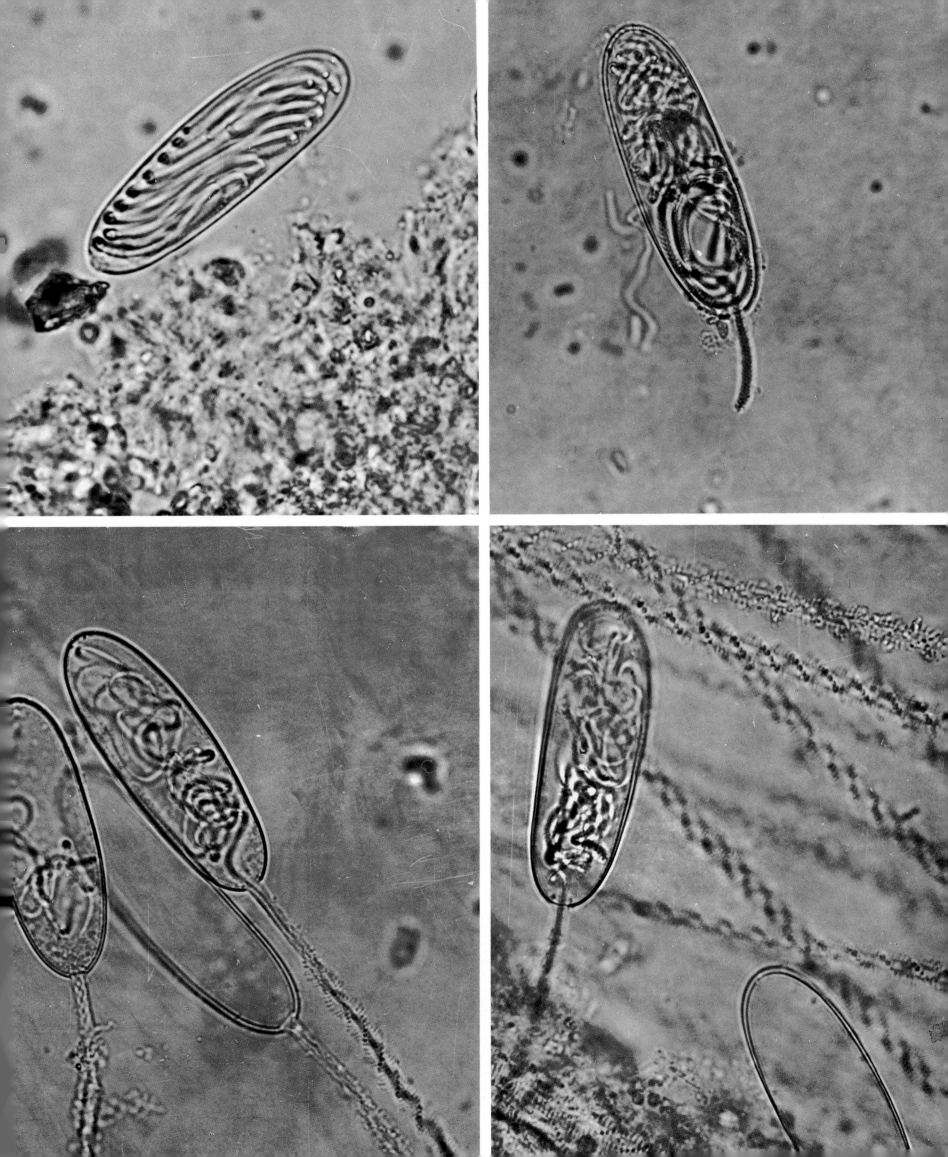

The Mushroom coral, *Heliofungia actiniformis*, is a solitary free-living species with extremely long tentacles. This photograph shows the tentacles almost completely retracted, with the mouth and a small part of the skeleton just visible. Dove Reef, Torres Strait.

Catalophyllia jardinei with its polyps fully expanded.

Staghorn corals, Wistari Reef, Capricorn Group.

Luxuriant growths of the staghorn coral, *Acropora*, along the edge of a marginal shelf reef.

Mauve *Acropora humilis*, Low Isles.

Colony of the massive coral, *Porites lutea*.

Typical 'micro-atoll' formation of *Porites lutea*, sandy reef flat, Wistari Reef.

Merulina ampliata, Wistari Reef.

Four different species of the Staghorn *Acropora* in shallow water along the edge of the reef. Green Island

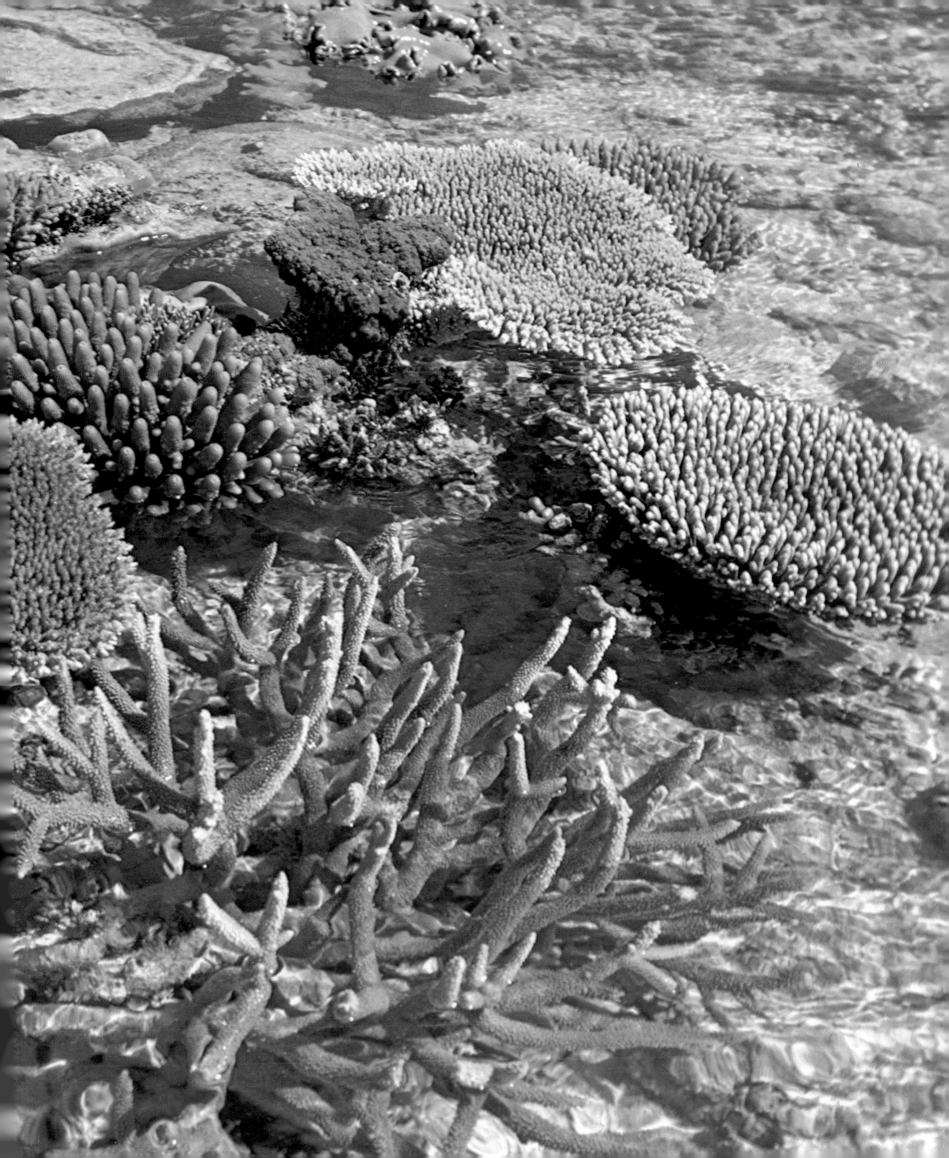

5. Diagrams to illustrate a coral polyp and its structure.
a. Single polyp of a colonial coral expanded above its thecal wall.
b. Vertical section through a solitary coral.

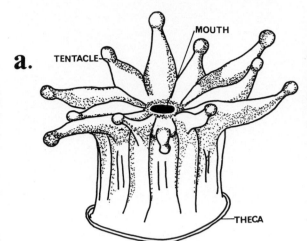

Colony of the delicate *Seriatopora hystrix*, with gall of the crab, *Hapalocarcinus marsupialis*. Heron Island.

axial structure, the columella. The upper, open end of the corallite is called the calix. Within the protective calix the polyp lies, as in a tiny cup, and it may vary in size from less than a millimetre to several centimetres in diameter, according to the species. In its simplest form, as a solitary individual, such as a cup coral, the resemblance to a sea anemone is obvious. The polyp itself is a very simple, small cylindrical structure, with a circular disc, the peristome, covering the top, in the centre of which there is a single opening, the mouth. Round this disc there arise one or more circles or rings of tentacles, either in a restricted position, or spread right across it. The tentacles vary greatly in size and number according to the coral species, but are usually in multiples of six. The outer layer of the oral disc is plentifully supplied with nematocysts and with mucous-secreting cells, both of which play an important part in the capture of prey.

The outer body wall of the polyp, which is covered with cilia, lies in contact with its protective corallum. The innermost layer performs all the functions of digestion and reproduction. The folds of this layer of cells of the body wall project into the central gastrovascular space of the polyp in a series of vertical partitions called septa—an elaborate arrangement which provides a very much greater area of cells to aid in the process of digestion. The septa are attached above to the inner surface of the oral disc and their free lower margins often bear filaments which, like the tentacles, also bear stinging cells, and may be projected through the mouth and aid in feeding. A second series of these vertical partitions arises from the base of this layer, and in between each of these soft septal folds, in the same radial pattern, there are secreted the calcareous partitions, the sclerosepta, arising from the bottom of the 'cup'. These sclerosepta are very important structures since they are still used primarily as the main basis for the classification of the stony corals into their respective families.

In the massive meandrine or brain corals, the corallites are often indistinguishable as single individuals since they tend to merge into one another. This type of skeletal growth is found in species in which there is a great elongation of the polyps, each of which develops a number of mouths, surrounded by a ring of tentacles. The skeleton is seen to consist of a complex arrangement of valleys and ridges, in which the sclerosepta are clearly distinguished, but the thecae, the walls, of the adjacent polyps have become merged into the ridges which separate the valleys. In a number of families of corals the thecal walls and other parts of the skeleton are

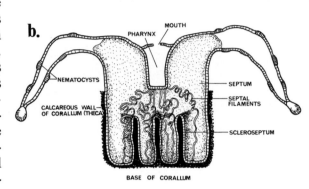

Fig. 5

Stylophora pistillata is also used as a shelter by the tiny gall crab. Heron Island.

A pink variety of *Pocillopora damicornis*, one of the more numerous species of the shallow reef flats. Heron Island.

very much perforated, so that the adjacent polyps are interconnected through pores in the thecal walls as well as lying on top of them. These are usually referred to as the perforate corals, and those whose skeletons are solid, as the imperforate. This factor, as will be seen later, plays an important part, ecologically, in the distribution of corals on the reef flat.

Whilst almost all the reef-building corals are attached, there are a few, such as the Mushroom Corals, which are free-living when adult, but attached to the substrate with a stalk when young, just like a mushroom.

Because of their ability to reproduce very rapidly by asexual means—by 'budding'—corals are predominantly colonial animals, and most of the solitary corals are deeper water, ahermatypic, species and not reef-builders. The intricate and complex structure which is the skeleton of a coral colony, is produced by these tiny polyps in the process of asexual reproduction, with each polyp budding off another individual next to it, which in turn secretes its limy skeleton, thus forming larger and larger

The tiny polyps of *Pocillopora* extended at night. Wistari Reef.

Extended polyps of a branching coral feeding at night.

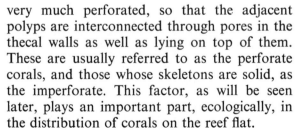

87

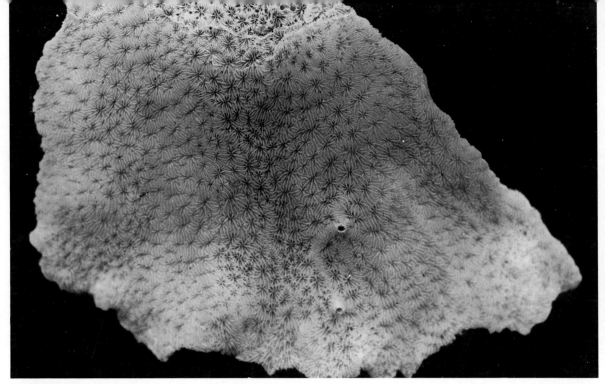

Skeleton of *Pavona*

Skeleton of *Goniopora tenuidens*.

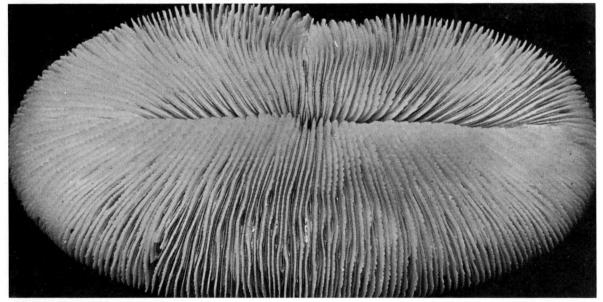

Skeleton of the Mushroom coral, *Fungia echinata*.

The extremely porous nature of the skeleton in the Family Poritidae is well illustrated in the genus *Alveopora*.

Skeleton of part of small colony of the meandrine *Platygyra*

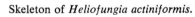

Skeleton of *Heliofungia actiniformis*.

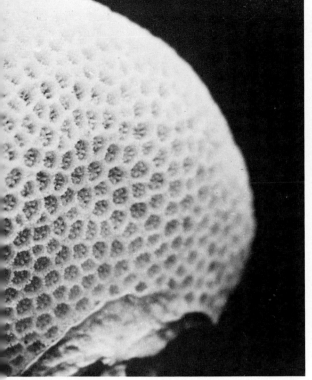

The Basket coral, *Sandolitha robusta*. This specimen from deep water off Tryon Reef, Capricorn Group measured 15 × 12 × 7 inches.

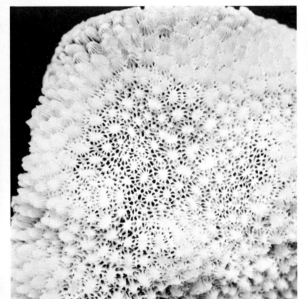

Skeleton of *Hydnophora microconos*.

Skeleton of *Hydnophora exesa*.

Colony of *Goniastrea benhami* on reef.

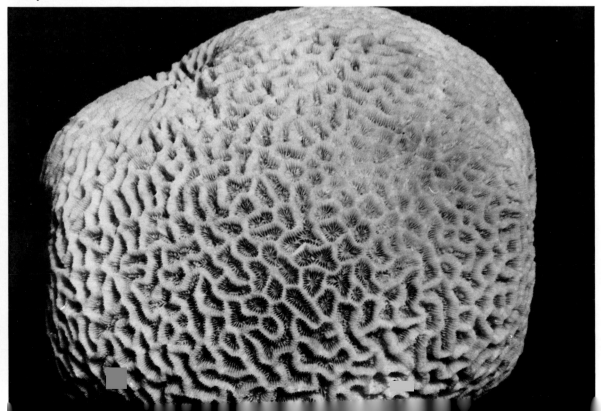

colonies as time goes on. The polyps of the colony-forming species are connected to one another laterally, the tissues of the body wall folding out over the top of the cup skeleton, and connecting with those of the adjacent polyps. Thus, in any living coral colony, all the polyps are horizontally connected with one another and lie as a thin film of living tissue on top of their protective skeletons.

In some species of colony-forming corals, the sexes are separate, and the polyps are male or female in any one colony. There is very considerable variation in the different species, for a single polyp may be either male or female at a given time, in which case the wholy colony is considered to be hermaphrodite. In other cases each polyp within the colony is hermaphrodite. The reproductive organs of the polyps are found attached to the septal folds. The polyp releases sperm freely into the sea water and some of these are eventually drawn into the body cavity of a female where the egg is fertilized. Here the tiny, free-swimming ciliated larva, the planula, is developed before being extruded into the sea. After perhaps a few days of being drifted round in the surrounding sea water, those larvae which are fortunate enough to elude predators, are able to survive provided they can find a suitable place on which to settle. If settlement does not occur within two or three days, the planulae of some species die, but others have been observed to settle after a period as long as 30 days.

In breeding experiments carried out at Low Isles by the Great Barrier Reef Expedition, it was found that in less than three weeks a planula larva had settled and produced an extra four buds surrounding the original polyp. As yet the life history is known only for a small number of species. Many years ago it was suggested by J. S. Gardiner, an English zoologist, that a regular phenomenon among some corals was for a whole series of colonies to die out after reproduction by a number of polyps of colonies of the same species in a single locality. Thus it is quite conceivable that a feature which is of normal occurrence could play a significant part in the appearance of the corals of any reef at a given time, and this appearance could easily be wrongly appraised. A very great deal is still to be learnt and verified in this regard.

Production of free-swimming larvae among the corals differs considerably. Some species breed for short periods only, others for up to six months and more. For many, nothing is as yet known. In common with numbers of other marine animals, there appears to a be close connection between the phases of the moon and the breeding cycle.

Perhaps the greatest impact on a first visit to a flourishing coral reef is one of vibrant colour. Against the intense blue of the sea with its white-capped waves, or the yellow-green of the shallower reef lagoon, are the purples and

Skeleton of *Galaxea*.

Colony of *Acrhelia horrescens* in pool on reef, Heron Island.

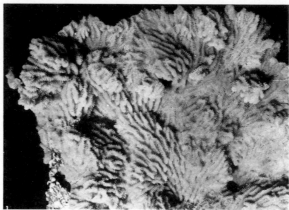

Skeleton of *Merulina ampliata*.

The elongated corallites of *Lobophyllia hemprichii*.

The beautifully sculptured skeleton of *Lobophyllia corymbosa*.

Skeleton of *Symphyllia* with the elongate corallites showing the long valleys and the position of the several mouths, and the thecal walls of two adjoining corallites merged into a ridge.

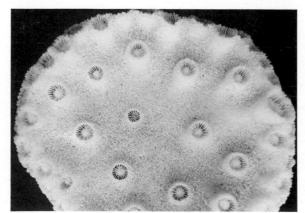

Skeleton of *Turbinaria peltata*.

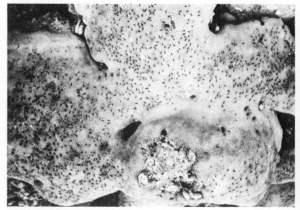

The small black marks are openings behind which there is a boring mollusc—an indication of the severity of attack to which a coral colony may be subjected.

A deep coral pool near the edge of the reef, dominated by species of *Acropora* and *Montipora*. Heron Island.

Acropora species dominate the scene taken by a diver in the Swain Reefs.

Plate *Acropora*, Lamont Reef.

 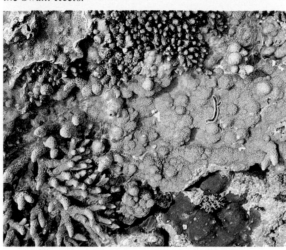  

These next eight photographs show some of the variation in shape and colour in the genus *Acropora*.

Acropora species sometimes also tend to form micro-atolls. Heron Island.

mauves, the yellows and browns of the massive coral species, the vivid greens, pinks, and yellows of the branching forms, often tipped with blue, white, pink, mauve, green and orange. The living colour of the coral colony has been traced to three different sources. Firstly colouration in the outer layer of cells is produced by fine granular matter in pigment cells, with a wide range of tints through black, red and orange. Secondly colour is sometimes indirectly caused by the red or green filamentous boring algae in the skeleton. Thirdly, the most common yellow, brown and green shades found in the reef-building corals are produced by the zooxanthellae, the minute single-celled dinoflagellates which live within the inner layer of tissue. The main function of these zooxanthellae is, however, of very much greater significance to the coral than the mere production of colour, and their presence has been the subject of controversy for more than half a century. Once it was realized that *all* reef-building corals possessed these symbiotic algae, and that the deeper the corals grew, the fewer algae were found in them, it was relatively easy to establish that sunlight and depth were correlated as operative factors for the presence of flourishing reefs.

Corals had long been known to be carnivorous. Among the experiments carried out at Low Isles in 1929, a number of physiological and growth studies were made, during which it was shown quite definitely that not only did the tentacles of the coral polyps reject anything which was vegetable in nature, but that the digestive enzymes of the animals were not capable of acting on it. At Low Isles it was noted that the corals fed on *Plankton*—the minute animals floating and drifting round in the sea water. They were, in other words, zooplankton feeders. And no evidence was found which militated against zooplankton being considered as their sole source of nourishment. Single individuals and small colonies were placed in the dark, and it was found that all the zooxanthellae disappeared—either they died or were expelled by the corals, but the colonies continued to grow without sunlight. Since the zooxanthellae as such, had never been found in a free-living state in the sea, it was considered that they were plant cells highly specialized and adapted to life within the tissues of corals, and a number of other related animals in which they had also been found. From these animals the algae not only received protection, but they also derived plentiful supplies of inorganic food as a result of the metabolic processes of their hosts. The algae liberated oxygen during photosynthesis, their chief life process, and they absorbed the waste products of the corals—carbon di-oxide in sunlight, and nitrates and phosphates at all times. Their numbers within any animal seemed only to be limited by light and the availability of inorganic food salts.

A foliose species of *Montipora* lines the side of a coral pool. Northern edge, Heron Reef.

A Faviid coral, and above it a species of *Astreopora*.

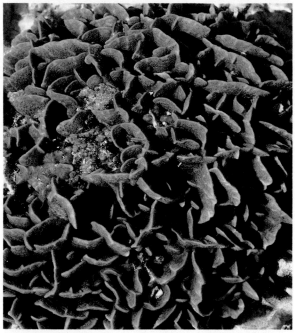

Colony of *Pavona decussata* on the southern shore of Heron Reef.

Pachyseris rugosa offshore at Magnetic Island.

Pachyseris speciosa, Darnley Island.

Leptoseris yabei, Gould Reef.

Micro-atolls of the species, *Porites andrewsi*, dominate the reef flat off the eastern end of the Heron cay.

Two micro-atolls showing two colour varieties of the coral *Goniopora lobata*. Northern edge, Heron Reef.

The Slipper fungiid, *Herpolitha limax*. Wistari Reef.

Goniopora is one of the very few corals in which the polyps are expanded during daylight hours.

Micro-atolls within a micro-atoll. *Porites lutea*, Heron Reef.

Some idea of the length of these polyps may be gained from this picture.

The Mushroom coral, *Heliofungia actiniformis*, a solitary species in which the long tentacles are often seen extended by day. Green Island.

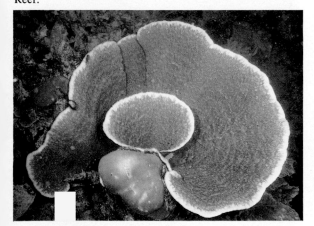

Exquisite shape of a species of *Podobacia*.

Underside of an old skeleton of the Mushroom coral, *Fungia fungites*, with a number of juveniles in various stages of development.

Thus there seemed to be substantial evidence that these minute organisms clearly benefited greatly from their association with the corals. The experiments mentioned above, however, had shown that corals could survive without zooxanthellae, so that it was difficult to determine just how the corals benefited in return, if at all. In darkness the zooxanthellae ceased to function, and this apparently terminated their usefulness to the corals. Since the association was of such universal occurrence among reef-building corals, it was felt that it must be of fundamental importance. The assumption was that the algae, by their rapid removal of waste products from the coral colony, were in fact contributing substantially to the metabolic efficiency of the corals. So this function could be extremely important to the reef-builders, if one took into consideration the complex nature of the total environmental conditions existing on a reef.

Until the publication of the Great Barrier Reef Expedition's work, tropical waters had been considered as being almost barren in their production of plankton, when compared with the colder waters of the world. And zooplankton, as the sole source of nutrition, sufficient to supply the requirements of the teeming millions of coral animals, would not have been considered as a possibility. In the colder seas of the Northern Hemisphere where, up till that date, most plankton studies had been made, there was an enormous peak of productivity in the spring months, followed by a smaller peak in autumn. However, the results at Low Isles seemed to indicate that the high temperatures so increased metabolic rates, allowing rapid development and replacement of planktonic animals in these tropical waters that, averaged over a year, the production there *was* comparably as rich as that of the colder waters.

The theory that radiant energy from the sun was the main factor restricting reef-building corals to shallow waters was accepted without question, since the importance of sunlight to photosynthetic algae was obvious. And as the zooxanthellae were clearly visible in the minute coral planulae as these were set free in the sea, this appeared to be the means by which the plant cells were 'handed on' from generation to generation of coral colonies.

It was not until the year 1955 that any query arose as to the validity of the second important finding of the Expedition, that zooplankton was the sole source of food supply of the massive reef-builders. A comprehensive analysis in 1944 had summarized the animals in which the zooxanthellae, the ' imprisoned phytoplankton' of tropical seas, occurred. Apart from the reef-building corals, they had been found in many of the other animals associated with coral reefs, such as the Foraminifera, sea anemones, soft corals (Chapter VI), and especially in the large clams of the Family Tridacnidae (Chapter VII). It was suggested that, since this association was

of such widespread occurrence, it might perhaps be attributed to the great competition on the part of the plants for the limited supplies of nutrient salts in these tropical waters, and so far as the animals were concerned, to the greater survival value owing to increased nutrient for the large clams, alcyonarians and others which were known to actually ingest their symbiotic algae. And, in the case of the reef-building corals, to the increased metabolic efficiency given to them by the rapid removal of their waste products.

After World War II, about 1946, the United States of America chose a remote group of atolls in the Pacific Ocean to test the effects of a nuclear explosion on the surrounding environment. In order to have comparable data, a comprehensive survey of the whole area was to be made, both before and after the explosion, so that a correct assessment of the total after-effects of the bomb could be gained. And so began the large scale studies on coral reef ecology which are still continuing today.

It is historically interesting that the islands chosen for the tests were the atolls visited in 1817 by von Kotzebue's Expedition to the South Seas during 1815–18 in the ship *Rurik*. From his observations on these islands, the naturalist on board, von Chamisso, was to put forward the first theory regarding the formation of atolls. The Marshall Islands, in the north Pacific Ocean, represent a unique community of coral atolls, situated thousands of miles from any large land mass, and exposed throughout the year to a steady one-directional, wind-driven current of oceanic water.

A large book and a long list of publications have already resulted from the work carried out on these islands. One extremely interesting fact discovered was that around an island there is a relatively closed local circulation of water which is controlled by local climatic variations. This could act as a very important conserving mechanism since it would restrict the dispersal of larval stages of the various reef animals, keeping them within the vicinity of the reef. This certainly appeared to be the case, since the biologists working at Bikini Atoll discovered that many of the planktonic animals found within the lagoon were not taken in the open ocean waters, except where there was a strong current flowing off a reef. Numbers of oceanic forms were, however, found to be concentrated in the lagoon. It is not difficult to appreciate how important, biologically, such a restricting mechanism would be in the case of an isolated reef, in order to ensure the stability of the populations of the various reef animals.

As a result of productivity studies carried out on Eniwetok Atoll, two biologists, in summarizing their work, suggested that corals, previously shown to be purely zooplankton feeders, *did* in fact, receive the greater part of their nutrition from their symbiotic algae. Their data indicated that in any coral colony there was actually a

greater amount of plant tissue than animal, and secondly, that there was *not* enough zooplankton in the surrounding barren ocean waters to have supported the huge mass of living corals which had developed and flourished there. It seemed very evident, therefore, that the algae must be involved in some way in supplying nutrients to their hosts.

This suggestion had indeed been made many years earlier, but the Great Barrier Reef Expedition's findings appeared to rule it out completely, so that an alternative reason for their presence had to be found. As is so often the case, scientific findings are inherently only progress reports and it becomes necessary to reassess them as new data becomes available.

The work at Eniwetok immediately sparked off further controversy and zoologists set to work in an endeavour to test the new theory using the most modern techniques available. In the first experiments, a sea anemone, known to contain symbiotic algae, was treated with radioactive isotopes which, when traced, appeared to indicate that there *was* an actual transference of material from the algal cells to the tissues of the anemone. It was not necessary, therefore, for the anemone to have ingested the plants at all. And if this were the case, there was every reason to assume that the reef-building corals could also derive nutrition from their contained algae.

Since 1958, when the results of this first experiment were published, a considerable amount of further work has been carried out with the aid of electron microscope techniques, both in Japan and the University of the West Indies. There appears no doubt that many organisms benefit from the photosynthetic productivity of their associated algae. But there is considerable variation, both in the digestive ability of many of the reef inhabitants with regard to their symbiotic algae, and also in the amount of nutrients received from them.

At the same time the experiments with the anemone and its zooxanthellae were published, scientists working at Jamaica were studying the growth of corals from a different viewpoint, that of skeleton formation. Radio-active calcium was used in order to trace the development of the coral skeleton which is not chemically quite the same composition as the carbonate dissolved in sea water. A suggestion had previously been made that there was some chemical exchange between the oxygen liberated by the symbiotic algae and the carbonate deposited by the corals in their skeletons. And the results of these experiments in the West Indies left little doubt that deposition of the skeletons was very materially aided by the presence of the algae. The isotope tracers certainly indicated that the skeletal carbonate was partly derived from metabolic processes and not directly from the sea water.

More recently, a detailed study in Hawaii of

A ' micro-atoll ' in the making, *Porites lutea*, Heron Island.

Turbinaria mesenterina, Rudder Reef.

Boulder regions of a reef may seemingly be devoid of life. The underside of a dead coral boulder showing luxuriant growth of sheltering species—Bryozoa tube-worms and compound ascidians, Heron Island.

The Basket coral, *Sandolitha robusta*, from a deep pool, Undine Reef.

Encrusting orange sponge hydroids and ascidians on the underside of a boulder, Green Island reef.

the development of the skeleton of the coral *Pocillopora damicornis*, a species widely distributed on reefs of the Great Barrier, has shown the presence of microscopic amounts (0·1%) of three organic compounds in the skeleton, one of which is a transparent matrix of chitin. Results indicate that synthesis of chitin depends on the activities of the zooxanthellae, and that the rate of chitin synthesis controls the rate of skeleton formation in the coral.

Slowly, year by year, the picture becomes clearer, although there is a need for far more experimental work. However, it seems impossible to over-emphasize the significance of the role played by these zooxanthellae in the living corals, if one adds the nutritional value to that of their part in the production of the skeleton. They must be considered to have been one of the major factors permitting the extensive growth and evolution of reef-building corals. The growth rate of corals differs considerably with the species, and also with the situation of the colony relative to the reef edge and highly oxygenated water. Water temperature, food supply and reproductive activity are important factors in the growth rate. Branching and foliose forms, and corals with very porous skeletons, like *Porites* grow very much faster than the solid massive species such as the brain corals. Upward growth has been estimated to average 25·6 mm. per year, but this would occur only under optimal conditions and possibly for only part of the life time of a particular species. Any reef as a whole would grow much more slowly.

Although both temperature and depth determine the original presence of a coral reef, once such a structure has begun to grow, a great number of other factors have to be taken into consideration, as having influenced the reefs as they are seen today. Not only does the coral grow outward and downward, thus increasing the size and shape of the reef, the latter being moulded by prevailing winds and currents, but it also grows upward. As mentioned in chapter III it will continue to do this until it reaches a level where it is exposed to air during periods of low water, when it will eventually die off on top. This results in a wide expanse of reef flat, all more or less at the same tidal level—an extremely important point to remember when out on the edge of a reef. Once the tide begins to flow again, most of the reef will be covered at the same time. To be caught out on the edge of a reef under these conditions can be very dangerous, especially if walking into the direction of the sun, for swift tidal currents make it impossible to be certain of one's foothold among the coral.

Corals, by their initial capacity for the buildings of reefs, have created an extremely wide variety of habitats over which the temperature and quality of the sea water—its oxygen, calcium and nutrient contents—will vary considerably. These habitats range from the open front face of the reef, to large and

Another slipper coral, *Polyphylla*, with its short tentacles extended. Heron Island.

One of the Honey-comb corals, *Favia lizardensis*.

A close-up of *Favia pallida*.

Leptastrea purpurea, Nara Inlet, Hook Island.

Favites complanata, Michaelmas Reef.

Favites abdita, with its conspicuous green oral discs of its polyps.

A species of *Goniastrea* Lizard Island.

As commonly seen on shallow reef flats, *Favites* colony. Michaelmas Reef.

small, deep or shallow lagoons and pools, and the differing substrates of the reef flat. To all of these, in the process of their evolution, corals have become adapted. It was at one time considered that they could only survive in very clear water, free of sediment. But these animals are highly specialized for its removal by means of the minute cilia which cover their bodies. Today, a number of species are found growing in quite muddy situations. Others have now become adapted to living in very shallow waters on the reef flat where temperature and salinity fluctuations may be extreme. The salinity of tropical waters in which reef corals have attained their maximum development is about 36 parts per thousand. Very few observations have been made on the salinity tolerance of corals but it is known that species like those of the genus, *Acropora*, the staghorn corals, which are very sensitive to temperature fluctuations, are unable to withstand a rise in salinity of only 4 parts per thousand for 12 hours, whereas many other species could stand at least a rise of 12 parts for the same period. Many are also able to tolerate a considerable drop in salinity for periods up to 24 hours, although, with the coincidence of low spring tides and continuous heavy rain during cyclonic storms, many reefs have suffered severe damage.

Other corals are found in the more strictly intertidal zone where problems of exposure and desiccation are added to the already complex nature of their environment. Structurally and physiologically they have become adapted to it. Ability to withstand exposure to air is related to the porosity of the skeleton and this has been shown to differ between the corals which are normally found growing out on the exposed reef face and those on the inner reef flats.

In any study of corals the whole reef as a marine community must be taken into consideration. It must not be forgotten that, although the coral polyps are the original founders of any reef, they are assisted in their construction work, as already mentioned, by the encrusting, lime-secreting coralline algae, which have played such an extremely important role in cementing and consolidating it. Apart from the zooxanthellae, there are the filamentous algae found within the calcareous skeletons of the corals. Brown and green algae use the dead coral as places of attachment, and their spores, with those of the coralline algae, compete with the corals and other attached species for space.

In its composition a reef is a conglomerate mixture of living and dead animals and plants, and a living reef today may be only a thin veneer, perhaps a few feet in its greatest thickness, estimated to represent less than 10% of its total mass. The greater bulk, in its final analysis, is composed of the dead remains—all the coral fragments, and coral sand and boulders, the skeletal remains of the multitudinous numbers of other animals and plants which, through geological time, have been part of its evolution to the stage at which it is seen today.

Should this surface cover of living corals be badly damaged or killed, the situation may change dramatically, for all the associated animals, invisibly bound to their coral realm, vanish and the picture is one of a drab grey desert of silt and rubble.

The corals themselves, once a reef has become established, form only a small percentage of the total number of species comprising its fauna. Not only are there hundreds of species of fishes, crustaceans and worms for example, which use the corals purely for protection, but there are fishes, starfish and worms which feed on the living tissues of the corals. There are a number of animals which bore into the corals, weakening their structure, such as sponges, worms, molluscs and echinoderms. Every available kind of habitat on the reef has been made use of by one species or another, whether free-living, attached, symbiotic or parasitic.

Apart from the minute, free-floating plants, the phytoplankton, the food supply in the sea surrounding and covering the reef is made up to a large extent of the planktonic larval stages of very many of these reef inhabitants themselves. A knowledge of the breeding, life-cycle, growth and behaviour patterns of all these interdependent organisms is essential in order to assess which of these form the greater bulk of the populations, and to establish their relationships to one another, and to the environment as a whole.

Very little is known of the factors which influence the settlement of the larval stages, the planulae, of the corals, or any of the other attached species of animals on the reef, although it has been noted that coral planulae bearing zooxanthellae move towards light, which would indicate that new growths do thus have a means of settling in positions of most favourable light. Experiments with barnacles, molluscs and tube-building polychaete worms indicate that light, water movement, and the previous settlement by the same species are all factors in the settling activities of their free-living planktonic stages. Usually the species present of each of these three groups of animals selects its own discreet tidal level. On the edge of a coral reef, and where water movement is always greatest, one may find at least half a dozen different species of coral within the space of a square metre, all competing in what *appears* an identical habitat. The next square may be composed of an entirely different set of species again. Why this should be so is one of the many questions awaiting an answer.

There is a very delicate balance between constructive and destructive forces on any reef. The greater number of reef organisms have become highly adapted to the complexities of their surroundings, but if one vital factor in the environment exceeds the limiting range, or some mass calamity occurs, the whole living reef may be in danger of extinction. Increases due to normal growth of the various members of the reef community, and the building up of skeletal remains by the coralline algae, are offset both by physical agencies such as cyclones, and by biological agencies. Boring organisms—algae, sponges, worms, molluscs and echinoderms—cause weakness and eventual breakdown of coral colonies, or parts of them. But one man walking across a reef of living *Acropora* could cause more damage in half an hour than any of these animals in a year! Cyclones are unpredictable, both in the time and direction of their occurrence. Many years may elapse with no damage. One storm, especially if it should coincide with low water and come from an unusual direction, may wipe out half a century of growth.

It has been estimated that a *normal* wave breaking against the windward side of a coral reef dissipates half a million horsepower! Yet it is to windward that the virile growth of corals is always found, stimulated by the surging waves with their high oxygen and calcium content and nutrient-rich water. The flourishing outer slopes of the reefs have withstood the battering of all but the fiercest storms. And growing there one finds not only the solid, massive species which one might expect, but also the stout branching staghorns which allow the force of the water to dissipate through them. The corals of the genus *Acropora*, which thrive in these areas, are known to have the highest rate of oxygen consumption and are amongst those most readily killed by heat or cold, and most sensitive to salinity fluctuations. Yet at least 300 species of this genus have been described from the Indo-Pacific Region and on the reefs of the Great Barrier they account for perhaps 80% of the corals of surface reefs, with 89 recorded species. Many of these are now being proved to be growth forms rather than different species. Dense growths of certain species of *Acropora* flourish in the relatively quiet waters at some distance below the reef crest, away from the influence of the stronger wave action.

Tough, massive forms, especially the porous species such as *Porites*, are found in the shallow moats where conditions are perhaps an even greater challenge to their survival. Free-living species such as the Mushroom corals of the Family Fungiidae are found either in pools or lagoons, or in the deeper waters off the reef edge where wave action is negligible. Fragile, branched and foliose species are typical of the more protected back-reef areas or the margins of the reef lagoons.

In the light of the accumulated knowledge of almost another century and a half, it is perhaps fitting to quote here the words of Charles Darwin, brilliant thinker and keen observant naturalist, written in his Journal on April 6th, 1836, during his first visit to a coral atoll—Cocos Keeling in the Indian Ocean—an historic

Meandrine corals on the edge of the reef flat. Heron Island.

Leptoria phrygia, Hardy Reef.

Unusual patterning on a colony of the meandrine *Platygra lamellina*. Heron Reef.

Platygyra zelli, Lizard Island.

A micro-atoll of the delicate *Echinopora lamellosa*.

Echinopora lamellosa, Heron Island.

A colony of the massive *Acropora pallifera* with *Galaxea fascicularis* below it.

Galaxea astreata, Heron Island.

One of the most beautifully sculptured of corals, *Acrhelia horrescens*. Heron Reef.

Cyphastrea sp. Lizard Island.

Montastrea valenciennesi, Lizard Island.

The Horse's tooth coral, *Lobophyllia corymbosa*. Heron Island.

occasion to prove of great significance to Darwin's future work:

> ' The ocean throwing its waters over the broad reef appears an invincible, all-powerful enemy; yet we see it resisted, and even conquered, by means which at first sight seem most weak and inefficient. It is not that the ocean spares the rock of coral; the great fragments scattered over the reef, and heaped on the beach, whence the tall cocoa-nut springs, plainly bespeak the unrelenting power of the waves. Nor are any periods of repose granted. The long swell caused by the gentle but steady action of the trade wind, always blowing in one direction over a wide area, causes breakers, almost equalling in force those during a gale of wind in the temperate regions, and which never cease to rage. It is impossible to behold these waves without feeling a conviction that an island, though built of the hardest rock, let it be porphyry, granite, or quartz, would ultimately yield and be demolished by such irresistible power. Yet these low, insignificant coral-islets stand and are victorious: for here another power, as an antagonist, takes part in the contest. The organic forces separate the atoms of carbonate of lime, one by one, from the foaming breakers, and unite them into a symmetrical structure. Let the hurricane tear up its thousand huge fragments; yet what will that tell against the accumulated labour of myriads of architects at work night and day, month after month? Thus do we see the soft and gelatinous body of a polypus, through the agency of the vital laws, conquering the great mechanical power of the waves of an ocean which neither the art of man nor the inanimate works of nature could successfully resist '.

Intensive collecting of coral by specialists has never been carried out over a wide range of reefs within the province, so it is not possible to state with any degree of accuracy the number of species to be found in these waters. The number represented in the collections of various scientific institutions is completely misleading, because those recorded for any particular locality will almost certainly be a reflection, partly of the amount of time spent there, and partly of the number of people involved in collecting, and their ability to realize the significance of differing growth forms of the corals. The final form of many of the mature coral colonies may be greatly influenced by the environment, especially where they are growing in crowded conditions, and it is often difficult to decide whether a given colony is a separate species or merely a variation in growth form of another. A colony near the exposed surface of a reef may have a short, stunted appearance whereas the same species growing free on the side of a deep pool may have long delicate branches.

A number of animals have been found to be specifically associated with one or another group of corals, but until the systematics of the corals are correctly understood it will not be possible fully to elucidate the complex problems of reef ecology.

In the literature, two authorities mention approximately 350 coral species recorded for Barrier Reef waters, belonging to about 60 genera of reef-building corals, which represents almost 75% of the genera known for the entire Indo-Pacific region. The number of species is known to fall off very significantly with increasing latitude and lower sea temperatures, but three quarters of the total Barrier Reef species are to be found in the Capricorn Group, almost at the southern-most limit of the Province.

Of the genera recorded, only about 25 play a really significant part in reef-building in Barrier Reef waters, and they have been illustrated in these pages.

On a first visit to coral reefs within the Great Barrier Reef Province generally, one should know and appreciate something of the requirements of the reef fauna as a whole. Luxuriant growths of living corals must be sought on the far seaward edges and deep pools along the edge of a reef, or the outer margins of a lagoon within a reef, not on a sandy or algal flat near a cay or larger island. Each part of the reef, be it deep coral pool, shallow sandy flat or mangrove glade, seaward slope or beach rock, has its own particular association of plants and animals, adapted to live under a given set of habitat conditions. Though there may be a certain amount of overlap, especially with the more mobile species, nevertheless, if one is interested in finding any particular species of animal or plant living on the reef, it is essential to understand something of its requirements in the environment.

Too often, a visitor expecting to see magnificent coral growths is bitterly disappointed. He does not realize that there are hundreds and hundreds of acres of dead boulder tracts, that it is possible to walk for miles at low tide along many of the reefs within the province without even seeing any

Shapely colony of *Echinophyllia* sp. Torres Strait.

Colony of the large brain coral, *Symphyllia cf recta.*

The coral, *Euphyllia glabrescens*, with polyps extended. Batt Reef.

coral at all, unless the correct zones are sought.

Beauty may *only lie in the eyes of the beholder. But it is there, everywhere among the fascinating reefs scattered over that vast expanse of sea, for all who have the eyes, and the soul, to see it.*

Since the above was written, the Australian Institute of Marine Science has been established at Townsville, and very extensive surveys, specifically of corals within the Province have been made by biologists specializing in this group of animals. Living coral colonies have been studied and photographed *in situ*, side by side with examination of their skeletons in the laboratory.

Four large monographs have already been published by the Institute (Veron *et al*, 1976-82) and work is still continuing, together with ecological and taxonomic studies of many other groups of associated reef organisms.

The last decade has, therefore, seen perhaps the greatest increase in our overall knowledge of the reefs, their fauna, flora and geological structure, since their original discovery.

Pectinia paeonia.

Mycedium tubifex.

Delicately fluted skeleton of Pectina.

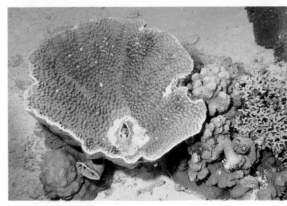

Colony of Turbinaria. Wistari Reef.

The diver's light attracted large numbers of small plank-tonic animals to the coral Clavarina triangularis. The response by the searching tentacles of the coral was in-stantaneous. Lady Musgrave Reef.

Numbers of Polychaete larvae met the same fate by the Mushroom coral, Heliofungia actiniformis. Lady Musgrave Reef.

CLASSIFICATION of the more important genera of hermatypic corals found in the Great Barrier Reef Province:

PHYLUM **COELENTERATA (or CNIDARIA)**
CLASS **ANTHOZOA**
SUB-CLASS **ZOANTHARIA (or HEXACORALLIA)**
ORDER **SCLERACTINIA**
SUB-ORDER **ASTROCOENIIDA—**
Family Thamnasteriidae
Genus *Psammocora.*
Family Pocilloporidae
Genera *Seriatopora, Stylophora, Pocillopora.*
Family Acroporidae
Genera *Acropora, Montipora, Astreopora.*
Family Agariciidae
Genera *Pavona, Pachyseris, Leptoseris.*
Family Siderastreidae
Genus *Coscinaraea.*
SUB-ORDER **FUNGIIDA—**
Family Poritidae
Genera *Goniopora, Porites, Alveopora.*
Family Fungiidae
Genera *Fungia, Podabacia, Herpolitha, Polyphyllia, Sandolitha, Heliofungia.*
SUB-ORDER **FAVIIDA—**
Family Faviidae
Genera *Favia, Favites, Goniastrea, Leptastrea, Plesiastrea, Leptoria, Platygyra, Echinopora, Hydnophora, Cyphastrea, Montastrea.*
Family Oculinidae
Genera *Galaxea, Acrhelia.*
Family Merulinidae
Genus *Merulina.*
Family Mussidae
Genera *Lobophyllia, Symphyllia*
Family Pectinidae
Genera *Pectinia, Oxypora, Mycedium.*
SUB-ORDER **DENDROPHYLLIIDA—**
Family Dendrophylliidae
Genus *Turbinaria, Tubastrea*

Chapter 6

Coral Reef Animals

Protozoa, Sponges, Coelenterates, Marine Worms and Crustacea

In the preceding chapters, brief mention has been made of some of the animals found on the coral reefs, and the complexity of the reef environment has been stressed. The immense diversity of the animal fauna in terms of number of species, and the ecological relationships between the component members represent both a fascination and a challenge to the marine biologist.

Unfortunately there is no list of the fauna of Great Barrier Reef waters, for on no reef has there been a comprehensive survey of *all* the animals associated with it, carried out scientifically and systematically by experts in the different groups. Large collections of some groups and the more obvious species of others have been made sporadically in isolated localities throughout the province by expeditions and by individuals. Museums, both in Australia and overseas, are over-crowded with specimens —possibly duplicated over and over again—all awating someone to study them. There are not enough trained zoologists in the world today available to work on the identification of some of these animals, many of which require detailed anatomical dissection and a knowledge of their growth forms, before their correct status can be ascertained.

One cannot name any one animal in the whole region, about which the full details of its life history, ecological relationships and geographical distribution are known. Much more attention has been paid to some groups of animals than to others. Some reefs have been almost completely denuded by collectors. This applies in particular to the molluscs. Both because of the intrinsic beauty of their shells, and their commercial value, these animals have suffered very heavily, especially on the more accessible reefs. In many instances the shells have found their way into private collections, large and small, across the world, and often because of the lack of data accompanying them, much of their scientific value has been lost.

The animals described and illustrated on the following pages represent only an infinitesmal part of the whole, but they are amongst those most easily seen, and so have been selected in the hope that they may give some indication of the diversity, the exquisite beauty of colour, form and design to be found among the marine inhabitants of the Great Barrier Reefs.

PROTOZOA

The minute, single-celled animals grouped together in the Phylum Protozoa undoubtedly occur in their billions on the coral reefs. The microscope reveals a new and undreamt of world in a handful of sand grains. But there is one group which is obvious even to the naked eye. The Foraminifera, usually referred to as forams and sometimes as "Star sand", occupy a singularly important place among the animals of the sea. They differ in two respects from most of the other Protozoa—firstly in their range of size, and secondly, in the possession of a ' shell ' or test. This is not a protective outer cover as in the case of the snail's shell, for it is more an internal skeletal structure except that there is living material both inside and outside the ' shell '.

Whilst there are perhaps only about a thousand species of forams living today, over 50,000 have been described, many of them as fossils. Their presence in cores drilled from reefs, and also from continental areas, is extremely important to geologists, as evidence of former sea level. They play an even more significant role for the petroleum geologist, who studies them to identify the materials through which he is drilling in order to locate the buried sedimentary layers which may contain the petroleum deposits he is seeking.

It has been estimated that there are millions of square miles of the abyssal ocean floor covered with foram shells which, in most species, are composed of calcium carbonate. These shells have come from planktonic forams which, when living, floated round in the surface waters of the sea. After death the tiny shells slowly drifted down to the depths where, over millions of years, they have accumulated as layer upon layer of sediment. So numerous is one species that it has given its name to great areas of deep sea sediments which are referred to as '*Globigerina* ooze'.

In shallow waters, on reefs and in coral sand, living forams may be found in enormous numbers. They range in size from less than half a millimetre to two or three centimetres. Some are just visible to the naked eye, closely resembling grains of sand, whilst others are extremely conspicuous, lying on the algal rubble of a reef flat. Hundreds may be found attached to a single clump of the alga, *Halimeda*. A handful of sand from a pool on the reef, when looked at under a lens, may be seen to be composed almost entirely of forams. On Bramble Cay (Map V), on a calm day, the tide-lines conspicuously left by each wave ripple on the sand were made up of shells of forams. On the sea floor of the Continental Shelf they are even more numerous. Here they are the dominant group of animals and again they are extremely important to the geologist in the interpretation of the bottom sediments.

The beautiful and delicate little shells have various structural arrangements internally, often with thin translucent walls containing minute perforations through which the proto-

The large foram, *Marginopora vertebralis*, as it occurs on the algal flat, Watson Island.
Numerous small forams of several species are often found attached to the alga, *Halimeda*.

plasm can pass. Many have tiny projections all over the shell during life, but these are usually broken off as the dead shells are rolled about by the waves. Some of the planktonic forms have long delicate spines and these again are invariably lost when the animal dies. There is great diversity in the shape and sculpturing of the shell which may be round and flat, globular, oval or star-shaped, elongated or tapering, or spirally coiled like a miniature snail.

When forams are feeding, the protoplasmic matter outside the shell is extended as thread-like processes which surround the food particles. These may be minute algae such as diatoms, or the living or dead forms of other tiny animals. They may even cluster on larger decaying animals ingesting small particles from these. And in their turn, in the complicated food web in the sea, they are consumed by bottom-dwelling animals such as the Holo-thurians (Chap. VIII) which pass considerable amounts of sand through their bodies, removing any organic matter in the process.

SPONGES

Sponges are among the more conspicuous organisms to be seen on some of the reefs of the Great Barrier which are exposed at low tide, but because of their inanimate appearance they are seldom recognized, even today, as living animals. Yet sponges have been well-known since the days of the ancient Greeks and Egyptians, and sponge diving must have been one of the earliest recorded industries of the Mediterranean Sea.

Like many of the other lower invertebrates without obvious animal features they were, until about a century ago, considered to be some type of plant growth. It is understandable that the early naturalists, with no microscope to aid them, were confused by the complete lack of any visible animal characteristics, a similar consistency throughout, and no internal organs of any kind. For a sponge fundamentally consists of a mass of living cells loosely held together by various means, and perforated by many small pores through which water may freely pass. And from the sea water the sponge obtains its food, filtering out the living and dead organic matter.

Sponges are sessile animals growing attached to a submerged substrate of some kind just like a plant, or anchored in the sediments of the sea floor. They vary in size from less than an inch to large masses several feet across. There are places where great beds of them flourish—long, slender and graceful, shapeless masses or delicate cylinders. They may be found as encrustations, thick or thin, where they may cover large areas on the sides of intertidal rock pools, under over-hanging boulders, in under-water caves, or under boulders on the reef flat where they occur as vivid splashes of colour, all the hues of the rainbow. Coloration may be due

to pigment cells or to the symbiotic algae within their tissues.

When torn from their anchorages by storm waves, and washed up among the flotsam and jetsam strewn along the shore, they may be recognized by their similarity to the once familiar bath-sponge. But the 'sponge' washed up on the beach, or the commercial sponge of the pre-plastic era, is only the skeleton, the framework, which supported the mass of cells which were the living animal. The classification of the sponges as a group of animals is based on the composition of this skeleton, which may consist of a tangled network of threads or fibres of a substance called spongin—the soft, durable sponges of commerce belong in this group. In the greater number of sponges, however, the body is strengthened and supported by many thousands of minute spicules composed of either calcium carbonate or silica. In some sponges both spongin fibres and silicious spicules may be found. The spicules are only visible with the aid of a microscope and are found in an infinite variety of shapes and sizes, exquisite in design. Depending upon the species of sponge, they may be arranged in a definite pattern, or scattered throughout the tissues.

Apart from being important in the classification of the phylum, sponge spicules are of value also to the palaeontologist, since they are amongst the most ancient animal remains, and their presence in cores drilled from great depths in the earth, tells its own story.

To the casual observer most living sponges appear rather drab, often slimy, inanimate objects, so completely unresponsive to the touch that it is difficult to accept them as living animals. Yet it has been shown that a small sponge little larger than a finger is capable of ejecting a thousand times its own bulk of water in an hour—a ton of water in eight days! This animated pump is just as efficient as a sieve for as the water streams out from the larger openings which may be seen on its surface, other water enters through all the minute pores covering the surface of the sponge, and in the process food particles are filtered out.

Although sponges have no separate body organs to carry out their various life processes, and are very simple in their structure, they are, nevertheless, unique in the porous nature of their bodies and the aggregations of cells which sustain them. The name of the phylum—Porifera—the 'pore-bearers' derives from the enormous numbers of pores to be found covering the living sponge.

The small pores on the surface of the sponge lead directly to the interior in thin encrusting forms or, depending on the species, into a series of canals of varying complexity. The interior of the sponge, or the walls of the canals, are lined with special flagellated 'collar' cells, each of which has at its free end a minute whip-like flagellum, surrounded by a collar of protoplasm.

Clusters of tiny vase-shaped sponges of the genus *Sycon* are sometimes found under boulders on the reef flat.

One of the more brilliantly coloured sponges which line the sides of caves over the reef edge.

Large brown 'cushions' growing among the seaweeds and coral rubble on the reef flat are the sponge, *Jaspis stellifera*. This sponge is bright yellow internally. Capricorn Islands.

The sponge, *Dysidia herbacea*, grows among coral and rubble on the surface of the reef flat. Heron Island.

The water currents throughout the body of the sponge are created by the beating of these microscopic whips and water is driven out through the excurrent openings, thereby causing water to enter through the small pores. The collar cells filter the food particles and the products of digestion are picked up by special wandering cells (amoebocytes), and distributed throughout the sponge, whilst the spicules and spongin fibres are laid down by a different set of cells again.

A most intriguing thing about these apparently highly specialized cells is that they are interchangeable in their functions. Sponges have been completely broken down to their component cells by passing them through a sieve and it has been found that isolated cells come together again, rearrange themselves and, under the proper environmental conditions, will continue to grow to form a new sponge.

Sponges are able to reproduce both by sexual and asexual means and possess great power of regeneration of their tissues. This has been utilized to good purpose by the sponge fishermen who have used the trick of cutting commercial sponges into small pieces and later collecting them when they have grown to marketable size. If the sponge is cut, leaving the base attached to the rocky substrate, this can grow again also to form a new sponge.

With the exception of three small families found in fresh water, all other sponges are marine. Mainly they are found from the intertidal zone down to a depth of 20 to 30 fathoms, although the so-called glass sponges range down to the ocean depths.

A large number of organisms from bacteria and microscopic algae or single-celled animals to worms, crustaceans, molluscs and echinoderms are found living in association with sponges. Some animals merely seek shelter whilst others take advantage also of the circulating water to obtain their food. These are, in other words, commensal forms which neither benefit nor harm their hosts. Zooxanthellae, symbiotic dinoflagellates, already described in corals, are also found in sponges, where they play a similarly important role, utilizing the nitrogenous and other waste products of the colony, removing carbon dioxide, and releasing oxygen which the sponge can use. At times enormous numbers of a single species of animal have been recorded from one sponge colony. Over 16,000 snapping shrimps were counted from a sponge a few feet in diameter. From a sponge as small as the palm of a hand we removed over 2,000 tiny polychaete worms.

Although sponges are susceptible to disease (a fungal blight almost wiped out the valuable fishery round Florida just after the peak year of 1938, when the annual production of commercial sponges was 1,750,000 lbs), they have few known enemies. Certain molluscs and a fish or two are known to feed on them, but

'Fire weed', *Aglaophenia cupressina*, growing in a coral pool.

The delicate, easily recognizable stinging hydroid, *Lytocarpus philippinus*, is found in deeper water over the reef edge.

Colonies of the tiny hydroid, *Cytaesis niotha*, are found on nassariid shells crawling on the sandy flat at low water. N.E. end Heron Cay.

their spicules would act as a deterrent to most animals.

They are, however, capable of causing considerable damage. Sponges of the family Clionidae bore into other animals and investigations in the Caribbean Sea have shown that the whole ecology of a Jamaican coral reef population, the movement of reef sediments and the structure of the reef edge, were all strongly influenced by boring sponges, which had caused considerable breakage among coral colonies. The very common West Indian sponge, *Mycale laevis*, on the other hand, has been found on these same Jamaican reefs, living in close association with corals on the reef slope. This sponge encrusts the lower sides of reef corals which grow as flattened colonies in more dimly lit reef areas, and the association is apparently beneficial to both animals.

Whereas in the West Indies approximately 300 species of shallow-water sponges have been recorded, the sponge fauna of the Great Barrier Reef Province is almost unknown, since little systematic collecting of this group has been done. Most of the species so far described are found throughout the Indo-Pacific region. It is notable that there is no commercial sponge fishery in Australian seas, and most species found there would be quite unsuitable owing to the presence of silicious or calcareous spicules. The number of living sponges has been estimated to be in the vicinity of 10,000 species, of which only about a dozen are valuable in industry. The distribution of the commercially valuable sponges with their skeletons of spongin fibres appears to be restricted to the Atlantic Ocean and the Mediterranean Sea.

COELENTERATA

This phylum must be considered as the most important of all the animal groups associated with reefs of tropical seas, since it contains not only all the reef-building corals, but also a large number of other forms, some of which are among the most prominent animals on the reefs.

There are many species of small colonial hydroids to be found on coral reefs, fragile, elegant plant-like growths whose beauty can only be appreciated with the aid of high power lens or microscope. The greater number are relatively inconspicuous since they usually grow out of sight under protecting boulders, or in rather inaccessible places in deeper waters. A character which distinguishes these animals from other coelenterates is that in addition to the polyp stage there is often produced a free-swimming medusa—a tiny gelatinous, transparent umbrella or bell-shaped jellyfish, often with tentacles round the margin, and with the mouth in the centre of the underside of the umbrella.

The minute polyp is a very simple tubular structure, closed at one end and attached to some object; at the other end it bears an elongated or cup-shaped expansion with a central mouth opening surrounded by tiny tentacles. There are two distinct groups of hydroids—one in which the polyp secretes a thin, transparent sheath of chitin around it which acts as a protective cover into which the the polyp can withdraw, and a second group in which the chitinous cover only extends along the 'stalks' of the colony, leaving the tiny delicate polyp exposed.

Colonies are formed by budding of the polyps, as in the corals, and there are usually three different types of polyp—defence and feeding, with tentacles armed with batteries of stinging cells (nematocysts) for the capture of prey which consists of any minute planktonic animals which come within their range—and the reproductive polyps which produce the medusae. These are the sexual stages which produce eggs and sperm, resulting in a planula larva which ultimately settles to form a new polyp and so begin another colony. Whilst most hydroid colonies are small, especially those found under boulders on the reef, others grow to several inches and because of their plant-like form are commonly mistaken for seaweeds. The most conspicuous species found in Barrier Reef waters is the stinging hydroid, *Aglaophenia cupressina*, which closely resembles a clump of small pale brown ferns growing on the side of a coral pool.

There is another colonial form which plays a far more important role on the reefs than the small hydroids to which it is related. This is the hydro-coralline, *Millepora*, the so-called stinging coral of which two species are found on reefs of the Great Barrier. These animals produce a massive calcareous skeleton and so play a part as reef-builders. This skeleton is quite easily distinguished from that of the corals and close examination will show it to consist, as its name implies, of thousands of minute pores which are of two different sizes. The larger accommodate the feeding polyps and they are surrounded by a circle of smaller pores for tiny polyps with batteries of stinging cells. Like the hydroids, *Millepora* has minute free-swimming medusae which, in this group, develop in special chambers within the skeleton.

Extensive colonies, sometimes several feet across, are to be found along the outer edge and in the deep grooves along the reef front in places of strong wave action. The colour in life varies in the species and is usually greenish- to yellowish-brown, often with white tips. To the naked eye, their similarity to several of the short branching coral species is so marked that it is understandable that they are usually mistaken for corals. The nematocysts of *Millepora*, of which there are two or three kinds, can produce a quite severe burning or stinging sensation. hence the common name.

The large jelly fishes are creatures of the open sea and are not therefore to be regarded

A species which is capable of causing irritation to the skin is the hydro-coralline, *Millepora platyphylla*, often mistaken for one of the corals because of its solid calcareous skeleton.

Large colony of *Millepora* in deeper water. Swain Reefs.

Small colony of *Distichopora violacea* under coral on the reef flat. Much larger colonies occur in caves and crevices down the face of the reef.

A related species, the delicately branching *Stylaster elegans*, from the sheltered back-reef area of Day Reef.

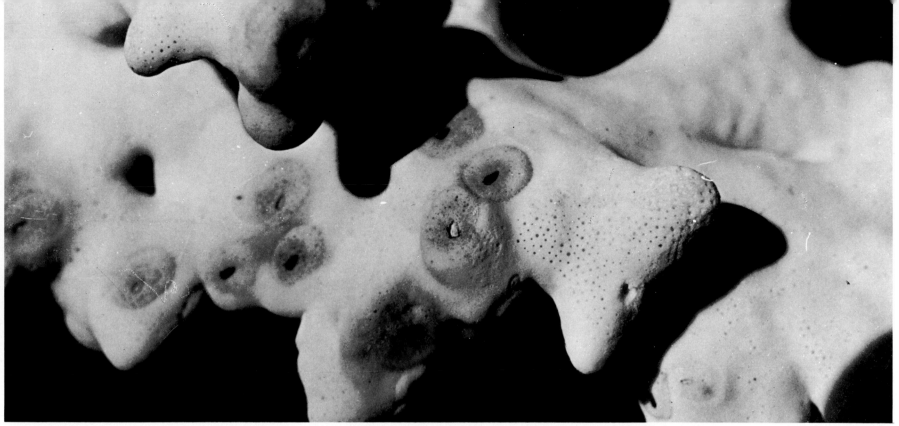

Small barnacles, *Pyrogoma millepora*, may be seen living within the skeleton of the hydro-corraline, *Millepora tenera*.

Part of a colony of the mauvish-purple hydro-coralline, *Distichophora*, in which the polyps are situated in rows along the edges of each branch. It favours the undersides of ledges on the reef slopes.

The underside of a dead coral boulder with colourful encrusting sponges.

The Comb jelly, *Bolinopsis*. These fragile relatives of the jellyfishes, are propelled through the water by the beating of minute ciliated paddles known as comb rows.

as part of the reef fauna, but they occur in numbers over the vast area of water contained within the Reef Province. At certain times of the year, some species have a tendency to congregate in enormous numbers, either in the more open waters, or along the coasts and in sheltered bays. They range in size from small translucent or highly transparent forms to the large *Cyanea capillata*, which may reach a diameter of three or four feet, and their colours may be tints of blue, pink, mauve, yellow or brown. Some jelly fishes are brilliantly luminescent at night, and may be seen pulsating gently along in the current near the water's surface.

The most obvious part of the animal is the rounded or bell-shaped umbrella, from the margins of which a number of tentacles, varying according to the species from four to many hundreds, trail out behind the animal as it swims. These tentacles are highly extensible and are usually heavily armed with stinging cells. The mouth lies in the centre of the underside of the bell at the end of a quadrangular tube which may be made up of four simple tapering oral lobes, or developed into a complex arrangement of 'lips' . In the case of *Cyanea*, these are extended into the most beautifully elaborate folds and frills which give the swimming animal an elegance unsurpassed in the animal kingdom. Jelly fishes prey mainly on small invertebrates of different kinds which are trapped by the tentacles and paralysed by the nematocysts of the tentacles and oral lobes, then carried to the mouth.

One group of jelly fishes which should be briefly mentioned is the Carybdeida—the Cubomedusae or box-jellies, which are widespread through-out the Indo-Pacific region. They are commonly referred to as sea wasps or fire-jellies because of their severe stinging powers, and in the far northern coastal waters of the Barrier Reef region have caused several fatalities in recent years. Fortunately, however, their occurrence is fairly seasonal and restricted to certain times of the year under a given set of weather conditions. This has now been well documented for the area concerned and bathers would do well to heed the warning restrictions, since these animals are usually highly transparent and difficult to see in the water.

The largest and most important group of the coelenterates, covering over 6,000 of the total number of species in the phylum, is the Class Anthozoa which contains not only the reef-building corals but most of the other well-known forms associated with the reefs such as anemones, 'soft' corals, and sea fans.

Whilst the basic structure is still that of a polyp, there is no medusa stage as in the hydroids, and it differs internally, as already described in the corals, since the gastric region is divided into numbers of radiating compartments by the longitudinal partitions, the septa (Figure 5). The other major difference is that many of the Anthozoa have either a solid skeleton of calcium carbonate, as in the corals, or there may be embedded in their tissues numerous microscopic spicules of the same material, differing in shape and size with the species. Others again have a skeleton which is composed of a hard horny or chitinous material.

On the basis of a number of characters but in particular on the nature of the tentacles, the Anthozoa are divisible into two easily distinguished sub-classes. The first, the Alcyonaria or Octocorallia, is comprised of colonial forms which are either tall and branching, elongate, or round and flattened. The polyps are basically of similar and uniform construction, invariably with eight septa and *eight* tentacles which are always pinnate, that is they are ' feathered ', having fine processes along either side of each tentacle. In the lobed and branching colonies,

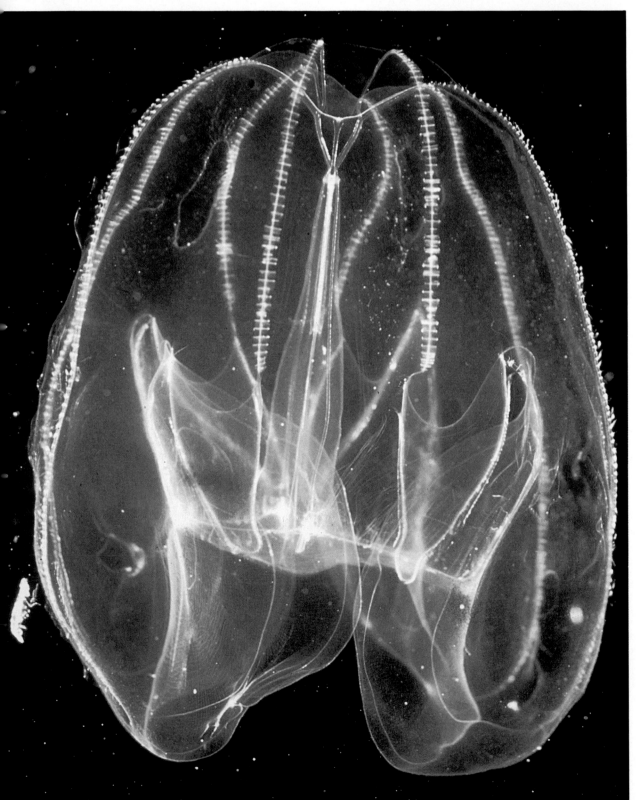

The stinging hydroid, *Aglaophenia cupressina* is locally known as 'Fire-weed' and is one of the few reef animals which should not be touched with bare hands.

At low water, areas of a reef flat may be found where sponges completely dominate the scene, as on this north-eastern edge of Undine Reef.

Small branch of a colony of the hydroid, *Pennaria australis*, showing the delicate polyps with tentacles extended, and the tiny medusae, almost fully developed and ready to be set free. Colonies are found on the undersides of boulders on the reef flat. (X 115).

The soft coral *Xenia elongata* with its pinnate tentacles fully expanded.

the polyps are found along the stems, but in the greater number of species the basal parts of the polyps are embedded in a gelatinous matrix into which they can withdraw completely. At low water, on some reefs, great areas of these so-called 'soft' corals may be exposed. The whole colony contracts as the internal network of canals connecting the polyps is emptied of water and the resultant mass of flat, tough, leather-like tissue is usually shunned by a visitor to the reef. But as the tide flows again and the colony is refilled with sea water, the polyps begin to expand. The drab, ungainly mass becomes again a vital living entity, covered with hundreds of exquisite tiny 'flowers' of the sea.

The requirements of the soft corals are similar to those of the reef-builders and they are found occupying the same kinds of habitats on the reef, so that there must always be a certain amount of competition between them for places of settlement. It is noteworthy that on reefs where areas of corals have been killed, either as a result of cyclonic activity or some disaster such as large-scale predation by starfish, that particular section of the reef may soon be recolonized by the Alcyonarians which are capable of much more rapid growth than the skeleton-forming corals. Symbiotic algae, Zooxanthellae, are found in these animals also, but it is not definitely known just how significant a part they play in regard to nutrition. Soft corals of the Family Xeniidae, for example, are apparently herbivorous, whilst other groups are known to be carnivorous although, like the corals, they possibly receive a certain amount of food material by way of their symbiotic organisms.

The minute spicules of calcium carbonate embedded in the matrix or the horny rods which give firmness to the branches of an Alcyonarian colony are among the most important characters used in the classification of the group. It will be appreciated that the skeleton of these octocorals, whether composed of separate or fused spicules, or horny axial rods, is always *internal*, thus differing completely from the stony corals in which the tissues lie *on top* of the calcareous corallite. There is another difference too, in that the skeleton of a number of species is itself definitely coloured and the colour is retained after the colony dies. The best known of these is the red Organ pipe coral, *Tubipora musica*. In suitable areas colonies several feet in diameter are found, but normally, on reefs of the Great Barrier exposed at low water, they are not more than inches across. *Tubipora* is easily identified by the red colour when the polyps are retracted within the fused cylindrical tubes. In sandy pools which retain water at low tide, the small grey-green polyps, fully expanded, may be found growing down among colonies of corals.

The Blue coral, *Heliopora coerulea*, which is found more commonly on the northern reefs of the Province, plays an important part in some

Soft corals exposed at low water, reef flat, Low Isles.

Soft corals, sandy reef flat, Double Island.

Soft corals, Michaelmas Reef.

Distinctive patterns are seen in some soft corals when exposed at low tide.

Soft corals, outer reef edge, Michaelmas Reef.

The soft coral, *Sarcophyton*, with polyps partially expanded.

The soft coral, *Lobophyton*, with a few polyps expanded.

Lobophyton now covered by the rising tide, with polyps fully expanded.

113

The Organ pipe coral, *Tubipora musica*, with its small polyps expanded, as seen in a coral pool on the reefs.

Section of the red 'skeleton' of *Tubipora musica* shows the appropriateness of its common name.

The 'Blue coral', *Heliopora coerulea*, as it occurs on the algal-rubble reef flat of Watson Island.

The skeleton of *Heliopora* remains a deep blue after the colony dies.

A colony of Sea Whips, *Junceela* sp. Pandora Reef.

areas as a reef-builder, since it also is capable of massive skeleton formation. In life the colour of the colony often tends to look a brownish grey-blue, but a piece of one of the branches, broken off, will reveal the very dense blue of the skeleton.

The Gorgonians, the sea fans, are normally not found on the reef flats, but grow in the deeper waters down the face of the reefs where they are collected by skin divers. Their skeletons are, however, often displayed among collections of corals and shells and so are familiar to most visitors to the reefs. The colours are generally variants of the yellow-orange tones, and close inspection of the dried branches will show the pores through which the polyps are protruded in life when they appear as tiny, fragile, white flowers scattered along the colorful stalk.

The Red or Precious coral, *Corallium rubrum*, so valued by the citizens of ancient Greece and Rome, is related to the sea fans.

The soft corals and the gorgonians not only act as protective hosts for numerous other small reef inhabitants, as for example the small crab, *Caphyra laevis*, which lives among the polyps of *Xenia*, but they are also preyed upon by various species. Small cowries of the family Ovulidae and other molluscs live on species of soft corals whose polyps are the sole source of food. Arthropods—pycnogonids or sea spiders, cope-pods, and barnacles—are all known to parasitize Alcyonarians.

The second distinct subdivision of the Anthozoa—the Zoantharia or Hexacorallia—includes the anemones and the reef-building corals, and the Black or Thorny corals. As has already been described for the corals, and as the alternate name implies, the tentacles and septa, in contra-distinction to the Octocorallia, are generally arranged in multiples of six.

Anemones are among the more numerous and most beautiful and colorful seashore animals and so are familiar to most people. Their internal structure is similar to that described in the corals except that the anemones completely lack any skeleton and therefore have no skeletal cup of any kind into which the animal can withdraw. The outer column in most species, however, is fairly tough and resistant, often covered with vesicles and nematocyst warts, and some species cover the column with sand grains and other materials. When exposed by the tide or when danger threatens the animal completely retracts its tentacles within the column and withdraws down into cracks and crevices or into the sandy substrate to which it is attached by a basal disc.

Between thirty and forty species are believed to have been collected from islands in the Capricorn Group, but there is no comprehensive published report on the sea anemones of the Great Barrier Reef and only a few species are easily recognized. The best known is the giant anemone, *Stichodactyla gigantea* which grows to a very large size.

A feature of scientific interest in connection with anemones of this group is the association, which is both common and widespread, between these animals and small fishes of the Family Pomacentridae, particularly the genus *Amphiprion*. These brightly coloured little fishes are to be seen darting in and out among the tentacles of the anemone, in no apparent danger of being stung whereas all other little fish in the vicinity carefully avoid the stinging tentacles. The relationship appears to be one which is mutually beneficial for the fish is protected from predators and possibly is also cleaned of any external parasites by the anemone's tentacles. At the same time it eats food wastes cast out by the anemone. In a series of experiments carried out in an attempt to discover the means whereby these little fishes gained immunity from the nematocysts of the anemone's tentacles, it was observed that an acclimation process was undergone which could take from minutes to several hours before immunity was complete.

The fish was seen to hover over the anemone, at times cautiously passing over and through the tentacles or settling in among them, and occasionally even nibbling at them. When no further adhesion occurred as a result of contact between the fish and tentacles acclimation was thought to be complete, and its was considered that some change had taken place in the mucus covering the surface of the fish resulting in its

Part of a large colony of the Gorgonian, *Melithaea squamata*.

A large blue anemone on the outer reef slope, Wistari Reef, *Heteractis magnifica*.

Large reef anemone in a coral pool, *Stichodactyla gigantea*. One of the small fish of the genus *Amphiprion*, so often found living as commensals with anemones, is seen emerging from among the tentacles.

One of the reef anemones commonly found partially buried in the sand.

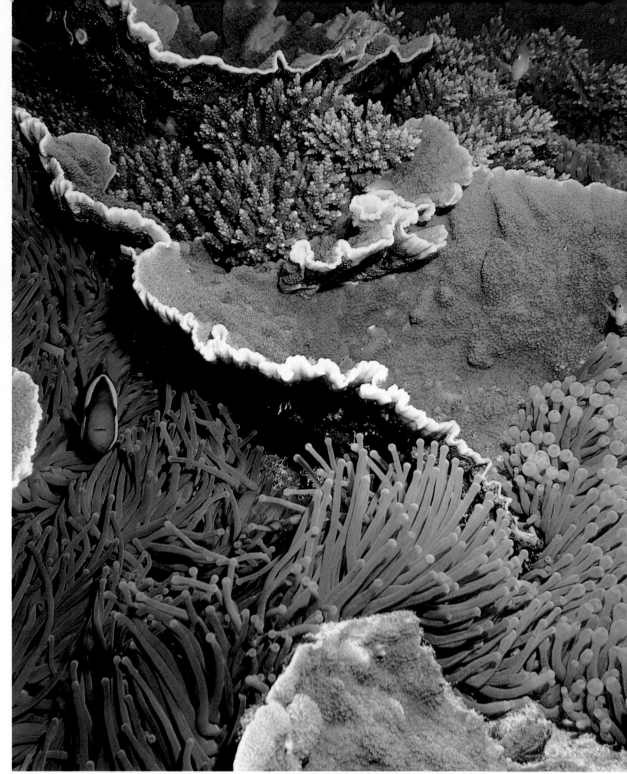

Surrounded by colonies of the corals, *Acropora* and *Montipora*, a large anemone with its sheltering Clown fish.

The beautifully marked little *Periclimenes brevicarpalis* live as commensals with the large anemones which burrow in sand.

On the algal crest on many reefs, great sheets of mustard-coloured colonies of the small zoanthid, *Palythoa caesia*, may be seen. When fully expanded they resemble clusters of small anemones.

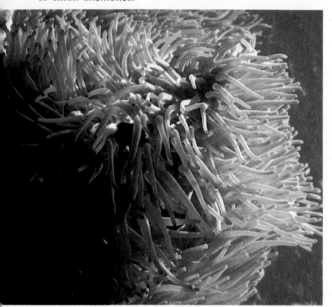

Stichodactyla gigantea, the largest of the Barrier Reef anemones. Marineland, Green Island.

The gorgonian, *Melithaea*, one of the fan corals, with its tiny polyps partially expanded—small section of a large colony.

The anemone, *Heteractis crispa*, lives among corals on the reef flat.

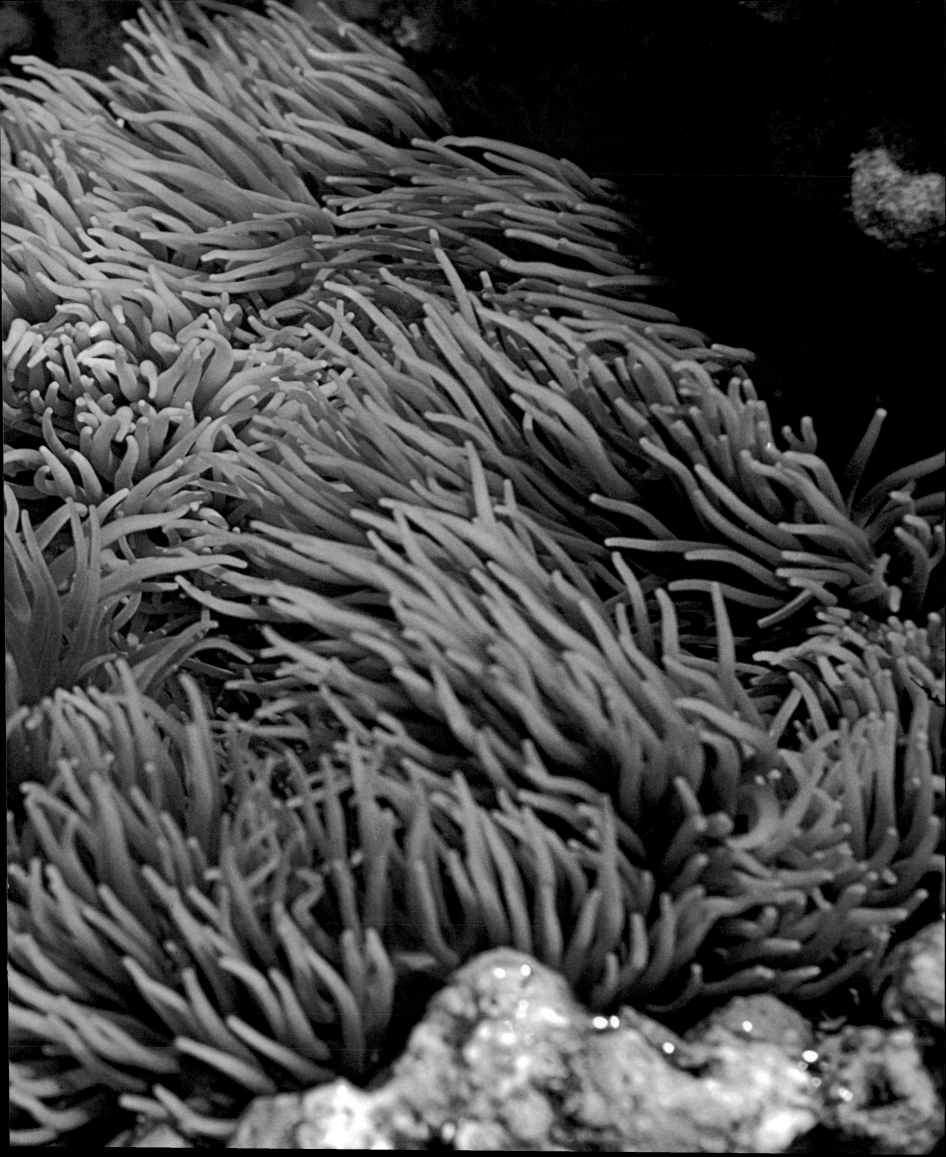

MARINE WORMS

protection from the effects of the stinging cells.

Another association which has been noted with some of the reef anemones is the presence of delicate little shrimps, often with beautiful markings on their almost transparent bodies. A very considerable amount of work has been carried out and observations made on the behaviour of small fishes and shrimps which act as 'cleaners' for other fish and larger animals, thus removing ecto-parasites, bacteria, mucus and unused food particles. This mutually benefiting behaviour is apparently world wide for it has now been noted wherever extensive diving observations have been made, and there is a list of published work from the Caribbean Sea and the waters off California and Mexico.

The small shrimps may be seen resting on an anemone which is fully expanded, but those photographed were caught by passing a very small net through the almost retracted tentacles of an anemone embedded in a crevice and only partially exposed at low tide. When removed and placed in a small pool of water, the shrimps remained stationary, seemingly at a loss in full sunlight and away from the protective host.

Although anemones are sometimes found in numbers fairly close together they are solitary individuals, but there is one small Order of the Anthozoa which plays quite a conspicuous part on many of the reefs, forming extensive colonies on the almost bare algal crests. Normally one sees them in the contracted state at low tide, sheets of mustard-yellow leathery looking substance, covered with small protuberances. When the tentacles are fully expanded, however, they closely resemble very small anemones packed tightly together over the coral substrate. This is the colonial zoanthid, *Palythoa caesia*.

A number of species of anemone are found burrowing in sandy areas of the reef flats, but they differ from the large slender *Cerianthus* found by skin divers from deeper waters. The latter has no basal disc for attachment to the substrate but lives in a protective tube of mucus and agglutinated sediments, buried down in the sandy mud.

The Black or Thorny corals of the Order Antipatharia are sometimes grouped with the cerianthids, but they are very different in their appearance, resembling the sea fans in their plant-like form with a main basal stalk attached to the substrate. The slender multi-branched colonies are normally inhabitants of deeper waters where they grow to heights of several feet. Numbers of more shallow-water forms have been found by skin divers in recent years among the coral reefs in various parts of the world. The tiny polyps which normally have only six tentacles, secrete a black, horny skeleton similar to the gorgonians, except that it is covered with minute thorns, hence the common names. The thicker, more solid sections of the skeleton are sometimes cut and polished to be sold as fashion jewellry.

The word 'worm' has been used to cover an infinite variety of animals, many of which are completely unrelated to one another, and which are classified zoologically into at least ten different phyla. Those most frequently found on coral reefs, and which are most easily seen and recognizable, belong in three of these phyla— the Platyhelminthes or flatworms, the Nemertea or ribbon worms, and the Annelida, the ringed or segmented worms.

These animals have attained a higher degree of organization in their body structure than the sponges and coelenterates, and most have eyes and well-developed respiratory, nervous, digestive and excretory systems. Many have larval stages which occur free-living in the plankton community in the waters surrounding the reefs. As adults they are to be found swimming, crawling on the sandy floor of a coral pool, burrowing in the substrate, sheltering under boulders or among coral rubble, or living in tubes which vary from temporary shelters of a soft, sandy nature to the permanence of solid calcium carbonate structures embedded in living coral colonies. There is great beauty of form and colour, and grace of movement to be seen in many of these worms, which range in size from less than an inch to several feet in length. The colour, in some instances, is due to pigmentation and in others to a brilliant iridescence caused by diffraction or interference of light on the chitinous outer layers of the worms.

The marine flatworms are usually only a few inches long, very flattened and leaf-like, and generally found sheltering under boulders on the reef flat, although the species *Pseudoceros bedfordi* occurs commonly crawling over corals or swimming in the sandy pools. It is often mistaken for a small 'Spanish dancer', a common name more usually applied to a large, brightly coloured nudibranch mollusc, *Hexabranchus sanguineus* (Chapter VII). This mistake is understandable for the highly muscular body of the flatworm permits it to move swiftly, whether gliding over sand or coral, or swimming for short periods with the most graceful undulations of the fluted margins of its body.

Flamboyant colourings in mosaic patterns, black, white and orange stripes, or pastel shades, are all found on the coral reef species. The colour can be due to symbiotic algae which give the brownish and greenish colours, or to pigment cells scattered in the tissue, or even to the prey which the worm has just devoured—especially clearly visible in the more translucent forms. In some species, seen against the light, the digestive organs may be quite easily discerned. There is a mouth, pharynx and many branched intestine. The mouth is on the ventral surface of the body, often surrounded by a frill-like structure capable of great expansion. These highly carnivorous animals prey not only

on dead animals but on all sorts of small invertebrates which they capture by wrapping themselves round them and entangling the victim with mucus. With the aid of the very expansible mouth apparatus, the inside surfaces of which secrete digestive juices, these small worms are capable of attacking larger animals.

The ribbon worms of the phylum Nemertea, although sometimes flattened, are usually soft bodied, elongate worms capable of tremendous expansion and contraction of their highly muscular bodies. Sometimes known as the proboscis worms, these animals possess a proboscis which is reversible through a pore which opens just above the mouth, and which is capable of great extension, being used by the worm in the capture of its prey.

The ribbon worms are capable of asexual reproduction by regeneration, of which they possess considerable powers. A new proboscis may be grown, or an anterior piece with the foregut is able to regenerate the posterior parts. In some species which may completely fragment themselves, each piece may form a new worm. The colours found on these worms vary from the very drab to bright orange, red, pink and greens, and they are very often either transversely or longitudinally banded. One species in particular, *Baseodiscus quinquelineatus*, is quite commonly found in Barrier Reef waters, among dead coral boulders or rubble on the reef flats, or among clumps of algae such as the calcareous *Halimeda*, which not only provide shelter for the worms but harbour many food organisms.

The majority of seashore worms, whether of tropical or temperate seas, belong in the phylum Annelida, and the segmented marine worms are grouped together in the Polychaeta—the many-bristled worms. This is a very apt name because each segment along the body of the worm bears clusters of chitinous bristles or setae (chaetae). There are two groups of these bristle worms, separated according to their mode of life. Firstly there are the free-living or errant forms, and those which are more or less sedentary, or tube-building species. It is often difficult, however, to make hard and fast distinctions because of the diversity of adaptation found in this group of animals which ranges from the burrowing, crawling, and free-swimming pelagic species and those which build temporary tubes, to the permanent tube dwellers.

These worms range in size from minute forms sheltering in coral clumps and sponges to the giant Australian beach worm which may reach a length of eight or nine feet when fully extended. On the reef flats of the Great Barrier, almost every boulder turned over on a sandy substrate will reveal the presence of one or more bristle worms, *Eurythoe complanata*. One of the most widely distributed species, this worm is found in all the world's seas. Handling it should be avoided, since its bristles, unlike those of

Where corals have died off on a reef, whether from natural causes, predation or storm damage, the whole area may be recolonized by the faster growing soft corals. Near-shore reef, Double Island with mainland near Cairns in background.

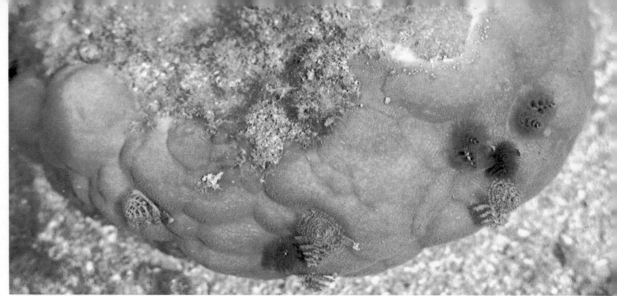

A solitary tube worm, with its double spiral fan extended, in a colony of the Staghorn coral, *Acropora*.

Large numbers of the tube worm, *Spirobranchus giganteus*, live embedded round the periphery of 'micro-atolls' of the massive coral, *Porites lutea*.

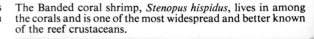

The Tongue 'shell' *Lingula* showing the stalk with which it attaches itself buried down in the sand flat of Brampton Island.

Pieces of pumice, wood or drifting logs washed ashore on the reefs, are often covered with numbers of the stalked barnacles, *Lepas*. These were floating in eastern Torres Strait.

This delicate little shrimp, *Periclimenes imperator*, was living beneath the protecting folds of the large nudibranch, *Hexabranchus*, on Undine Reef. This species has been recorded with the same nudibranch as far away as Zanzibar and Mozambique, and is known from the Red Sea to Hawaii.

One of the most colourful of the reef crabs is the red, white-spotted *Lophozozymus pictor*.

The largest and gayest of the Barrier Reef Hermit crabs is the red *Dardanus megistos*, seen here occupying a large Triton shell at Green Island.

The Banded coral shrimp, *Stenopus hispidus*, lives in among the corals and is one of the most widespread and better known of the reef crustaceans.

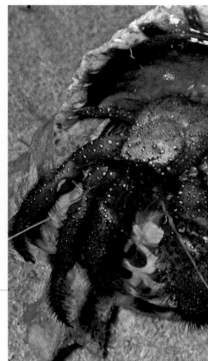

The flatworm, *Pseudoceros bedfordi*, is often seen swimming in pools on the reef flat.

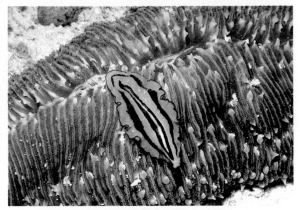

A strikingly marked flatworm of the genus *Pseudoceros* crawls over a Mushroom coral.

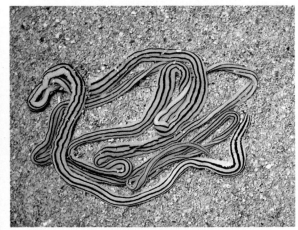

Ribbon worms such as the long black and white *Baseodiscus quinquelineatus*, live among coral rubble.

The Bristle worm, *Eurythoe complanata*.

most other polychaetes, are composed of calcium carbonate and are very brittle. The needle-like setae break off very easily and cause considerable irritation.

The free-living worms are usually extremely active animals, with a distinct head and tail. They may be seen in numbers when breaking up clumps of rubble or turning boulders. They move with graceful sinuations of the body, propelled often at considerable speed, by means of a pair of muscular locomotory feet, or swimming paddles, on each segment of the body. The head region bears palps, tentacles, and one or more pairs of eyes, although in some of the burrowing forms the head region may be very considerably reduced. Carnivorous by nature, many of the errant species have a protrusible pharynx which may be completely everted through the mouth, and used in the capture of prey.

The sedentary polychaetes, especially those which secrete tubes of calcium carbonate, seldom if ever leave their tubes, and exhibit as great diversity in their form, structure and adaptation as their free-living relatives. The nature of the tubes they occupy is just as varied both in structure and composition—they may be soft, fragile, mucous-lined tubes, felted of sand and mud, or they may be highly complex structures of sand grains arranged in beautiful design, or of hard calcareous material cemented to the substrate or embedded deep in coral boulders.

The mode of feeding in the tube-dwelling worms differs greatly from the errant and burrowing forms. The distinct head may be completely lacking, and the head region highly specialized into a food-collecting apparatus. In some species there are numbers of long highly extensile ciliated tentacles which are spread out over the substrate, and by means of which particles of organic detritus suspended in the sea water, or accumulated on the sandy bottom, are carried along to the mouth of the worm. One of the most characteristic sights on the reef flat among algal-covered boulders, is the network of white thread-like tentacles of the tube worm, *Reteterebella queenslandia*, spread out among the algae or over the dead coral. If the boulder is turned over, the worm and its fragile muddy tube, together with a great tangled mass of tentacles and bright red gills, will be found.

Perhaps the best known, and certainly the most conspicuous of all the Barrier Reef polychaetes is the fan worm, *Spirobranchus giganteus*. This brilliantly coloured little worm builds its tube in living colonies of coral, particularly in the micro-atoll forming *Porites lutea*, and as the coral grows the tube becomes completely embedded. The beautiful double spiral of delicate pinnate processes, each with a ciliary groove along its length, acts as a food-trapping mechanism, and occurs in multicoloured array—from white, fawn, brown and black to reds, blues, orange and yellow. At the

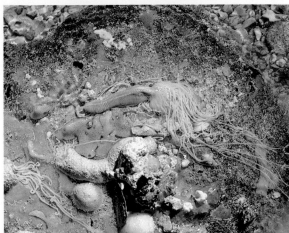

Creamy white threads spread out over coral rubble are a common sight on some of the reefs. Turning over the boulder reveals these as the tentacles of the tube worm, *Reteterebella queenslandia*.

Three colonies of the tiny tubeworm, *Filograna implexa*, commonly found under boulders on the reef flats. Heron Reef.

slightest approach of danger the worm withdraws at lightning speed within its protective tube.

CRUSTACEA*

Crustaceans such as lobsters, crabs and prawns or shrimps are familiar to most people, but the tremendous importance of this group of animals in the economy of the sea is not generally recognized.

The Crustacea belong in the Phylum Arthropoda which is one of the largest and most diverse in the animal kingdom, and which includes such well-known land animals as insects, ticks, spiders, scorpions and centipedes. Despite the dissimilarity in size and form, all these animals have segmented bodies with jointed legs—hence the name of the Phylum—and all are covered by an external skeleton of chitinous material, differing considerably in its thickness and texture within the various groups.

There is perhaps a greater diversity of form within the Crustacea than in any other Class of animals. They are found in the sea from the top of the tidelines to the abyssal deeps, and throughout the world's oceans they are a major component in the marine fauna. Just as the Insecta, with their mastery of flight and their enormous numbers, must be considered the most successful group of land animals, so the Crustacea may be regarded in the sea. And here it is not, as might perhaps be expected, the larger, well-known edible species commercially valuable to man, which are of major importance.

Of the twenty six thousand known species, of which the greater number are marine, the small copepods, only just visible to the naked eye, play one of the most significant roles of all animals in the food-web of the sea. For they convert the phyto-plankton—the microscopic plants of the sea—into animal proteins, fats and carbohydrates and, in their teeming millions, are in turn the food of other animals from the corals to the edible fishes.

Crustaceans range in size from microscopic creatures to the giant spider crabs of Japanese seas, with legs five feet in length, and they include such unlikely forms as the delicate little water fleas and the large barnacles with their heavily calcified 'shells', found on wave-beaten rocky shores. With such a bewildering array of diversification in colour, shape, size, habitat, life history and feeding mechanisms, they are one of the most fascinating groups of animals and would constitute a life study in themselves.

Apart from the segmented body and jointed appendages possessed by all members of the Class, the most outstanding character common to them all is the method of their growth. The crustacean exo-skeleton, whether it be a thin, transparent sheath of chitin as in the tiny water fleas, or heavily calcified as in many of the crabs and lobsters, acts as a suit of armour in which

*The Crustacea are now considered to be a separate phylum (Manton, 1977).

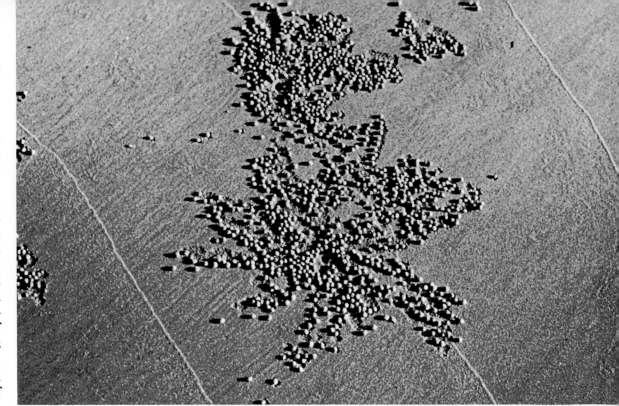

Sand patterns. A very characteristic sight on many of the wide flat northern beaches, is the radiating cluster of balls of sand made by the little Sand bubbler crabs as they feed. Alexandra Reefs.

Very flattened and with long legs, the crab, *Percnon planissimum*, is found under coral boulders.

The small olive-green crab, *Atergatus floridus*, is to be found in numbers among coral-algal rubble on reef flats.

the plates are moveable on one another. This firm, inelastic cover which encloses the animal as in a vice, must be shed at intervals for it is only when the new 'skin' beneath is still soft and flexible that the animal can increase in size. Thus, throughout their growing period of life, all crustaceans periodically moult, or cast off their outer 'skins'. The number of moults, which may be very frequent in the early stages of the life cycle, decreases and in some instances ceases altogether as the animals reach maturity. Moulting is controlled by hormone mechanisms and is part of the normal physiological processes of these animals. By the reduction of muscles and other structures the animal is able, when the new exo-skeleton is fully developed beneath the old, to withdraw itself completely from its old 'skin'. The whole performance is a most intriguing phenomenon to watch, and if one is fortunate enough to witness it, it will be seen that the cast-off cover is perfect in every detail down to the finest bristles on the jointed appendages.

The smaller, more primitive, crustaceans possess large numbers of appendages of a similar structure, which together perform a number of different functions, whereas in the so-called 'higher' Crustacea the appendages are fewer and are modified for different purposes. Basically the crustacean form consists of a head, thorax and abdomen, all consisting of a number of segments. Each of the segments bears a characteristic pair of appendages. The number of segments varies in such forms as the small water fleas and copepods, and in the barnacles, but in the larger Crustacea such as prawns, lobsters and crabs, the number is normally twenty, of which the first five are fused to form the head. Here five characteristic pair of appendages are found, the antennules and antennae, which are sensory in function, the mandibles and two pair of maxillae, used in the capture and masceration of food. On the thorax, there are eight segments which may be fused or free, bearing eight pair of appendages. In forms such as the lobsters, prawns and shrimps and crabs which are grouped together as the Decapod Crustacea, because they each possess five pairs of 'walking legs', the head and thorax region is covered by a protective carapace, heavily calcified in the case of most crabs and lobsters, and often armed with strong spines, especially in the Spiny lobsters. The abdomen has six fused or free segments with six pairs of swimming appendages. In the lobster and prawn-like forms the last abdominal segment, the telson, together with the last pair of appendages, forms a broad and often powerful 'tail fan' which is extensively used in evasive action, enabling the animal to propel itself backwards at very considerable speed. In the crabs the abdominal appendages are modified, and hidden from sight beneath the abdomen which is folded back under the body as a narrow flap in the males, and a much

Although it is rarely seen, the Mud lobster, *Thalassina anomala* is a common inhabitant of the mangrove flats of the far north. It makes very large mounds of mud, up to a foot in height above its burrow.

On many reefs, notably on some of those fringing continental islands, the only obvious inhabitants are swiftly moving, mottled green crabs. Fiercely aggressive, they stand up prepared to battle with a would-be collector. Three species belonging to the Portunid genus, *Thalamita*, are commonly found.
The Red-eyed crab, *Eriphia sebana*, is found among beach rock and under stones on the inner reef flats.

One of the many species of Xanthid crabs found among rubble and under boulders on the reef flats. *Leptodius sanguineus*.

Small crabs of the genus *Trapezia* are found in pairs sheltering among corals such as *Pocillopora damicornis*.

broader flap for the protection of developing eggs in the female.

It is perhaps in their feeding habits, and the multiplicity of structures which make up the food-catching apparatus, that the Crustacea display to the full their greatest adaptations to all the varied habitats in which they are found in the marine environment. There are the filter-feeding species with an exquisite array of fine setae or bristles on the head and thoracic appendages which act as sieves, trapping organic particles and small animals drifting in the water. Some are scavengers eating any organic matter they can find, others are herbivores or carnivores. The habitat may be the open ocean where planktonic and free-swimming pelagic species spend either part or the whole of their lives. But the greater majority of crustaceans live at varying depths in the sea, on or in the sandy or muddy substrate, or under boulders or corals on rock platforms, beaches and reefs.

Of the smaller forms, perhaps only the Amphipods, the sand-fleas or sand-hoppers, will be obvious to a visitor to the reefs. These small animals which may be up to about half an inch in length, are flattened from side to side, and may be found under piles of seaweeds or other organic matter washed up on the shore. They leap about swiftly when disturbed, and rapidly disappear from sight beneath the sand.

The other Crustacean inhabitant of the sandy beaches is the Ghost crab, *Ocypode ceratophthalma* but during daylight hours its large burrow will be the only obvious indication of its presence. After dark the scavenging crabs emerge and then, with the aid of a strong torch light, it is possible to see them.

Where there are areas of beach rock with broken boulders along the edge of a reef, small flattened crabs of the genus *Petrolisthes* will be found, sometimes occuring in considerable numbers. Hermit crabs are found here too. In tiny borrowed shells, they scuttle for safety when boulders are turned over, and under larger stones and in crevices the Red-eyed crab, *Eriphia sebana* is often seen. This crab may also be found among boulders in coral-rubble areas of the reef flats.

The swift-footed crab, *Grapsus albolineatus*, is sometimes seen along the deeper cracks of the beach rock area, but it is more numerous on rocky shores of the continental islands and the high, jagged limestone platforms of the more northern islands, where a brilliant flash of green may be seen disappearing over the edge to safety.

On some of the higher reefs, completely uncovered at low water, especially in algal-coral-rubble areas, highly aggressive crabs, in mottled patterns of green, blue and black, may occur in numbers. They belong to the genus *Thalamita* and by their nature and colouring and the characteristic swimming 'paddles' of their last pair of legs, these crabs are easily recognized. The strong claws, often predominantly bluish in

The Painted Spiny Lobster, *Panulirus longipes*, and other closely related species, although more usually caught by skin divers, are sometimes seen in pools. The waving of the long antennae among coral colonies is often the only indication of their presence.

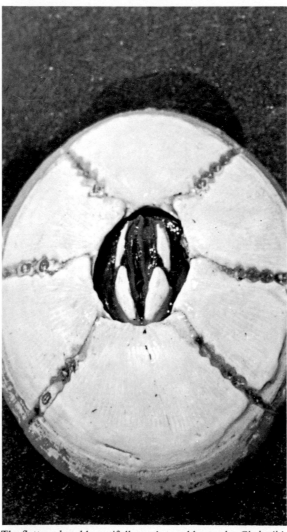

The flattened and beautifully sculptured barnacle, *Chelonibia testudinaria*, as its name implies, is found attached to the large reef turtles.

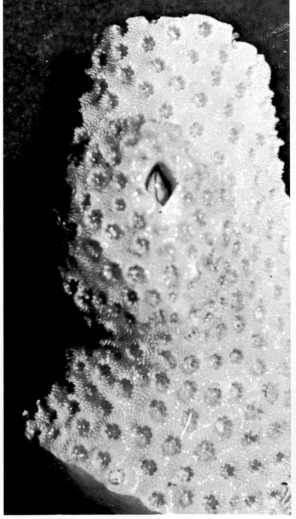

Among the many animals which harbour in coral is the small barnacle *Creusia spinulosa*.

colour, and capable of inflicting a nasty bite, are immediately thrust upwards at any attempt to catch them.

Small, extremely fast-moving animals ranging in size from about an inch to four inches in length, will be seen on these same reef flats, darting for cover among boulders and rubble as one walks across the reef. These are the Mantis shrimps, *Gonodactylus*.

Many other crabs will be found sheltering under boulders on the reef flats. One of those most often seen, perhaps because of its spectacular colouring, is the Red, white-spotted *Lophozozymus pictor*. And finally there are the Hermit crabs, those most comical of reef characters which belong in a group between the prawns, lobsters and the true crabs. They have a soft, unprotected abdomen and use the dead shells of molluscs as a covering. With every few moults the Hermit crab must of necessity find a larger shell. To watch the house-hunting is a most amusing pastime as the small crab tests each shell it finds for size. During these periods it is of course very vulnerable to attack from predators.

All the above animals are basically dwellers on or in the various substrates of the reef flat or the beach. Other small crabs are to be found sheltering among the various plants and animals of the reef. The small crab, *Huenia proteus*, has a carapace shaped like the alga, *Halimeda*, and blends so well against its background that it is difficult to find. Where the crabs are found with animals they are most frequently living as commensals with their protective hosts, and they are fairly specific in their choice of habitat. In the case of the gall crab, *Hapalocarcinus marsupialis*, however, the situation is an extremely interesting one. A young female crab settles at a growing point of a branch of coral, almost invariably a species of the Family Pocilloporidae. The currents produced by the crab cause the growing coral branches to arch and produce a gall or chamber which eventually encloses her completely, although a series of small apertures remain through which the crab causes currents of water to circulate, from which she filters minute food particles. The male crabs are extremely small and thus are enabled to gain access to the female which eventually is permanently immured.

Shrimps and prawns are among the free-swimming crustaceans and normally are much more difficult to find on the reefs. The Hunchback Prawn, *Metapenaeopsis lamellata*, lies among the corals and on the sea bottom in the immediate vicinity of the reefs, and the Banded coral shrimp, *Stenopus hispidus*, is a dweller among the corals of the deep pools, lagoons, and the reef face. A small shrimp, mottled green and cream, *Saron marmoreus*, is frequently seen in shallow pools under boulders. Others are found living as commensals with a variety of animals.

The painted spiny lobster, *Panulirus versicolor*.

A number of the Turtle barnacles seen here on the carapace of a Hawksbill turtle.

Hermit crabs which use dead mollusc shells as protection, are often seen with one or more commensal anemones, *Calliactis polypus*, attached to the shell.

The Ghost crab, *Ocypode ceratophthalma*, lives in large burrows high up on the sandy beach of the coral islands.

The small flattened crab, *Petrolisthes lamarckii*, is exceedingly common in shingle areas on the reefs.

The swift-footed rock crabs, *Grapsus albolineatus*, are found high up at the top of the tide line among the beach rock.

The small crab, *Caphyra rotundifrons*, is found in pairs among the green Turtle weed, *Chlorodesmis*.

A related species, *Caphyra laevis*, lives among the polyps of the soft coral, *Xenia*, its colour pattern blending with its protective host.

Chapter 7

The Mollusca—the Sea Shells

In their relationship to the general ecology of the reefs, the Mollusca as a group of animals play a highly significant role. Because of the nature of their shells, mollusc remains may be found among the limestone debris of a reef dating back from its very earliest stages of evolution in the geological past, and may, therefore, be considered as having aided in its construction. Yet, as boring organisms, in both living and dead coral, certain species of molluscs rank among the most destructive agents to be found on the reefs. They are part of the whole economy of the reef in terms of its productivity, for mollusc eggs are laid in tens of millions and the floating larval stages form a very important part of the zooplankton in the waters over the reefs. In their vast numbers, as herbivores and carnivores, the molluscs are both prey and predator on the reefs.

The 'Shells' are probably the most widely known and highly prized of all seashore animals and throughout history they have undoubtedly played a more important role in relation to human beings than any other group of marine invertebrates. Primitive man used molluscs as food and their shells formed part of his everyday life, in domestic use they served as his cutting tools, fish hooks and water carriers, they were his currency, and in many instances, his most prized possessions, either in their original form or as elaborately carved ornaments for sacred and ceremonial rites. From the time of the earliest known civilizations the shell motif appeared in art, sculpture and architectural form.

In a different way, perhaps, molluscs are equally important to modern man. Since the hard, calcareous shells have lent themselves to preservation as fossil remains, they are a valuable aid to the scientist in his interpretation of the geological history of the Earth, and in the study of evolution. The cultivation of edible species

such as oysters, clams, mussels and scallops, is extensively carried out in many parts of the world, and the pearl culture industry alone is today estimated in millions of dollars. The exquisite natural beauty of sculpturing, form and colour, and the tremendous diversity of shape and size of molluscan shells have fascinated man from his earliest childhood to old age. Very extensive and extremely valuable collections are to be found in Natural History Museums and private collections throughout the world, and shell collecting still remains a most popular hobby.

Therein, however, lies the danger. Indiscriminate and unrestricted collecting can lead to extinction in any group of animals, and despite the huge reproductive potential of most marine molluscs there may well come a time when this will no longer suffice to preserve a species against man's predation. Ever since the year 1770, when the first recorded shells from Queensland waters were collected by the naturalists on board Captain James Cook's ship, *Endeavour*, the reefs and islands of the Great Barrier have been regarded as a shell collector's paradise. The plastics industry, perhaps fortunately, has replaced much of the old-time trade in *Trochus* shell and pearl oysters, once so much in demand for their beautiful mother-of-pearl. There was a period when Trochus shells, weighing in all over 1,000 tons, were removed in one year from Barrier Reef waters, and it is difficult to realize that nearly one hundred years ago, in the year 1878, the value of pearl shell alone gathered in Torres Strait (Map V) was over $224,000 at a price of $800 a ton.

Ten years earlier the captain of the brig, *Julia Percy*, from Sydney, fishing in the vicinity for *Bêche-de-mer*, had by chance seen preparations at a nearby island for a ceremonial dance. This first discovery of pearls and pearl shell in

Torres Strait led to an exchange for tomahawks! To the fierce, head-hunting warriors with their great war canoes, eighty feet long with twenty foot outriggers on either side to make them unsinkable, the tomahawks and iron were priceless by comparison with mere ceremonial ornaments. It seems ironic that, down the ages, something so intrinsically beautiful as a pearl—such perfection in itself—should have been the cause of massacre, savage reprisals and criminal exploitation, quite apart from all the inherent dangers encountered in obtaining it from its natural environment.

Those historic days have gone but the present upsurge in popularity of shell collecting, very unfortunately, has brought in its wake the ruthless commercial collector. The great fascination, the stimulation and aesthetic reward, of a private collection should lie in the personal gathering of the shells by its owner. The appreciation of the living animal which created the shell and a knowledge of its habitat and perhaps its life history, must surely lead to a greater awareness of the destructive consequences, to the habitat, and to the animal, of careless and indiscriminate collecting and, hopefully, to a strong desire to further in every way the preservation and conservation of both.

The devastation which can be caused by one small boatload of people during the few hours of one low spring tide on a reef flat can be quite appalling. By their thoughtless depredation the whole productivity of that reef flat and the natural habitat of thousands upon thousands of its inhabitants can literally be ruined in a matter of hours. To appreciate the truth of this statement fully one must have traversed such a reef —far from human habitation and the normal shipping lanes—where the trail of destruction

The largest animals living on the beach rock along the edge of a reef. or high up on boulders along its outer zone. are the Coat of mail shells—the chiton, *Acanthopleura gemmata*. which may reach a length of six to eight inches.

126

across the reef was glaringly apparent and easy to follow. Boulders, not one, but many hundreds, had been overturned in the blazing tropical sun. They once gave life and protection to untold numbers of plants and animals, large and small, and, in the spring breeding season to millions of eggs. Multiply this by a few more boats and a few low spring tides, and the result is not difficult to imagine. Only when the full significance of the very simple act of turning back a boulder is realized by *all* visitors to a reef, will there by any future for many of its marine inhabitants.

There are today some eighty thousand described species of molluscs, making them the second largest group of invertebrate animals. Generally speaking, they are recognized only by their shells, but there exist large numbers in which the shell is internal and covered by the tissues of the animal, or there is no shell at all. The name Mollusca means soft bodied. By considering only the various parts of the animal's body and ignoring the shell, zoologists have been able to recognize an underlying uniformity of structure and function which has enabled them to link together this extremely diverse and fascinating group of animals.

Molluscs range in size from minute snails to the giant clam with shell valves over three feet in length and weighing up to five hundred pounds. The great squids of the deep ocean waters have an overall length, including tentacles, of sixty feet and more, and propel themselves at speeds estimated at up to twenty knots. The phylum includes not only the familiar garden snails and slugs, the edible oysters and mussels, but also the periwinkles of the seashore, the lovely volutes and cowries, poisonous cone shells, and the octopus, cuttlefish and Pearly Nautilus. There are both land and freshwater molluscs, found from the arid regions to the tropical rain forest, from small ponds to large lakes, rivers and streams. They live from the depths of the ocean right up to the sandy shore and mangrove swamp, ranging from polar seas to the coral reefs of the tropics. Some are permanent dwellers in the surface waters of the open ocean, others are found only on rocky ocean shores, mobile or firmly attached to the substrate. There are molluscs which burrow into sand or mud, and these have streamlined shells and a specially modified 'foot' for burrowing. Others bore into wood, rock and coral boulders. Some species are so specific in their food requirements, as for example the carnivorous nudibranchs, that they are only found living on or among their prey. Certain species may be found in pairs during the breeding season, others occur as isolated individuals scattered sporadically over reef or sandy flat. Or they may aggregate in numbers as a means of conserving moisture.

In the process of their evolution the molluscs have adapted themselves in shape, size and in

the function of the various parts of the body to all these diversified habitats. Four of the six Classes of the Phylum are well represented along Australian coasts, and especially on the reefs of the Great Barrier, where several thousand species have been recorded. These Classes are the Amphineura, the Chitons or Coat-of-mail shells; the Gastropoda, the univalves including such forms as periwinkles, cowries, cones and many others together with the shell-less sea slugs; the Lamellibranchia or Pelecypoda, the bivalved shells such as clams, oysters and cockles, and the Cephalopoda—the octopus, cuttlefishes, squids and their relatives.

Despite this great diversity there are a number of features which are common to molluscs in general, and one of the most significant of these is the mantle. This special structure consists of a flap or fold of tissue covering the outside of the soft body and lying next to the shell (in those species which possess a shell). It encloses a cavity known as the mantle cavity in which the gills and other organs are situated. The cells of the mantle edge also perform the very important function of secreting the shell. Mollusc shells differ very considerably and range from fragile, transparent, thinly calcified forms to the highly polished, multi-coloured shells of cowries and volutes, and heavily sculptured *Murex* shells and the huge solid valves of the Giant Clams. In a typical univalve shell such as a marine snail, the shell consists of three separate layers, the outermost of which, the periostracum, is very thin and composed of a horny material, conchiolin. In many shells this layer is rather opaque and until it has been removed the colour pattern of the shell remains obscured. There is a middle prismatic layer of the shell, followed by an inner nacreous or pearly layer. These two inner layers are of calcium carbonate which has been laid down in different ways. In the prismatic layer the crystals are vertical, and thin lamellated layers of a crystalline form of calcium carbonate, known as aragonite, form the pearly layer.

Another distinctive feature possessed by all molluscs, except the bivalves, is a remarkable file-like apparatus, the radula, used by the animals when feeding. It consists of a long, thin, flexible ribbon covered with rows of minute recurved teeth, which the animal is able to replace as they are worn down. By means of the radula, which works over a cartilaginous structure within the buccal cavity, the mollusc is able to rasp or cut its food from the surrounding substrate. The number of teeth varies from a highly specialized few to many hundred thousand on a single radula ribbon, depending to a large extent on the carnivorous or herbivorous nature of the animal. In shells such as the poisonous Cones the teeth are long and hollow with barbed ends, arranged in pairs in the radula sheath. When a Cone attacks its prey, its extended proboscis shoots out a

The most obvious and numerous of the beach rock inhabitants are the small shells, *Planaxis sulcatus*, as they are found typically in clusters.

Whilst most species of the Family Littorinidae live at the top of the tideline on the high shore rocky slopes, the tropical *Littorina scabra*, climbs high up on the trunks and branches of the mangroves.

The boulder zone on some reefs, especially Near-Shore reefs of the Whitsunday Islands, may carry large populations of the small boring clam, *Tridacna crocea*, almost completely embedded in the solid coral rock.

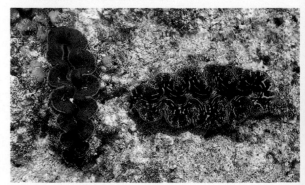
With the rising tide, the small clams magically colour the otherwise drab coral boulder.

There is extraordinary variation to be seen in the mantle colours of *Tridacna maxima*, from drab greyish browns and black to vivid greens and blues, Undine Reef.

Cryptoplax larvaeformis, easily recognized by the minute shell valves embedded in its girdle, is found under coral boulders on the reefs.

Cypraea arabica, one of the most commonly found cowries on the reefs, and its egg capsules.

The porcelain-white of the beautiful shell of the Egg cowrie, *Ovula ovum*, contrasts markedly with its black, white-flecked mantle. The shell of this species, often found in pairs on the reef flat, was of great significance on ceremonial occasions in the Pacific Islands. It is usually found on soft corals on which it feeds.

Fully grown Spider shells—the larger female and the smaller male.

A large clam with its mantle fully expanded and showing the inhalent and exhalent apertures by which water enters and leaves the body of the animal.

The Magic Carpet, or Spanish Dancer nudibranch, *Hexabranchus sanguineus*, one of the largest and most spectacular species on the reefs, especially when seen swimming. Undine Reef.

Unlike the Spider shells living among hard coral rubble, those found in sandy algal flats have very long slender spines.

The Barrier Reef Abalone, *Haliotis asinia*, with a mantle far larger than its small shell.

The Elephant snail, *Scutus antipodes*, completely covers its small shell with its large black mantle.

The Purple-mouthed *Strombus gibberulus* is found on the inner sand flats of the reef. The smaller shell is a species of *Nassarius*.

The Red-lip strombs, *Strombus luhuanus*, are the most numerous shells found in the open on semi-solidified rubble areas of the reefs.

radula tooth rather in the manner of a harpoon, and the prey is rapidly drawn to the mouth, at the same time becoming immobilized by a toxic secretion from a poison gland which opens into the mouth cavity.

In the Class Gastropoda which is both the largest and most diverse among the molluscs, the marine species can be broadly separated into two big groups, the snail-like Prosobranchia with shells, and the slug-like Opisthobranchia which are mostly either shell-less or possess only a thin internal shell, and which are among the most highly coloured and ornamental of all the marine invertebrates. In most species there is a well-defined head region, often with eyes at the base of a pair of sensory tentacles, and the animals crawl or glide over the substrate by means of a muscular foot, in some instances secreting a sheet of mucus which considerably aids their movements. An important structure possessed by many of the gastropods is the operculum—a hard, calcareous or horny flattened plate attached to the foot. When the animal withdraws into its shell the operculum, which fits tightly into the shell opening, closes the door as it were, and acts both as a protective mechanism, and also as a means of retaining moisture within the shell. The latter is especially important in the case of species living on reef areas uncovered at low tide which may be exposed for many hours to the tropical sun.

As with all other groups of animals associated with the coral reefs, it is necessary to know something of the habits and requirements of the various molluscs, if one is desirous of finding a particular shell without too much difficulty. The actual number of species to be found on the reefs depends to a certain extent on latitude, since there are some which do not range as far south as others. Again some molluscs migrate into shallower waters over the reefs during the breeding season. But generally speaking, abundance depends very largely upon the accessability of any reef and the amount of collecting to which it has been subjected. This does not, of course, apply where reefs are already proclaimed faunal reserves. For the visitor interested in the fauna of the reef as a whole, a general description of mollusc species likely to be seen as one crosses from shore to outer edge of a reef is perhaps the most useful.

On reefs along an island shore, there are often areas of beach rock or broken boulders which may support populations of animals not found elsewhere on a reef. One of the most interesting molluscs found here is the Chiton, *Acanthopleura gemmata*, the largest of the Australian Coat-of-mail shells. Two distinctive characters of the chitons are the shell, which is made up of eight separate transverse plates overlapping one another, and the girdle which is actually a fold of the mantle into which the sides of the shell valves are fitted. This very flexible shell not only enables the animal to move over rough surfaces,

Juvenile of the Spider shell, *Lambis lambis* (underside) showing the thin lip and ridges where spines will develop on the shell.

The small cowry, *Cypraea cribraria*, easily identified by its brilliantly coloured mantle.

The small Ring cowries, *Cypraea annulus*, often show a colour variation in the shell. Magnetic Island.

Cypraea vitellus with its creamy-white egg capsules.

but also to roll itself into a ball if dislodged, when the shell valves act as a protective armour. The very broad flat foot is strongly adhesive, and this together with the girdle, enables the chiton to clamp down so firmly on the substrate that it is very difficult to remove the animal without damaging it. These chitons seek shaded cracks and crevices during daylight hours, creeping about at night rasping small algae from the beach rock by means of the radula.

The small periwinkles, *Planaxis sulcatus*, and five or six species of Nerites are also found in these rocky areas along the beach. Where a sloping beach adjoins the sandy flats of a reef the small burrowing bivalve, *Atactodea striata*, may be found in numbers. It lies buried a few inches below the surface of the sand, and its dead shells are strewn along the tidelines. Typically the small white shell is often partially stained green by various species of small algae which utilize it as a substrate.

The near shore sand flats usually support a number of species of the Sand-plough snails of the Family Naticidae, easily detected by the trails they leave as they make their way through the sand. Their egg masses are commonly found on the flats in the spring months.

Even more obvious and more numerous on these inner sand flats are the purple mouthed *Strombus gibberulus*, which may be found lying scattered about on the open surface of the sand. Dead coral boulders in this region may be found to shelter several small molluscs, by far the most spectacular of which would be the swimming Lima, *Promantellum parafragile*, easily recognised by the conspicuous colour of its long, fragile mantle processes. These shells, one of the only two families of bivalves which are capable of rapid movement by swimming, clap the two valves of the shell together, and the water forced out of the shell cavity jet-propels the animal over the bottom.

Seawards on the reef flat, and especially in areas of semi-consolidated rubble, large numbers of the Red-mouthed Stromb, *Strombus luhuanus* are found. In these animals, the solid shell is banded with fawnish brown and has a highly polished, vivid orange-red aperture. Because of their shape the Strombs are sometimes mistaken for poisonous Cone shells, but the characteristic notch near the anterior end of the outer lip of the shell is quite unmistakable. As are the large stalked eyes, and the sharp serrated 'hook', which is a modified operculum, on the end of the slender, highly flexible foot.

The Strombs are amongst the most active of the shelled gastropods, moving by a series of jerks which are achieved by thrusting the claw-like operculum into the sand and contracting the muscular foot. A notable fact about the family is that they are almost without exception found lying in the open on the reefs. The best known member is probably the Spider shell, *Lambis lambis*, which gets its name from the number of tapered spines borne along the

A pair of mating Bailer shells, *Melo amphora*, from deeper water in the reef lagoon. Wistari, January, 1970.

Female and male Bailer shells.

The Razor clam, *Atrina gouldii*, lies in sandy muddy areas of the reef flat, almost completely buried. Low Isles.

The Sea Hare, *Aplysia dactylomela*, found in both temperate and tropical waters in Australia, grows to a very large size on the reefs where it may be seen crawling among the algae and coral rubble in pools. Heron Island.

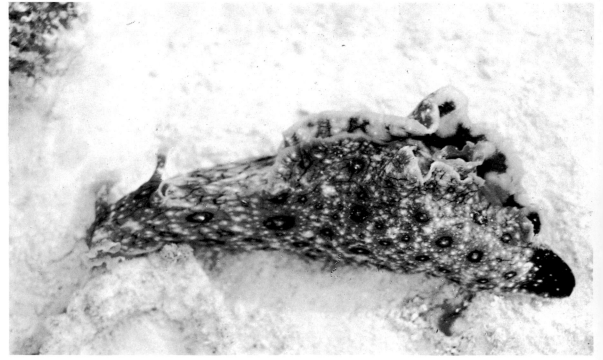

Periglypta reticulata and Periglypta puerpera. Solid white shells with brown markings, from shallow water sand flats.

The Cockle shell, Fragum unedo, has solid, beautifully sculptured shells, yellow and white with red markings, and is very common on Barrier Reef sandy flats.

The pink and white Tellinella virgata lives deep down in sandy areas, but its dead valves are often picked up on the reefs.

The sand snails, species of Polinices, plough through the sand along the tide line at low water.

Conspicuous objects of the sand flats on the reefs at certain times of the year—spring and early summer—are

the sandy smooth or scalloped coils of eggs of the Sand-plough snails of the Family Naticidae.

extended outer lip of the shell. The animal itself is a mottled green and cream, combining well with the colourful, highly polished underside of the large spiked shell. Usually, in the adult form, the shell on its upper surface is so eroded, or covered with encrusting forms that it is barely recognizable against its background.

There are at least eighteen species of Strombs found in Barrier Reef waters, ranging in size from two inches to about a foot in length, and most are widely distributed throughout the Indo-Pacific Region.

Another group of shells often found lying out on the outer semi-consolidated rubble areas of reefs is that of the Cones. Because of their widespread reputation as dangerous marine animals, these shells are often referred to as poisonous Cones. At least seventy or eighty species have been recorded for the Barrier Reefs and their shells may be very beautiful, with their characteristic shape and diversity of colour pattern. In addition to the highly specialized radula and poison gland, the Cone shells possess a more powerful sensory organ than most other gastropods, all of which combine to make them dangerous predators in their environment. Since human beings have been partially paralysed, or have died, as a result of handling Cone shells, considerable research has in recent years been carried out on the toxic effects. Studies to date indicate that the food of Cone shells consists mainly of small fish, molluscs and marine worms, varying according to the species, and evidence seems to show that only those species which eat fish, and whose venom has, therefore, a toxic effect on vertebrates, are harmful to man. A number of the Cones retreat under cover of dead coral boulders during daylight, and this seems to be a preferred place for the laying of their egg capsules. The species, Puncticulus arenatus is a sand-dwelling animal, found on sandy outer reef areas, often only uncovered by low spring tides. Here molluscs of several other families are also on occasion to be seen. Sometimes it is possible to trace them by the slight trails they make when feeding. This applies especially to the Creeper shells, the Augers and their relatives, notable for the beauty of their highly glossed surfaces and their lovely tapered shapes, and also to some of the smaller Volutes. Many of the Volutes lie buried during the day and emerge to feed at night. Shells of this group are amongst those most popularly sought by collectors, for they are beautifully marked, usually with colour tones ranging from dark- to reddish-brown, through pinkish, orange to golden yellow, and they are normally highly polished. Fortunately for the Volutes many live in deeper water and are thus difficult to find and collect.

The largest and most handsome members of the Volutidæ are the Bailer shells. Where there are deep sandy pools on an outer reef, or lagoons within a reef, there is always the chance

The swimming bivalve, *Promantellum parafragile*, with its long brightly coloured mantle processes, lives under boulders in sandy areas of the reefs and when disturbed swims with rapid jerky movements. Langford Reef.

Colourful little Bubble shells, *Haminoea cymbalum*.

of an exciting find, such as a pair of mating Bailers, or a large female laying her eggs in a great mass of capsules. These carnivorous animals have an extremely powerful foot which serves a dual purpose. It enables the animal to plough through the sand in search of prey—usually other molluscs—which it then completely smothers by this enormous foot. By this means Bailers are able to attack such large and seemingly invulnerable animals as the Horse-shoe Clam, with its solid shell valves held together by powerful muscles. It is only a matter of time, then the muscles give and the clam succumbs. Immediately the Bailer inserts its long extensile proboscis in which the radula is situated, and tears away at the flesh of the clam.

The Helmet Shell, *Cassis cornuta*, is another large mollusc to be found in deep sandy pools along the edge of a reef. Often the only indication of its presence is the rounded, eroded top of the shell projecting a few inches above the sandy substrate, looking very like a small boulder embedded in the sand. The Helmet Shells have a long history of association with man. Not only are their beautifully marked shells prized by collectors, but the large Helmets of Mediterranean seas have for centuries been used in the making of cameos, exquisitely carved from the shells by highly skilled craftsmen.

The Helmets are also carnivorous in their habits, and the related King Helmet of West Indian seas is known to prey consistently on the large Needle-spined urchin, little daunted by the sharp spines which can cause so much pain to the human flesh. Examination of the animal's foot reveals little if any damage after the urchin has been captured and consumed.

Also occurring in deeper waters off the reef edge are the large Trumpet or Triton shells, *Charonia tritonis*, although small specimens may sometimes be seen on the reef flats. This is one of the most spectacular of the tropical shells, reaching in mature individuals a length of eighteen inches and more. In life, the distinctive markings of the shell are sometimes obliterated by the outer layer of periostracum, but the wide mouth with its characteristic orange to gold markings is highly polished.

Amongst the world's best-known shells are the members of the Family Cypraeidae, the cowries. They seem to epitomize all the qualities that appeal in a shell and their highly polished elegance has always placed them amongst collectors' items. The beautiful lustre seen on these shells is due to the protection given to them by the lobes of the mantle which normally cover the external surface. The mantle itself is not unattractive—often highly coloured and ornamented with various processes on its outer layer.

In shape the cowrie bears little resemblance to a typical coiled gastropod shell since it has a flattened base and a long narrow opening whose

A pair of Bailer shells.

A juvenile Bailer shell, with the animal fully extended as it crawls over the sand.

Volutes of northern sandy reefs—*Cymbiolacca wisemani*.

The large Helmet Shell, *Cassis cornuta*, may sometimes be seen in deep sandy pools at the edge of the reef. Normally only the eroded top of the shell is visible.

Creepers of the sandy reef flats—the large *Terebra maculata*, *Terebra muscaria*, and two creamy *Cerithium vertagus*.

A Tun shell of the genus *Tonna*, taken at night showing the strikingly marked animal.

Caroli's volute, *Amoria maculata*, with its strikingly patterned mantle partially showing as it moves through the sand of the reef flat.

Conus marmoreus with siphon and foot partially extended. This is one of the cone shells commonly found on coral rubble areas of the reef.

The cone, *Conus textile* and its egg capsules found on the underside of a boulder. Watson Island.

The Giant Triton shell, *Charonia tritonis*.

solid, rolled, highly polished lips are often toothed or grooved. The cowries are particularly plentiful in warm tropical waters and are among the most common shells occurring on some of the reefs, where they may be found under boulders or in crevices among the corals. In a few instances, however, especially the small Money Cowries, and their relatives the Ring Cowries, they seem to prefer the open reef flat, browsing on small algae and other organic matter among the rubble.

The Opisthobranchia, the Sea slugs and Sea Hares and their allies, represent a very large group of the Mollusca, but because of the difficulty in collecting and preserving them, they have perhaps fortunately been left to the specialists. These animals must really be seen alive, for only then can their delicate beauty, flamboyant colours, and elegance and grace of movement be fully appreciated. Only with colour movie film is it possible to capture their elusive charm. Their shells are generally very reduced, internal, or completely lacking, and both colour and shape are lost when the animal is preserved. In the various species of Bubble shells, there is an external and obvious shell, which is sometimes almost completely hidden by the large frilled mantle. In the Sea Hares the thin fragile shell is internal and in the colourful sea slugs, the Nudibranchs, there is no shell at all.

Although the gastropod molluscs are undoubtedly the most beautiful from the point of view of their shell coloration and sculpture, the bivalves nevertheless outclass them in one family at least, in size, the colour of the animals themselves, and in their extraordinary adaptation to life on tropical reefs.

One of the most vivid and unforgettable sights of a visit to a coral reef is that first glimpse of one of its most characteristic inhabitants—a large clam. Seen through the clear shallow water, the clam lies with its valves apart and the beautiful mantle—like the richest velvet in its brilliant colouring—fully expanded in the sunlight. From dull fawns, brown and black, the colours range through olive greens to purple, peacock blue and ultramarine, in all possible combinations. The clams of the Family Tridacnidae vary in size from the small boring *Tridacna crocea*, only a few inches long, to the Giant Clam with its huge, heavy valves up to three feet and more in length.

Each member of the Family has its own preferred habitat on the reef and is always to be found in that particular locale. Whilst the Giant Clam, and the Horseshoe Clam are always free-living animals lying in the open, the Giant Clam often in slightly deeper water along the edges of a reef, and the Horseshoe Clam on sandy or rubble areas of the open reef flat in the more northern region, the small *Tridacna crocea* is always to be seen embedded to the top edges of its valves in solid coral boulders. The larger *Tridacna maxima* is usually found more or less

The nudibranch, *Phyllidia ocellata*.

The Sea Hare, *Aplysia dactylomela*, found in both temperate and tropical waters in Australia, grows to a very large size on the reefs where it may be seen crawling among the algae and coral rubble in pools. Heron Island.

The side-gilled sea slug, *Pleurobranchus forskali*.

The small green *Elysia bennettae* are usually found in clusters among algae on the outer reef flat. Heron Island.

The nudibranch, a species of *Halgerda*, from Carter Reef.

The clam, *Tridacna maxima*, is usually found embedded among living corals or rubble and there is extraordinary variation to be seen in the colours of the mantle.

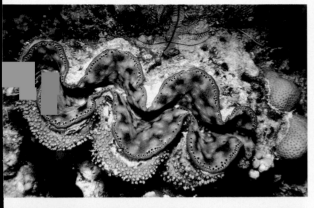

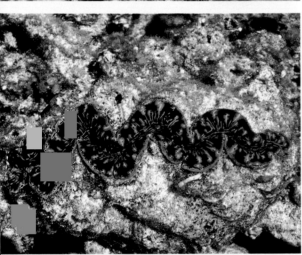

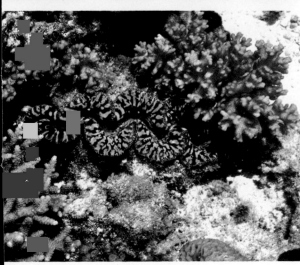

A Giant Clam, *Tridacna gigas*, lying fully uncovered at low tide among corals and rubble, Michaelmas Reef.

The Giant Clam is usually seen in deeper water. The valves of the shell are only partially open and their projections together with the tough and very solid mantle which fills the opening, make it practically an impossibility for a human foot to be trapped, as often reported.

loosely embedded in coral rubble or among living corals in pools and outer reef areas.

Most molluscs obtain their oxygen directly from the sea-water by means of gills in the mantle cavity. In the bivalves these gills have become developed to such an extent that in many species they also act as the food-catching apparatus. Most bivalves are filter-feeding animals, sieving minute organisms from the surrounding sea water and because of this method of feeding, they have no differentiated head region and no radula.

It is in the method of feeding that the clams of the Family Tridacnidae display their remarkable adaptation to their environment. In the course of their evolution the various members have become structurally modified in such a manner that best enables them to develop in the particular habitat they have selected on the reef. Considerable difference may be seen in both shell shape and internal organs between the burrowing and free-living species of the Family. There is, however, a unifying similarity in these clams, all of which normally live with the animal lying on the hinge side of the shell, and the edges of the shell valves pointing upwards. The result of this mode of living is that the internal organs in their relationship to the mantle and shell differ from those of all other bivalve molluscs. The mantle-tissue, by reason of the animal's way of life, is capable of considerable expansion, and is exposed to the direct rays of the sun to the greatest possible extent. This is undoubtedly associated with the most unique feature of all displayed by these remarkable molluscs, for within this mantle tissue there are to be found millions of tiny Zooxanthellae, closely resembling the symbiotic algae found in the corals and the alcyonarians. (Zooxanthellae have recently been cultured from several species of clams from Barrier Reef waters and their identity has been definitely established as the symbiotic dinoflagellate, *Gymnodinium micro-adriaticum*, originally recorded from coelenterates in the Caribbean Sea.)

On the surface of the mantle there are large numbers of small lens-like structures, usually in rows, which allow penetration of light deep into the tissues of the animal. It has been definitely established that these zooxanthellae form a considerable part of the diet of the Tridacnas, and the modifications found in these molluscs indicate that they are not only specialized for harbouring these minute algae, but that they also deliberately 'farm' them. This must surely be one of the most fascinating examples of symbiosis to be found in nature. The whole ecology of the clams, bound exclusively to warm, shallow waters of tropical seas, appears linked to an increase in the efficiency of that symbiosis which gives food and protection to the algae and very considerable additional nutrient from its symbionts to the clams.

On the whole, the bivalved molluscs, apart from the large clams, are not conspicuous members of the reef community, except perhaps where there are islands with limestone ridges or areas of large boulders in the intertidal zone when massed encrustations of oysters may be found. The oysters and the Chamas are permanently attached to their rocky substrates to which they have become firmly cemented. Boring forms are found within rock or coral boulders. Some bivalves, and notably among these are the well-known mussels, attach themselves to the solid substrate by means of special threads secreted by the animals, which form an anchoring attachment known as the byssus. On outer rubble areas on some reef flats small mussels may occur in large numbers forming quite extensive beds. The greater number of bivalve species are found in sandy or muddy areas of the reef flats where such shells as the Cockle, *Fragum unedo*, and others may be collected.

The large and very beautiful Golden Lip pearl oyster, *Pinctada maxima*, and the slightly smaller Black Lip, *Pinctada margaritifera*, have for many years formed the basis of a valuable commercial fishery in Barrier Reef waters for Mother-of-Pearl. The Black Lip is sometimes found as an isolated individual attached by its byssus to a coral boulder on the reefs, but the Golden Lip is brought up from deeper waters by the pearl divers. Today both species are being used extensively in the 'cultured' pearl industry in northern Australian waters. The shells are collected by Torres Strait Islanders and brought back in their luggers to bases on the various islands such as those in the vicinity of Cape York (Map V).

The Class Cephalopoda of the Molluscs is regarded as one of the most important and most highly developed groups of all marine invertebrates. Aristotle, in his famous *Historia Animalium*, was writing of octopuses, cuttlefish and squids of the Mediterranean more than 300 years before the birth of Christ, but it remained for the French novelist Victor Hugo, nearly two thousand years later, to bring the octopus and its relatives to notoriety in the eyes of the world. To the zoologist there are so many fascinating features about the cephalopods that it is difficult to share the general feeling of repulsion towards them. As a group, however, they are far more creatures of the open sea than of the coral reefs and so their part among the members of the reef community is small. Octopuses are sometimes found in coral pools and their egg capsules, and those of some of the cuttlefishes are laid under the shelter of boulders on the reef flat. The very delicate little Ram's Horn Shell, *Spirula spirula*, lives in the mid-deep layers of the ocean, but the empty shells are familiar objects along the strandlines of some of the coral cays after heavy storms. On the more northern reefs of the Great Barrier, the beautifully marked shell of the Chambered or Pearly Nautilus is occasionally found, again

tossed up on the shore by gale-force winds. The story of the Pearly Nautilus, last living genus related to a vast array of fossil forms, is a long and fascinating one, from its original discovery in Indonesian waters in 1705 through a series of large zoological monographs in the 19th century to Dr. Willey's entertaining description of living animals kept in captivity in New Caledonia waters, at the beginning of this century.

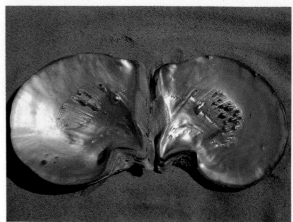

The Golden Lip pearl shell, *Pinctada maxima* (half-grown specimen). Numerous 'pearl blisters' may be seen.

The Black Lip pearl shell, *Pinctada margaritifera*.

A cuttle fish, a species of *Sepia*, at Lizard Island.

Only in the very small, uneroded shells of the Horseshoe Clam, *Hippopus hippopus*, is the colour of the valves and the very characteristic shape of the horse's foot, which gives it its name, to be clearly seen. North Barrow Island. ▶

speaking, is far less familiar to most people than sea shells or fishes, for example.

The phylum Echinodermata contains some of the most spectacular, colourful and fascinating animals of the seashore, and its five Classes link together an extraordinary assemblage of animals which are quite distinct from all others in the sea. These Classes are: the Crinoidea, the sea lillies and feather stars; the Asteroidea, the star-fishes or sea stars; the Ophiuroidea, the brittle stars or snake stars, the Echinoidea, the sea urchins, heart urchins, and sand dollars; and the Holothuroidea, the sea cucumbers, *Bêche-de-mer*, or Trepang.

The five thousand or so known species, of which between 900 and 1000 have been recorded from Australian coastal waters, are found on rocky shores, sandy beaches and coral reefs, down to the depths of the ocean, but never in fresh water. Whilst a small number of species are pelagic, spending their lives swimming about in the sea, most are bottom-dwellers—slow-moving animals which may occur on the sea floor in enormous numbers. With the exception of a few of the sea lillies which are permanently attached to the substrate by a stalk, the echinoderms are free-living animals each of which has selected its particular habitat in the sea.

Although superficially the various Classes may bear little resemblance to one another, there are several unique features which unite them together in the one phylum. One of the most important of these is the radial symmetry shown by the arrangement of the five divisions of the body around a central region. The body is supported by an internal skeleton consisting of calcareous plates, known as ossicles, which either articulate with one another or are more or less rigidly joined together, as in the sea stars and sea urchins, or there may be scattered plates and spicules embedded in the outer tissues as in the holothurians. Again, in many species, the skeleton will be seen to be covered with spines, a feature which gave rise to the name of the phylum—the spiny skinned animals. As in the case of molluscan shells, the calcareous remains of echinoderms play a quite considerable part in adding to the detritus which, when consolidated by agencies such as encrusting algae, helps in the building up of the reef surface over geological time, counter-balancing to a certain extent the boring activities of these animals.

Because of the radial symmetry of the echinoderm body there is no anterior "head" end, and the area surrounding the mouth is known as the oral surface whilst the opposite side is the aboral surface. Thus a starfish, or a sea urchin, creeps about, usually rather slowly, mouth downwards, on the sea floor. The means

A Feather star among coral on the reef flat.

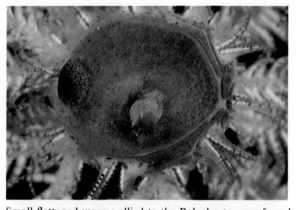

The feather star, *Comanthus bennetti*, in its characteristic position on top of a boulder. Swain Reefs.

Small flattened worms allied to the Polychaetes, are found living as commensals on the oral region of feather stars.

The starfish of tropical reef sandy flats, *Archaster laevis*. Very often the only indication of the presence of these starfish is a slight depression in the sand. All the starfish in this picture disappeared beneath the surface within a few moments. Cairncross Reef.

The feather star, *Himerometra robustipinna*.

Starfish of the flat reef. Heron Island.

The starfish, *Nardoa rosea*.

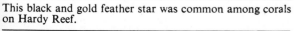

This black and gold feather star was common among corals on Hardy Reef.

A colour form found under boulders on sandy reef flats

145

whereby these animals move is one of their most fascinating features. All echinoderms possess appendages known as tube feet, delicate structures which exhibit an extraordinary variety of structure and function. Not only are they the means of locomotion, but they also act as sensory, feeding and respiratory organs. And the mechanism by which these tube-feet are operated is one of the most amazing and unique in the animal kingdom. Within the body of all echinoderms there is a water-vascular system which consists of a ring-shaped tube or canal encircling the mouth region, and from it five radial canals lead into the five sectors of the body. In a starfish or a sea urchin sea water enters through a small button-like structure on the aboral surface and passes through the radial canals to an extensive series of fine tubes, each of which has an internal muscular bulb, and a long hollow *tube foot*. Extension of the tube feet is brought about by contraction of the bulbs which force liquid into the cavities of the tube feet. By the relaxing of the bulbs, and contraction of the muscles within the walls, the tube feet are drawn back. The muscles also control the direction in which the tube feet are extended. Thus, in starfish, sea urchins and in the holothurians, this water-vascular system is responsible for all movement by the animals, which progress by means of these tube feet—a built-in hydraulic system evolved millions of years before man invented them for his everyday use. Small suction discs at the tips of the tube feet enable an echinoderm to adhere to solid objects, thus resisting the force of the waves. In some species the disc is so efficient that it may be torn away from its tube foot if one attempts to dislodge a starfish or sea urchin clinging to the substrate. There are no discs on the papillate tube feet of feather stars or brittle stars, which have somewhat pointed ends and are not used in locomotion.

The crinoids represent the most ancient group of the Echinodermata and are very numerous as fossil species. The stalked sea lilies are mostly attached animals living in deeper waters, but the feather stars occur mainly in the tropical waters and they may be found on most coral reefs where they are commonly to be seen sheltering under boulders, or among corals in deeper waters over the reef edge. In the feather stars the aboral surface bears whorls of jointed appendages known as cirri, by means of which the animal clings to the substrate. The body is drawn out into slender, pinnate or feathery arms—hence the common name—and these surround the mouth on the oral surface. Thus the mouth, in the crinoids, is found on the upper surface and not on the underside as in the starfish, sea urchins and brittle stars.

The cirri, arms and the tiny pinnules all have a characteristic 'jointed' appearance which is given by the internal, calcareous plates of the skeleton. Both the colour and the number of arms in these tropical feather stars are very

In its juvenile stage, the Pincushion Star *Culcita*, is much more easily recognisable as a starfish. Low Isles.

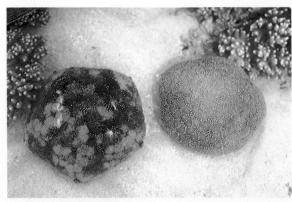

Three colour varieties of the large Pincushion star, *Culcita novaeguineae*.

The underside of the starfish *Culcita*, showing the teeth surrounding the mouth.

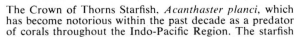

The Crown of Thorns Starfish, *Acanthaster planci*, which has become notorious within the past decade as a predator of corals throughout the Indo-Pacific Region. The starfish as seen in massed aggregation, The Slashers Reef Complex, north-east of Townsville, August 1970.

The starfish, *Leiaster leachii*.

Two starfish most often seen on the open reef flat, *Nardoa novaecaledoniae* and *Nardoa pauciforis*.

The Rhinoceros starfish, *Protoreaster nodosus*, is one of the best-known and most colourful species with a wide Indo-Pacific distribution. The colour of the body and arms varies from cream to bright red, with black-tipped spines.

Echinaster luzonicus, with colours ranging from a bright to rusty red and brown to almost black, is another starfish easily found on the open reef flat or under boulders.

Two colour varieties of the starfish, *Pentaceraster regulus*, trawled in 25 metres east of Wistari Reef.

Acanthaster planci. Close-up of part of the upper surface of the starfish, showing respiratory papulae and the tiny pincers (Pedicellariae), by means of which the animal is able to remove foreign particles. This starfish, from Fitzroy Reef, measured 28 inches from arm tip to arm tip across the body.

The edible sea urchin, *Tripneustes gratilla* and the poisonous *Toxopneustes pileolus.* The whole surface of the latter is covered with colourful, flower-like pincers (pedicellariae) which are hollow and connected with venom glands at their bases.

Needle-spined urchins, *Diadema setosum,* among rubble in a moat area, Low Isles.

variable. An animal may be dark red or almost black, with a small number of arms, usually in multiples of five. It may be found in soft creamy, orange, yellow, fawn or other pastel shades, with as many as two hundred arms. By movement of these arms the feather star swims with graceful undulations through the sea water.

Quite apart from the notoriety surrounding the Crown-of-Thorns, starfishes or sea stars are perhaps the most familiar of the echinoderms, well-known to all who visit the seashore. All shapes, sizes and colours, they are found from cold deep waters of polar seas to tropical coral reefs. Whilst a typical starfish has a body consisting of a central disc with five arms radiating from it, the number of arms may vary in the different species between five and fifty. In some species the number is always constant. In others it differs considerably, as in the Crown-of-thorns which may be found with seven or seventeen arms.

The mouth of a starfish will be seen in the centre of the under, oral surface of the body and is usually surrounded by sculptured teeth. Along the centre of the oral surface of each of the arms there is a groove, usually bordered with spines, which contains from two to four rows of tube feet. Not only does the starfish move about by means of these tube feet, but they also enable it to right itself if turned over, or to hold its prey. Whilst a few of the starfish are detrital feeders, most are carnivorous, preying on other marine animals such as corals, crustaceans, worms and molluscs. When attacking a bivalve mollusc, the starfish attaches its suckered tube feet to each valve and exerts pressure, pulling until the muscles holding the valves together finally give way under the continued strain. The thin sac-like convoluted stomach of the starfish is then protruded through the mouth and completely envelops its prey, secreting enzymes to digest it.

Close examination of the upper surface of a starfish will reveal the presence between the spines or plates, depending on the species, of small soft filaments known as papulae which are scattered over the body and along the arms and which aid both in respiration and excretion. Here, too, another unique feature, found in both the starfishes and the sea urchins, may be seen. Small pincer-like 'jaws' known as pedicellariae are used to remove all foreign particles which, by covering the epithelial tissues and the vital soft parts, could prove a menace to the metabolic efficiency of the animals. This explains why these echinoderms, whose often large and rigid bodies otherwise offer excellent places of settlement for the larval stages of sedentary species, are never found covered with encrustations of various sorts.

It is fascinating to watch, under high power lens or microscope, the almost uncanny 'robot-like' movements of these minute structures at work, activated as it were by remote control

from deep within the body of the starfish.

Although reproduction among starfish takes place in the usual way with males and females shedding sperm and eggs into the sea where the fertilized egg develops into a planktonic larval stage, a number of starfish also reproduce asexually, by simply splitting the central disc in two. Each part is capable of regenerating new arms and the remainder of the disc. The power of regeneration is so great in these animals that most are able to replace lost or damaged arms. One of the most beautiful of the reef starfish, the vivid blue *Linckia laevigata* is even capable of regenerating a whole new disc and set of arms on each severed arm.

Whilst many of the starfish of the Barrier Reef Province are found in deeper waters surrounding the reefs, some species such as the large and colourful *Protoreaster nodosus*, migrate into the shallower waters at certain times of the year and may be seen in large numbers on reef flats uncovered by low spring tides. One of the most unusual and interesting starfish which is very often seen on the reefs is the large Pincushion star, *Culcita novaeguineae,* The common name is very apt, and seen from above as it lies among the corals or in pools, the animal bears little resemblance to a typical five-armed starfish.

The now notorious Crown-of-Thorns starfish, *Acanthaster planci,* was originally described by the famous Swedish zoologist Linnaeus as long ago as 1758. Its appearance in plague proportions as a predator of corals throughout the Indo-Pacific region had been sudden and dramatic. The living veneer of any reef represents such a very small percentage of its total structure that any threat to the living corals and, therefore, to the whole ecological structure of any reef community, must be regarded as a very real danger. It was argued that the outbreak was a natural phenomenon occurring periodically throughout the evolutionary history of the reefs. Since there are so many reefs within the Great Barrier Reef Province, partial destruction of some (and this was shown to be only a small percentage on many of the reefs attacked) was no great threat to the whole.

There is now some geological evidence indicating that the outbreak *is* an episodic occurrence, a natural if infrequent phenomenon.

From observations made to date, the starfish appears to be a nocturnal feeder, and during daylight hours seeks shelter in the deeper waters along the reef edge under and in among the corals. There is the remote possibility, therefore, that its presence in large numbers may have been overlooked in the past—and has only been revealed in recent years, with the advent of modern skin-diving techniques used by trained observers.

All the theories put forward, all the opinions expressed, were mere speculation, both as to cause and effect. Quite simply, no one knows. Whether the infestation by the starfish over the past 20 years is cyclic or not, a natural phenomenon occurring may be once every hundred or two hundred years, one *very certain* fact remains. With vastly expanding human activities, the environmental conditions of the waters of the Reef Province will never again return to the undisturbed and unspoiled state of bygone days—conditions which, a century ago, would have permitted rapid and extensive regrowth of devastated corals.

It is an ironic situation where the corals, now severely threatened by the adult starfish. must themselves be considered as amongst its greatest predators. During the starfish breeding season in the Australian summer months of December and January, a massed aggregation, such as that shown on page 146, would release millions upon millions of eggs. The searching tentacles of the equally teeming millions of carnivorous coral polyps could hardly fail to capture a large percentage of the resulting larval stages drifting about in the waters covering the reefs.

Although the Brittle stars are not nearly so well-known as the starfish and the sea urchin, there arc many reefs throughout the Great Barrier, where they are amongst the most numerous and conspicuous inhabitants of rubble areas of the reef where they may be seen lying in the open or partially hidden under coral fragments. Although there is some resemblance between the brittle stars and the starfish, it will be noted that the central disc of the body of the brittle star is very clearly defined and the arms radiate at a wide angle from it. The brittle stars are the fastest moving and most active of all the echinoderms, and by using the five arms are able to move with considerable speed in any direction. The structure of the arms also differs considerably from those of the starfish. The jointed appearance is given by the four rows of calcareous plates or shields which form the internal skeleton of the arms, which are extraordinarily flexible. The sinuous movement of a brittle star is fascinating to watch. Often two side arms are used to push the animal along with oar-like movements—one arm, or maybe two in front keeping the disc slightly raised, and the fifth arm trailing behind. Alternately there may be only one arm in front, thrust forward by the other two pair.

Brittle stars are quite harmless, but should be handled with care for they are well named, and the arms break off very easily. As with the starfish, however, their powers of regeneration are such that a new arm is soon grown again. One very common reef species, *Macrophiothrix longipeda*, is almost impossible to collect with all its arms intact. This animal has a habit of secreting itself in crevices among the coral rubble with one long arm protruding, weaving conspicuously about over the surrounding area, and it is extremely difficult to extricate.

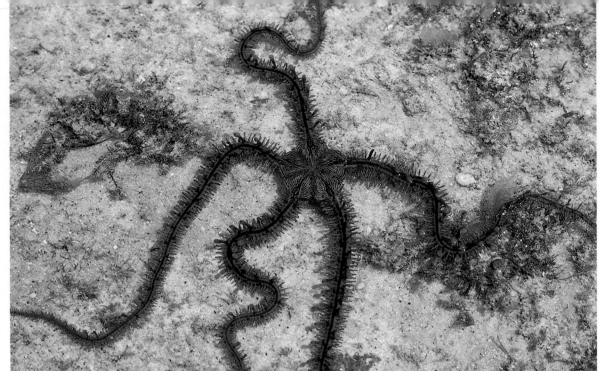

Brittle stars of the genus *Ophiomastix* are extremely common on the more northern reefs. They are often seen in numbers among coral rubble on the open reef flat.

A closer view shows the characteristic club-shaped spines on the arms. These brittle stars move very rapidly.

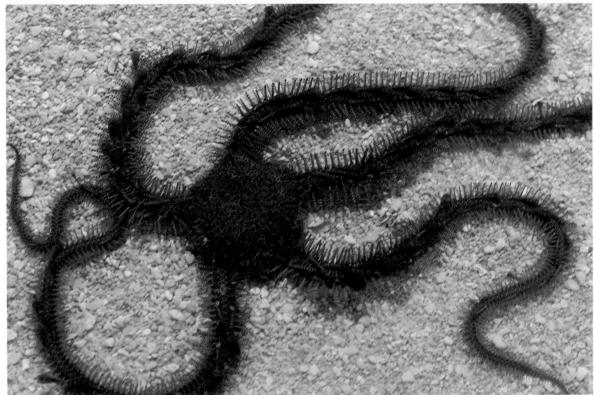

The beautifully coloured body and spines of *Ophiarachna incrassata*.

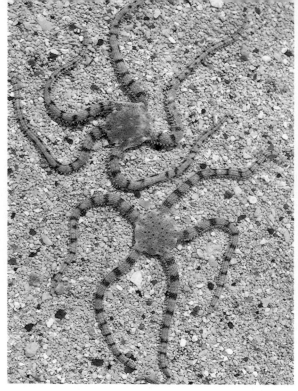

A pair of Brittle stars from Hook Reef, *Ophioplocus imbricatus.* On the more northern reefs juveniles, pale green and white in colour, are commonly found under boulders in sandy areas.

Macrophiothrix longipeda, a large brittle star with extraordinarily long arms. The animal is rarely seen fully exposed on the reef, but one long arm is often visible projecting from beneath coral rubble in search of food.

The largest of the Barrier Reef Brittle stars is the beautiful green *Ophiarachna incrassata.*

Ophiolepis superba, with its distinctive marking, solid body and arms, and its habit of lying inert on the reef, make it easily identifiable.

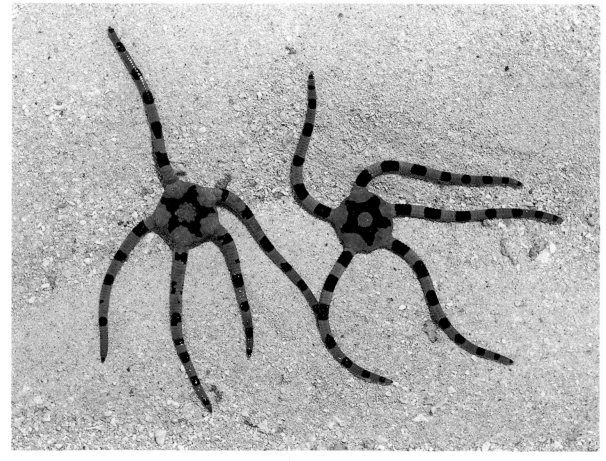

A wide range of colour patterns, sculpturing of the skeleton, and arrangement of spines on the arms and discs is to be found on the brittle stars. And under a high-powered lens or microscope, they will be seen to be amongst the most exquisite designs found in the animal kingdom.

Whilst large, rather solid forms such as *Ophiolepis superba* may be found lying on the surface of a reef, many others in their countless thousands shelter during daylight hours in the sandy substrate among rubble and under coral boulders.

Unlike the echinoderms already mentioned, the sea urchins, the heart urchins and the sand dollars have no arms at all, and the body, which may be rounded, oval shaped or flattened, is densely covered with long or short moveable spines, the most conspicuous and characteristic feature of these animals. The internal skeleton is a solid structure, known as the test, and is made up of calcareous plates which are fused together. Dead tests may often be picked up on the reefs, and if one of these is examined the surface will be seen to be clearly marked in ten radiating sections, five of which are perforated for the rows of tube feet. The five alternating sections bear tubercles of different sizes over which the concave bases of the spines are fitted, making a perfect ball and socket joint and allowing free movement of the spines in any direction.

The spines, all of which are covered with a very thin layer of tissue, vary considerably in both size and sculpturing. Whilst in some species the spines are either all long or all short, most have both long (primary) and short (secondary) spines. These may be smooth, or sculptured, circular, triangular or flattened in cross section, blunt tipped, or needle sharp. There are a few species which have poison sacs on the spines, but all sea urchins should be handled with care for the spines are not only extremely brittle but their nature is such that it is very difficult to remove a piece and especially its covering tissue, embedded in one's finger, so that even non-poisonous spines can inflict painful wounds.

The sea urchins are herbivorous animals, and the large mouth on the underside of the body, the oral surface, is surrounded by five strong teeth or jaws, which are supported internally in a complex calcareous structure, known as Aristotle's Lantern, after its discoverer. The sea urchins use these powerful jaws to scrape the algal film from the rubble substrate or coral boulders. In species such as *Echinostrephus aciculatus* and *Echinometra mathaei*, which are found in hollowed out areas in the coral, the animal sometimes fits so tightly into its hollow that it is impossible to remove it without breaking the spines. They are among the boring species which cause considerable damage to the reefs. It is not known how long it takes to make these holes, which could be the result of the scraping action of jaws and spines of many generations of sea urchins.

Large numbers of small jaw-like pedicellariae are to be found usually round the bases of the spines of the sea urchins. Most consist of three tiny 'jaws' borne on a stalk, and in some urchins as many as four different types may be found. In species such as *Toxopneustes pileolis* a poison gland surrounds the jaws.

One of the largest, best-known and certainly the most conspicuous of the sea urchins of the coral reefs is the Needle-spined *Diadema setosum*. This sea urchin is widely distributed in tropical waters throughout the world. Sometimes it is found wedged in among corals in pools, but quite often numbers may be seen clustered round dead coral boulders in shallow moats on the reef flat. Among the very long primary spines, series of very much finer secondary spines may be seen. A closely related *Diadema savignyi* occurs on the reefs and it is reasonably easy to distinguish between them in the field, since in *Diadema setosum* the large anal tube which protrudes among the spines on the upper surface of the body is tipped with reddish orange and the body itself is flecked with white spots. In the adult urchins the long slender spines are a dark reddish purple but in the juveniles the spines are characteristically banded with white.

Small fish of at least three different species have been found living in close association with these long spined urchins, darting down among the spines at the approach of danger. A pair of small shrimps, beautifully coloured to match their background, are also on occasion found among the spines.

A third Needle-spined urchin, found more commonly on reefs in the Northern Region of the Great Barrier, is the beautiful *Echinothrix calamaris*. Another large and very spectacular species of the reefs is the Slate pencil urchin, *Heterocentrotus mammillatus*. Its heavy blunt spines may be up to half an inch in diameter and five inches in length.

Whilst the sea urchins are generally among the more conspicuous animals on the reefs, the little heart urchins, the sand dollars and their relatives, because of their mode of living, are not often seen, although they may be present in considerable numbers. They are to be found in sandy areas of the reef flat, and they have become specially adapted for a burrowing existence, with the result that they are all more or less flattened. The spines which cover the body are usually all very short, but they differ in length, some being used as an aid in burrowing. Two species commonly found on the sandy flats are the small round Dollar urchins, *Arachnoides placenta*, and the Sand Dollar, *Laganum depressum*. Their presence is sometimes indicated by faint trails and depressions on the surface of the sand.

The holothurians, the sea cucumbers, are the least known of all the echinoderms and they are

Needle spined sea urchins, *Diadema setosum*, Porites Pond. Low Isles, August 1954.

One of the most numerous and widely distributed sea urchins of the reefs is the oval shaped *Echinometra mathaei*. The colour varies from fawn and olive-green to purple, but the spines are most invariably tipped with white.

The Cake urchin, *Clypeaster telurus*, sand flat, Heron Reef.

Sand dollars, *Arachnoides placenta*.

The Prickly Red Fish, *Thelenota ananas*, from northern reefs, was once the most valuable of the commercial species which formed the *Beche de mer* fishery of the Torres Strait region. The largest of the holothurians, its very solid body with only minute calcareous granules made it highly prized by the fishermen.

A holothurian, taken in typical spawning position at night. Heron Island, February 1979.

The long, slender *Synapta maculata,* is capable of considerable extension of its body. When picked up, these specimens measured over 6 feet. The body has a prickly consistency when touched, caused by the minute, anchorlike spicules embedded in its tissues.

The related *Holothuria leucospilota* as it is usually seen feeding with its tentacles extended over the sand.

The small *Chirodota rigida* is common just below the surface along the edge of the reef flat where it abuts the sand cay. Heron Island.

The black *Holothuria atra* with its characteristic covering of sand.

The beautiful blue *Linckia laevigata*, which occurs in numbers on some of the reefs, stands out brilliantly against the background of coral rubble amongst which it is usually found.

Tripneustes gratilla—showing the colour of the body and spines, and with its tube feet fully expanded—moving across a small sandy pool on the reef. Barrow Island.

In juvenile specimens of the Needle-spined urchin the larger primary spines are banded with white.

Echinometra is generally found in holes which it has bored in coral rubble and boulders.

Close-up of the rasping teeth used by the sea urchins to remove algae on which they feed, from the rocky surrounds where they live.

A large boulder overturned on Rudder Reef, showed three species of urchins, a dark *Echinothrix*, *Tripneustes* and *Echinometra*, as well as numerous molluscs, encrusting sponges and other forms.

The tropical Slate pencil urchin, *Heterocentrotus mammillatus*. The urchin which was found among clusters of *Palythoa* near the reef crest, has been overturned to show the mouth. Heron Island.

Large colony of Heart urchins, *Maretia planulata*, at a depth of 25 metres on the sandy substrate between Heron and Sykes Reefs. Decmber 1978.

Echinothrix calamaris, perhaps the most beautiful of all sea urchins, exhibits varying colours on its larger spines, ranging from pure white, with few or numerous banded spines, to almost jet black. The finer clusters of needle-sharp spines are bronze coloured, and amongst them as the animal moves, splashes of the brilliant emerald green of the body may be seen. The translucent gelatinous sac on the upper surface appears in the sunlight to be studded with tiny pearls.

Echinostrephus aciculatus, another of the sea urchins which bores into the solid coral. The boulder was broken apart to show the tube feet and the hollowed out portion in which the urchin was living.

shunned by most visitors to the reefs. Whilst at a casual glance they show little or no resemblance to the starfish, brittle star or sea urchin, nevertheless they possess the characteristic water vascular system of the phylum, and in most species the tube feet are responsible for their sluggish movements. In these animals the body is so elongated that they actually lie on one side as it were, rather than on the oral surface so that the mouth appears to be at the "front end". The radial symmetry, so obvious in the other groups, is seldom apparent and the body has become differentiated into an upper and a lower surface, the animal moving along on a "sole" which is quite clearly marked in some species but not in others. In some species the sole may be made up of three of the five areas of the body with rows of large tube feet and well-developed sucker discs. In others small tube feet may be found all over the body, and in one group there are no tube feet at all.

Between sixty and seventy species of holothurians have been recorded from Barrier Reef waters. They vary in size from an inch or so in length to the long snake-like *Synapta maculata*, which is capable of expansion to several feet. The body may be very solid, quite tough and leathery to the touch, it may be soft and flaccid or it may appear to be very sticky, as in the case of *Synapta*. The stickiness is caused by the invisible spicules of calcium carbonate embedded in the skin, which in this particular species, are shaped exactly like miniature anchors. The skeletal support in this group, unlike that of the other members of the phylum, is composed only of very small spicules which are microscopic in size. The classification of the holothurians, which is difficult even for the expert, is largely based on the formation of the spicules which vary immensely in number, shape and size.

The colours on the body surface range from white, pink, and yellow, through orange, fawn and brown to black. The black species, mostly belonging to the genus *Holothuria*, predominate in exposed areas of the reefs where they may be seen in numbers lying on the sandy substrate with feeding tentacles extended.

A crown of tentacles, varying in number between ten and thirty according to the species, surrounds the mouth. These tentacles which may be pinnate or branched, are retractible like the tube feet and are part of the water-vascular system. Species with multi-branched tentacles are usually plankton feeders and minute animals and organic particles in the sea water are trapped and swept into the mouth. The greater number of holothurians are, however, detrital feeders living in the sandy mud of the reef flats and the tentacles are used to sweep across the substrate. This is swallowed, the food particles are removed, and the animal as it feeds, leaves either a thin round core of sand trailing behind it, or a characteristic coiled mound.

These animals, like those of the rest of the

A small, beautifully-marked *Euapta godeffroyi* feeding among the rubble, Rudder Reef.

The ' Curry-fish ', *Stichopus variegatus*, in a pool on the reef flat, Heron Island.

Stichopus chloronotus, one of the most numerous and most easily recognized of the Barrier Reef holothurians. A glossy dark green in colour, it is usually found lying in the open on rubble areas of the reefs.

Small commensal fishes of the genus *Carapus* are commonly found sheltering within the bodies of holothurians. This fish which was almost as large as its host, emerged into a bucket of water when the holothurian was picked up, then it unsuccessfully attempted to return to its shelter. Normally the fish enters tail first, and its tapered body is adapted to fit into the body cavity of its protective host.

The large *Bohadschia argus*, easily identified by its conspicuous markings, ejects its very sticky Cuvierian organs when irritated. This very effective defence mechanism will trap any aggressor.

The brilliant red, blue and yellow holothurian, *Pseudocolochirus axiologus* from northern reef waters, is like a highly coloured football.

This animal is fascinating to watch when feeding. The feathery white tentacles trap minute organisms in the sea water, the mouth opens, and the whole branch is inserted into the opening. As one branch is withdrawn, another bends over. Marine Gardens, Magnetic Island.

An easily recognised species, the brown and pink *Holothuria edulis*.

phylum, also possess considerable power of regeneration, although it is used in a different way, to replace parts lost as a result of defensive action. If handled, or disturbed in any way, many species react in one of two ways. Either they will shoot out from the anal aperture great masses of orange, red or white, exceedingly sticky threads, called the tubules of Cuvier, after their discoverer, which completely entangle an intruder such as a crab. If touched with one's foot, it will be found extremely difficult to remove the threads from a shoe. Or else they may practically eviscerate themselves, throwing off many of the internal organs. Experiments have shown that the latter may take four to six months to regenerate.

Holothurians have a very definite effect on the substrate in which they live and in any one year are responsible for an extraordinary turn-over of sandy mud. The common and wide-spread large black species, *Holothuria atra*, has been estimated to occur on different reefs in the Pacific Ocean in numbers ranging from fifty to over three hundred per hundred square metres. As this is only one of the sixty and more species found within the Barrier Reef Province, it will be appreciated that these seemingly moribund animals have, in fact, a very significant effect on the bottom sediments of the reef flats. The various species are fairly selective in their requirements, some being found to prefer coarse sand, others mud and others again areas in which there is a considerable amount of ooze. The range of movement, which depends to a certain extent on the species and on the condition of the substrate, has been found in some places to vary from about four to over fifty metres and more where feeding grounds are poor.

Whilst the *Bêche-de-mer* fishery of Barrier Reef waters is not an important one today, it was of considerable commercial value at the beginning of the century when numbers of boats were engaged in the collection of holothurians. The most valuable species taken was the Prickly Red Fish, *Thelenota ananas*, the largest of all holothurians. Its large solid body and small spicules made it highly desirable and the demand for it was such that it was practically exterminated in some of the areas fished.

With the re-opening of the Chinese market, there are now signs of a revival of the industry in northern reef waters.

The Echinodermata, with their wheel-like spicules, ball and socket joints, suction discs, built-in hydraulic system, and miniature robot-arms, might well have been the basic example for the newly created branch of Science—Bionics—which will test the use of natural models in modern technology.

The undersides of large coral boulders along the outer edge of the reef provide protection for incredible numbers of small to microscopic species.

Fragile, gelatinous, yellow-green in colour, *Ecteinascidia nexa*.

Didemnum molle, showing the tiny incurrent openings on the surface of the colony, with only a single excurrent opening.

Herdmania momis, a much larger species.
Many of the reef animals lay their eggs in the shelter of the boulder. A cluster of Cuttlefish eggs.

A cluster of colonies of *Didemnum molle*.

Colonies of Ascidians, tiny sea-squirts, are amongst the most numerous species. The red *Polyandrocarpa latericius*.

Chapter 9

The Reef Fish

One cannot think of a coral reef without visualizing the myriad shoals of colourful and elegant little fishes flashing by, darting in and out among the coral branches. Great shoals of brilliant emerald green are seen, floating like a cloud over large plate-like heads of coral, disappearing as if by magic at the slightest sign of danger. Deep down in sandy pools, against their coral-covered sides, fishes slowly and gracefully swim in and out among the branches. As the rising tide covers the reef, shoals of large bright blue and green parrotfish, vivid in the tropical sunlight, invade the flats.

The fishes, of infinite variety in shape, size and colour, are as much a part of the reef community as the corals which bring them there, and they are amongst its most fascinating members. Their appeal to the visitor is perhaps greater than that of any other group of reef animals. The number of tropical marine species recorded for Barrier Reef waters is in the vicinity of 1400, but when it is realized that, in a very comprehensive survey, Australian Museum workers are reported to have found some 500 different species of fish from one reef alone—that of One Tree Island in the Capricorn Group—some idea may be gained of the extraordinary diversity within *one* single group of animals in the reef habitats.

The fishes are gill-breathing, aquatic vertebrates, much more highly organized animals than the Invertebrates mentioned in the preceding chapters. They are an extremely ancient group of animals whose fossil remains date them back hundreds of millions of years. In the evolutionary tree they are ancestral to all terrestrial vertebrates, and far outnumber them in known species, of which about 25,000 have been described.

Since the greater number of fish, during their normal lives, move *through* water, one of the basic problems which they have had to over-

come has been the means whereby they are able to progress in their incompressible environment. As a fish swims it displaces water, pushes it aside as it were, and just as quickly the water closes in behind it. And so their shapes and structures have evolved, broad and flattened in those species which live on or near the bottom of the sea, stream-lined and torpedo-shaped with highly developed muscles and powerful tail in the large, swift-swimming fishes which roam the world's oceans. With fins, paired and single, they achieve balance, steering and movement through the water.

They have developed great differences in physical features. Small mouths, large mouths, upturned mouths with greatly enlarged lower jaws, elongated snouts, or a mouth completely hidden on the underside of the head, as seen in those species which dwell on the bottom of the sea. Teeth for biting, cutting, rasping and grinding, and teeth that are replaceable and continue to grow, as in the large aggressive sharks. Spines—sharp, serrated, and sometimes toxic—for defence. Bony scales, all shapes, sizes and thickness, covering their bodies, both protecting them and aiding stream-lined movement through water. Various means of camouflage including a built-in mechanism for changing colour. Gills adapted for every kind of water in which a fish may be found, and in some cases modified as a sieve-like mechanism for plankton feeders, such as the Basking shark and the Manta ray. Swim bladders filled with gas, able to be controlled by the fish, preventing its sinking and aiding its buoyancy at the water level in the sea at which it lives.

By all these means and many more, the fishes as a group of animals have continued to thrive throughout their long evolutionary history.

Each species, through the process of natural selection, has become beautifully adapted, both physiologically and in its shape and colour

pattern, to meet all the stresses of its environment. Most of the structural variations to be seen in the different families are modifications which adapt the fishes for their particular habitat. It has been found that once they are established, few species ever move out of or far from their chosen grounds.

There are, of course, a number of migratory species—fishes like the salmon which enter large fresh-water rivers to spawn, and the eels which move down from the rivers to breed in the distant ocean. Cold water species move to warmer waters with the approach of winter. In tropical seas, where the temperature remains relatively stable, there is little migration.

By far the greater number of species are to be found in the waters marginal to the land masses, that is in the shallower waters overlying the continental shelves. Here light penetration and abundant nutrient salts in well-oxygenated waters provide the basic requirements for the plants—large and small—the producers which, with the aid of sunlight, convert the inorganic compounds in the sea water into the foodstuffs on which all other life in the sea ultimately depends.

It is not surprising, therefore, that a huge area of continental shelf such as that covered by the Great Barrier Reef Province, with its hundreds of massive reefs, their luxuriant coral growths, and extensive areas of reef flats with all their varied habitats, should support such an enormous diversity of fish species.

The fish which usually inhabit the different regions of the sea differ considerably, but there is a certain amount of overlapping and no hard and fast lines of division can readily be drawn. Large oceanic fish such as the tunas—dark blue above and silvery beneath in the colours so characteristic of the animals living in the upper

Shoal of Blue Pullers, *Chromis atripectoralis*, among coral, Heron Island.

waters of the high seas—are to be found at certain seasons of the year in the deeper, more open waters of the Province, following the movements of the smaller shoaling fishes on which they prey.

Whilst great shoals of fast-swimming species akin to the tunas, such as mackerels and bonito, the barracudas and swallow-tails, trevally and mullet, roam freely throughout the Province, most of the fishes live in fairly restricted areas, seldom moving far from shelter. To a great extent their food consists of the life to be found on the reefs and rocky areas or in the sandy-muddy substrate (Text figs. 7 and 8), and they are usually dependent on some kind of shelter for their survival. Many are not capable of prolonged, swift swimming, nevertheless they are able to achieve considerable speed, and dart among the corals with lightning rapidity at the approach of danger.

The fishes are divided into two major sections, basically on the nature of their vertebrate skeletons. The more ancient and primitive Elasmobranchs include the many species of sharks and rays which characteristically have a skeleton composed only of cartilage, with no true bone, and which lack a gas-filled swim bladder. The second very much larger group comprises all the Teleost or bony fishes whose firm internal skeleton is composed of true bone, and most of which possess elaborate swim bladders.

With the exception of an Order of flat fishes in which both eyes are placed on the same side of the head, a fish in its body structure is a bilaterally symmetrical animal in which its right and left sides are mirror images of one another. Through its more or less cylindrical or disc-shaped body there runs an alimentary canal from mouth to anus, and associated with this are all the various digestive organs. Above these lies the vertebral column, made up of separate discs, or vertebrae of cartilage or bone, with spinous supporting processes, all attached to and moved by powerful muscles which control the swimming movements of the fish.

Apart from a few species of fish a common feature is that the body is covered with scales. In the sharks and rays, the scales are of quite a different type from those of the bony fishes. If one runs a finger over the skin of a shark the sensation is like rubbing very coarse sandpaper. The minute scales, referred as placoid because of their shape, are embedded in the skin over most of the body, separated from one another by only a small space. They have a very minute, backward pointing spine coated with enamel and a flattened base of dentine which lies embedded in the skin. Shark's skin is so tough and resilient that it was once used as an abrasive by cabinet makers and a shark leather, shagreen, has been used commercially.

The scales on the bony fishes are thin, trans-

In a deep sandy terrace over the reef edge, lined with coral boulders, a school of Surgeon fish swim over two White-tipped sharks, *Triaenodon apicalis*. These greyish-brown sharks, easily identified by the rounded snout and white tips on dorsal and caudal fins, grow to a length of about four feet, are harmless to man, and are among the characteristic inhabitants of these areas round the reefs.

A shoal of Black-spotted Dart or Swallowtails, *Trachinotus bailloni*. Like the Trevally and other members of the Family Carangidae to which they belong, they are good sport fish. Active and fast swimmers, they congregate in schools along the edges of reefs.

Epaulette shark, *Hemiscyllium ocellatum*.

Beautifully banded, a small Wobbegong shark, *Orectolobus ornatus*.

Stingarees and rays are often seen in the shallows on the reef flats. In the algal-coral rubble near the mangrove grove on Watson, these dark, longtailed Mangrove rays, *Himantura granulata*, were very common. These bottom dwelling fishes have a pair of spiracles on top of the head through which water enters to pass over the gills. This mechanism prevents the intake of sand or other detritus which would occur if water were drawn in through the mouth.

Blue-spotted Lagoon Ray, *Taeniura lymna*.

parent layers of bone, varying in size and thickness, but generally rounded in shape. They are embedded in the skin at one side, overlap one another in the manner of roof tiles, and are highly flexible, permitting completely free movement by the fish when swimming.

Scales may be modified by calcification into hard bony plates which in some species are fused into a solid bony casing as in the little Box Fish and Cow Fish. Other scales project through the skin as sharp spines which are used in defence, as in the large jack-knife spines situated in front of the tail fin on the sides of the Surgeon Fish.

In addition to scales, the body of most fishes is covered with numerous mucous-secreting glands. The mucous slime produced by these glands not only helps to keep the body surface well lubricated, aiding movement, but it also has antiseptic qualities which help also in keeping the body of the fish clean.

The scales of certain species have been used extensively by scientists in attempting to discover the age of fishes—an extremely important fact when trying to estimate fish stocks, and ensure good fisheries management by preventing overfishing of commercial species. The use of the technique has been applied more specifically to fishes of temperate waters than those of the tropics because it was discovered that fish grow faster during summer months than in the colder winter months. As they grow new growth laid down by the layer of skin covering the scales forms distinct rings. By counting these rings on many scales of many different size groups within a given population it has been possible to make reasonable estimates of yearly growth and age of a number of important food species throughout the world.

A notable difference between the cartilaginous sharks and rays and the bony fishes is their mode of swimming. The movements of fishes may appear the same, a locomotion brought about by the action of powerful trunk muscles and flexible fins, but closer examination will reveal a fundamental difference in both action and propelling force in these two basic groups. The tail fin of a shark is referred as being heterocercal, that is it is asymmetrical, made up of two unequal lobes, the upper one being always the larger. The vertebral column, instead of ending at the beginning of the tail fin as it does in the bony fishes, continues along to a point in the upper lobe, thus giving it considerable support and great propulsive power. The lower lobe is membranous and thus more flexible, bending almost to a horizontal plane against the pressure of the water as the animal swims.

Sharks are amongst the most beautifully streamlined of the fishes, capable not only of tremendous speed but also of long-distance swimming. If one watches a shark in a large pool, it will be noted that it moves by lateral undulations of its long muscular body and

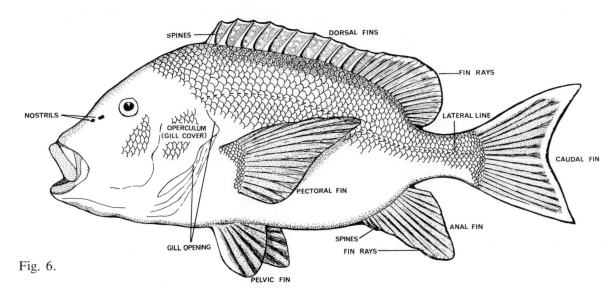

Fig. 6.

The Red Emperor, *Lutjanus sebae*, (considered one of the finest edible fish of the reefs), showing the chief external characters used in the classification of the teleost fish.

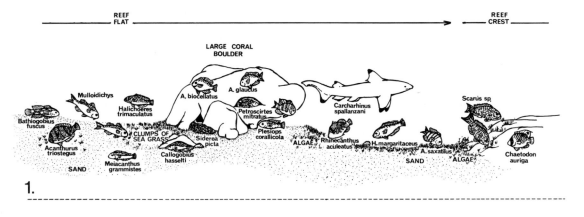

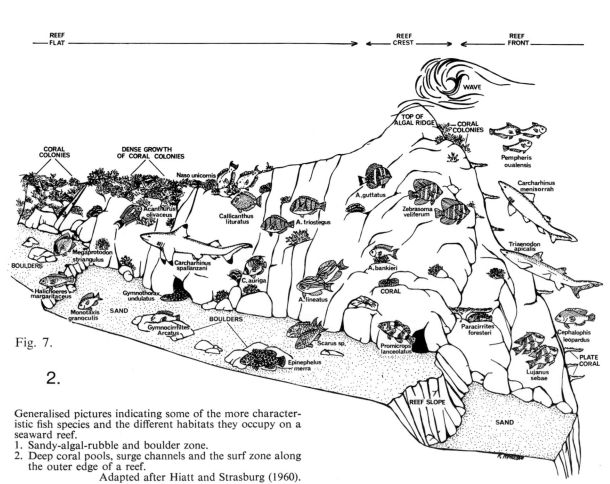

Fig. 7.

Generalised pictures indicating some of the more characteristic fish species and the different habitats they occupy on a seaward reef.
1. Sandy-algal-rubble and boulder zone.
2. Deep coral pools, surge channels and the surf zone along the outer edge of a reef.
Adapted after Hiatt and Strasburg (1960).

powerful tail. The particular shape of the latter produces a downward thrust as the shark swims, a tilting of the body with the head pushed down at an angle and the tail lifted up. This is counteracted by the paired front, or pectoral, fins which are not used in swimming and are relatively inflexible, acting as planes rather like the vanes of a submarine. By alteration of the angle of the pectoral fins the shark can rise or fall, exercise effective turns in wide circles, rapidly diving down or shooting up to the surface. It is, however, unable to stop or back away as many fishes do—it must always continue forward, swimming ahead, sweeping towards its prey, swerving in to attack. If it misses it must circle to return to the attack, hence its reputation for circling movements. Since a shark has no swim bladder to counteract its specific gravity in the water, it must keep swimming or it would sink to the bottom.

The shark's ray-like relations have gone a step further, suffering as they do from the same limitations of Elasmobranch construction. The tail is reduced to a thin, elongated, often whiplike structure, in some species armed with poisonous barbs, used as a rudder. The paired front pectoral fins are attached to the head region. They are both elongated and considerably expanded. Many species use these great flattened 'wings' for their flapping movements, and others for the beautifully synchronized undulations along the body, both of which produce a forward gliding motion. As a large, harmless Manta ray swims along with graceful undulations of its huge fins, it far more closely resembles a bird flying through air than a fish swimming in water—hence the group as a whole are sometimes known as sea-bats.

Like the sharks, the rays must also keep swimming forward to prevent sinking. Since, however, their flattened structure is an adaptation to a bottom-dwelling existence, browsing along in search of molluscs and other invertebrate animals living in the substrate, the absence of a swim bladder is of far less significance than to the sharks, which spend most of their time foraging in the upper waters of the sea.

The true bony fish, are of very different design. Buoyancy and angle of body axis are controlled by a pair of longitudinal gas-filled sacs which lie in the gut cavity beneath the vertebral column. These tough, air-tight swim bladders are supplied with glands which can draw gases from the blood vessels of the fish, precisely selecting the exact amount necessary for the buoyancy needed to keep a fish at its preferred level in the sea, and at the same time enabling it to carry out all possible vertical manoeuvres. Some fishes when caught by line and pulled up very quickly, will be seen with the swim bladder forced outside the body. Both water pressure and the speed with which the fish was pulled through the water, act to prevent physiological adjustment. Some bony fishes, like slowmoving, bottom-dwelling species and the deep-sea fishes, do not have swim bladders.

Although the tail of the bony fish is responsible, like that of a shark, for a certain amount of forward thrust, it is not the sole organ of locomotion. The many-rayed paired and unpaired fins of every Teleost fish. (Text figure 6), by their oscillations, act in a multitude of different ways. They assist in propulsion, as vertical and horizontal rudders, or as brakes. A bony fish can thus rapidly tilt and turn in any direction, executing its movements with grace and accuracy. It can immediately stop any forward movement by extending its paired fins, and it can swim backwards.

The sharks and rays, from an evolutionary viewpoint, are considered to be more primitive than the bony fishes, they are nevertheless more advanced in some ways, such as in their method of reproduction. In both the shark and rays, fertilization is internal, and either solitary eggs, often in protective and elaborately formed horny capsules, are laid, or the young are born alive. An extremely wasteful external fertilization process is carried out by the majority of bony fishes, some of which literally produce eggs by the million. Very few eggs survive to the stage of adult fishes.

These eggs vary considerably in size. Some are pelagic and float among the plankton community in the upper layers of the sea. Others are demersal and sink to the bottom. The eggs of the flying fish have a filament which is attached to or becomes entangled among floating objects. Some of the Blennies attach their eggs to empty mollusc shells or other objects on the sea floor, and other fish attach them among the fronds of seaweeds. Elaborate forms of courtship are practised in some groups of fishes. Some build nests, others carry the eggs in the mouth, or, like the seahorse, in a male brood pouch, until the young are hatched.

Although the brain of a fish is small, the nervous system is well developed, and fishes possess the senses of hearing and smelling, taste and touch as well as sight. Eyes vary considerably in the different kinds of fish, but in most species they are placed well apart, on either side of the head rather than in front, so that they can see in two directions at once. The optic nerve from each eye passes to the opposite side of the brain so that an object seen on the right side registers on the left side of the brain. This is referred to as monocular vision.

Eyesight in sharks has been found to be very poor but to compensate for this they have developed the highest olfactory sense among the fishes—a factor of great importance to these voracious, highly carnivorous animals.

Fishes also possess a sixth, very important sense. In most fishes, along the sides of the body, there is a very obvious line running from the head region to the tail. This is actually a row of scales differently shaped from the rest, and known as the lateral line. Beneath it there is a

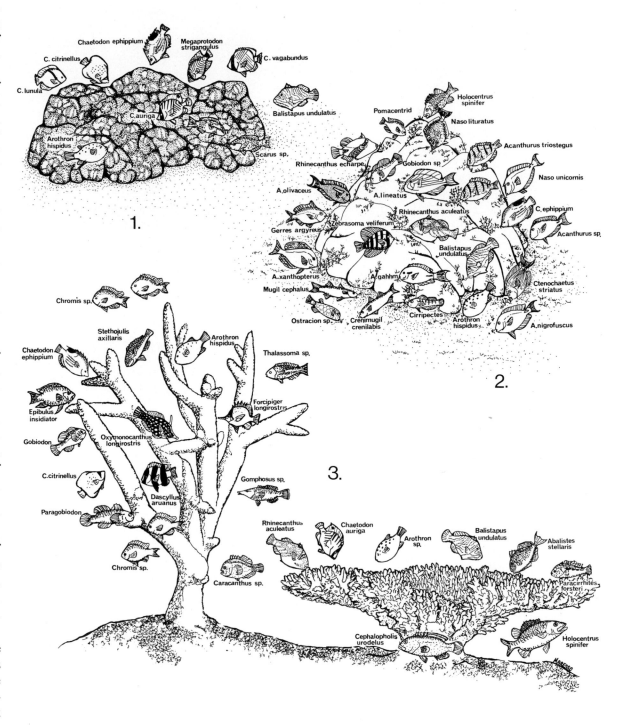

Fig. 8.

1. Butterfly fish, Parrot fish, Trigger fish, and Puffers are amongst the species most commonly found grazing on large massive corals such as *Porites lutea*
2. Herbivorous fishes of the reef flats.
3. Fishes usually found associated with branching and plate corals. These fish are not all coral feeders. For example, the Humbug fish, *Dascyllus aruanus*, is a plankton feeder. Whilst some of the Butterfly fish nibble the coral polyps, others use the elongated snout to catch minute worms and other animals sheltering among the corals.
Adapted after Hiatt and Strasburg (1960).

163

system of canals connected by nerves with the brain. So sensitive is this organ to the slightest movement or current in the water that a fish is thought to use it for a number of purposes instead of its poorer vision. For example, a Butterfly fish, as it darts for shelter deep in cracks and crevices among the corals, is guided by its sensitive lateral lines rather than its power of eyesight. The lateral line is considered to play an important part in keeping the individuals of vast shoals of fish together in perfect formation. Watching a huge shoal one must marvel at the perfect rhythm with which the fish move, never touching but keeping their distance constant from one another, regardless of the direction in which they swing.

One of the most outstanding features of the many reef fishes—one which makes a lasting impression on all visitors to a coral island—is that of colour. There are the characteristic countershading colours of blue and silver of the pelagic fishes, every variation of muted pastel tones, and brilliant, vibrant colours which cover the range of the spectrum and may even be found on a single fish. There are fishes with poisonous flesh which are thought to flaunt their dazzling colours as a deterrent to would-be predators. Others use colour as a weapon of defence, camouflaging them against their background, and many of these have the power to change colour at will to resemble that background. This is done by means of pigment cells beneath the transparent scales, which are capable of expansion and contraction, giving more or less of certain colours as required.

On the coral reefs, however, brilliant colours and distinctive markings serve to draw attention to the fish rather than divert it. Since these features apply to so many of the more important families of fishes associated with reefs in these clear tropical waters, they have been considered to serve as a function for recognition among themselves of the different species. Many of these extremely brightly hued little fish rely solely on the branching corals for their protection. One can often lift a whole colony of branching coral from the water and the small fishes will come with it, tightly wedged down among the branches. Since the reefs provide such vast areas with excellent cover in the many interstices of the coral colonies, the necessity for blending with its surroundings to escape predation is not nearly so pressing for the fish as it would be in a different environment.

The visitor to the reefs, whether using diving gear or viewing the corals from a glass-bottomed boat, is confronted with an almost bewildering array of fishes—kaleidoscopic in colour, bizzare or elegant in shape—all breath-takingly lovely in the grace and speed of their movements. In the seeming chaos of myriads of small fish there is in fact well-established order, with each fish fitted precisely with the means to survive as a species—to live, eat and grow and reproduce.

 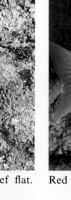

Moray Eel, *Gymnothorax*, in shallow pool on reef flat.

Red throated Sweetlip *Lethrinus chrysostomus*.

Anemone and Clown fish, *Amphriprion akindynos*.

Anemone and unusually marked *Amphriprion melanopus*.

A Threadfin Coral fish, *Chaetodon auriga* and two Angel fishes, *Chaetodontplus personifer*, round the 'Bommie', Heron Island.

A shoal of Black-backed fish, *Chaetodon melannotus*.

Fishes of the Family Pomacanthidae are amongst the most brilliantly marked of the coral reef fishes—the Imperial Angel fish, *Pomacanthus imperator*.

164

No longer does the marine biologist have to use his knowledge of anatomy to postulate how or why a fish uses certain structures—he is able with free-diving gear to observe at first hand—to find the reason for shape and arrangement of fins and spines, to observe the various methods of feeding, to see how all features blend to fit in with the chosen habitat.

The colourful red or gold Goatfish of the Family Mullidae uses the pair of barbels below its head to probe in the substrate for its food. These modified portions of its pelvic fins are covered with taste buds which sense out food as the fish shoal sweeps over the reef flat or through channels to a lagoon. Little coral fish, which feed on minute organisms living among the corals, have the mouth produced into an elongated snout enabling them to probe in among the branches. The teeth of the Parrotfish have become fused into a beak-like structure, making it a perfect tool for scraping its algal food from the coral boulders. The body of a Stonefish is so covered with rough, wart-like protruberences, that it is able to lie amongst coral rubble on the reef, absolutely invisible against its background.

In 1960 the results were published of a very comprehensive ecological study of the relationships of the various fishes associated with coral reefs. This was carried out by American scientists in the Marshall Islands as part of the U.S. Atomic Energy Commission's research programme in the Pacific. This study has added very considerably to our knowledge of the food organisms utilized by the fishes, and the prey and predator relationships among them in the reef community. Since many tropical species are widely distributed throughout the Indo-Pacific Region, it is not surprising that the same kinds of fish, in a number of instances, are to be found both round the Marshall Islands and in the waters surrounding the reefs of the Great Barrier. Figures based on the above results, should be helpful in giving some indication not only of the different habitats on any reef where one might look for the fish inhabitants, but also of their feeding habits (Text figures 7 and 8).

A similar study has since been carried out in East African waters, and work is currently in progress within the Great Barrier Reef Province itself. Together with productivity studies in various reef areas throughout the world, this work is leading to a better understanding, and adding to our knowledge of the complicated structure of the food web within a reef community. The fishes, because of their diversity, and as very active, mobile members of that community, undoubtedly play an extremely important role, both as herbivores and carnivores. The greater number of reef fishes are found to be carnivorous. Not only do the larger fish prey on the smaller, but many of them feed on the various invertebrates of the different reef habitats, including among these the living polyps of the corals. It has been suggested that

The Beaked Coral fish, *Chelmon rostratus.*

Amongst the most commonly occurring fishes over the shallow reef flats are the colourful Parrot fish.

The beautifully marked Peacock Wrasse, *Halichoeres argus.*

A squirrel fish, *Adioryx,* shelters among a branching coral.

The Blue-banded Angel fish, *Pygoplites diacanthus.*

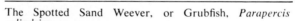
The Spotted Sand Weever, or Grubfish, *Parapercis cylindrica.*

The Rabbit fish or Spinefoot of the Family Siganidae are herbivorous fishes found among weeds on the reefs.

The short snouted Unicorn fish, *Naso brevirostris*.

The Unicorn Fish, *Naso unicornis* (c.f. Fig. 8 (2)).

Conspicuous banding of the juvenile of the Red Emperor, *Lutjanus sebae* — often referred to as the Government Bream. (c.f. Fig. 6).

The Harlequin Tuskfish, *Lienardella fasciatus*.

The Queensland Groper, *Promicrops lanceolatus*, (weight approximately 400 lbs.).

The Two-spot Coral fish, *Chaetodon plebeius*.

the presence over the reefs of such enormous numbers of carnivorous fishes has, through geological time, been responsible for the cryptic habits of so many of the reef invertebrates. Not only do many of these seek shelter in the substrate, among and under boulders, and even in other animals, but there are also the species which, as mentioned in previous chapters, actually bore into coral. These include such forms as sponges, barnacles, bivalved molluscs and various kinds of worms. And the plankton feeders are responsible, by consuming enormous numbers of eggs and larval stages of both the fishes and the invertebrates, for helping to maintain the natural balance among the reef populations.

Reference has already been made to grazing by herbivorous species such as parrotfish and the Surgeon fishes, and their effect on algal-covered reef areas. Evidence of grazing by parrotfish is very obvious in some places where the whole surface of a colony of a massive coral such as *Porites lutea*, may be almost completely covered by the rasp-like marks made by the sharp, beak-like teeth. As the parrotfishes scrape off the algae, however, they also take in part of the calcareous skeleton of the coral itself, which is later extruded as a fine sediment. Since these fish are amongst the most numerous of the larger species frequenting the reef flats, their role in the deposition of sediments there must, over geological time, have been very considerable.

As with all the other animals of the reefs, some knowledge of the habits of the fishes is of great assistance to the visitor if he wishes to find any particular kind.

Fortunately, although ferocious carnivores like the extraordinary Hammerhead shark and the Whaler sharks, together with the enormous but harmless, plankton-feeding Whale shark, occur in the waters of the Great Barrier Reef Province, they are rarely seen by the reef visitor. By far the most numerous species are the Black-tip, *Carcharinus spallanzani*, and the smaller dogfish-like White-tip shark, *Triaenodon apicalis*. As the rising tide covers the reefs, bringing with it all the various fishes which normally feed there, black-tipped fins may often be seen cutting swiftly through the water. These sharks, especially on the shallower reefs, are seldom more than a few feet long, and are considered harmless to man. The White-tip shark is to be found more in the deeper waters round the reef edge.

Manta rays and large Eagle and Devil rays cruise slowly along over the reefs, and smaller bottom-dwelling rays are frequently seen as one wades across the sandy shallows. The Lagoon ray, *Taeniura lymma*, identified by its tan colouring with bright blue spots over its body, lies on the sandy floor of a pool buried to the eyes. It may startle by shooting out from underfoot, but it will rapidly make for shelter beneath a coral boulder.

Coral Trout with attendant Cleaner Wrasse, *Labroides dimidiatus*.

A shoal of Soldier fish, *Holocentrus cornutus*.

Tiny carnivorous fishes of the Family Apogonidae occur in shoals round the coral reefs.

The White-barred Trigger fish, *Rhinecanthus aculeatus* (c.f. Figs. 7 (1) and 8 (2)).

One of the most striking small reef fish, the Moorish Idol, *Zanclus canescens*.

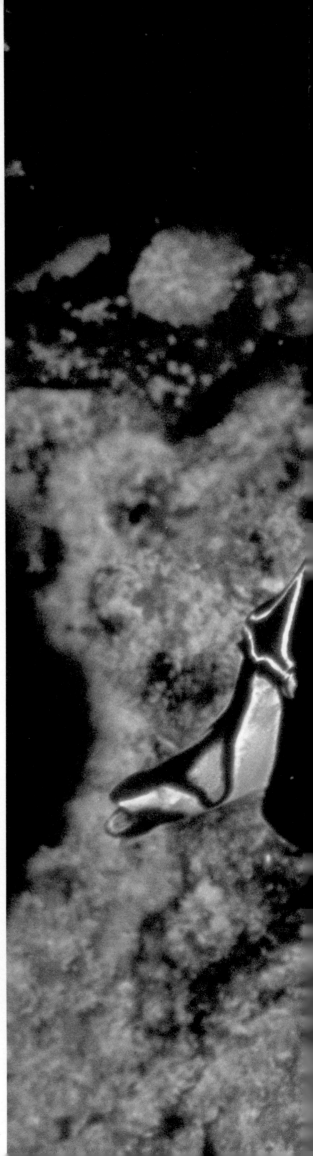

The Rabbit fish or Spinefoot of the Family Siganidae are herbivorous fishes found among weeds on the reefs.

The short snouted Unicorn fish, *Naso brevirostris*.

The Unicorn Fish, *Naso unicornis* (c.f. Fig. 8 (2)).

The Harlequin .Tuskfish, *Lienardella fasciatus*.

The Queensland Groper, *Promicrops lanceolatus*, (weight approximately 400 lbs.).

Conspicuous banding of the juvenile of the Red Emperor, *Lutjanus sebae* — often referred to as the Government Bream. (c.f. Fig. 6).

The Two-spot Coral fish, *Chaetodon plebeius*.

the presence over the reefs of such enormous numbers of carnivorous fishes has, through geological time, been responsible for the cryptic habits of so many of the reef invertebrates. Not only do many of these seek shelter in the substrate, among and under boulders, and even in other animals, but there are also the species which, as mentioned in previous chapters, actually bore into coral. These include such forms as sponges, barnacles, bivalved molluscs and various kinds of worms. And the plankton feeders are responsible, by consuming enormous numbers of eggs and larval stages of both the fishes and the invertebrates, for helping to maintain the natural balance among the reef populations.

Reference has already been made to grazing by herbivorous species such as parrotfish and the Surgeon fishes, and their effect on algal-covered reef areas. Evidence of grazing by parrotfish is very obvious in some places where the whole surface of a colony of a massive coral such as *Porites lutea*, may be almost completely covered by the rasp-like marks made by the sharp, beak-like teeth. As the parrotfishes scrape off the algae, however, they also take in part of the calcareous skeleton of the coral itself, which is later extruded as a fine sediment. Since these fish are amongst the most numerous of the larger species frequenting the reef flats, their role in the deposition of sediments there must, over geological time, have been very considerable.

As with all the other animals of the reefs, some knowledge of the habits of the fishes is of great assistance to the visitor if he wishes to find any particular kind.

Fortunately, although ferocious carnivores like the extraordinary Hammerhead shark and the Whaler sharks, together with the enormous but harmless, plankton-feeding Whale shark, occur in the waters of the Great Barrier Reef Province, they are rarely seen by the reef visitor. By far the most numerous species are the Black-tip, *Carcharinus spallanzani*, and the smaller dogfish-like White-tip shark, *Triaenodon apicalis*. As the rising tide covers the reefs, bringing with it all the various fishes which normally feed there, black-tipped fins may often be seen cutting swiftly through the water. These sharks, especially on the shallower reefs, are seldom more than a few feet long, and are considered harmless to man. The White-tip shark is to be found more in the deeper waters round the reef edge.

Manta rays and large Eagle and Devil rays cruise slowly along over the reefs, and smaller bottom-dwelling rays are frequently seen as one wades across the sandy shallows. The Lagoon ray, *Taeniura lymma*, identified by its tan colouring with bright blue spots over its body, lies on the sandy floor of a pool buried to the eyes. It may startle by shooting out from underfoot, but it will rapidly make for shelter beneath a coral boulder.

Coral Trout with attendant Cleaner Wrasse. *Labroides dimidiatus.*

A shoal of Soldier fish, *Holocentrus cornutus.*

Tiny carnivorous fishes of the Family Apogonidae occur in shoals round the coral reefs.

The White-barred Trigger fish, *Rhinecanthus aculeatus* (c.f. Figs. 7 (1) and 8 (2)).

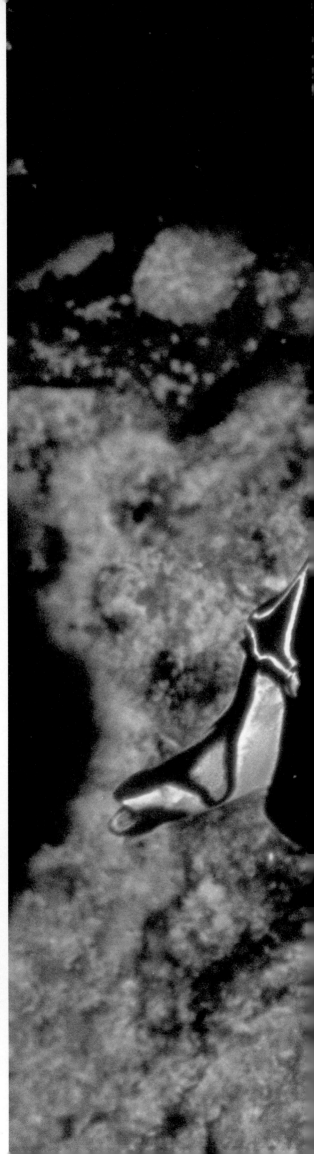
One of the most striking small reef fish, the Moorish Idol, *Zanclus canescens.*

Gregarious, plankton-feeding species such as the little sardines and sprats of the Family Clupeidae may be seen in enormous shoals at high tide, cruising along the shore. Others may be seen from a boat, hundreds of small slivers of silver, flashing by along the edge of a reef, inevitably with larger fish in their wake.

Shoals of larger pelagic fishes, usually powerful, fast-swimming species, forage around the reefs or follow in the wake of the shoals of smaller fish on which they prey. They may be fierce Barracudas or Sea-pike of the Family Sphyraenidae or one of the many related mackerel-like fishes—Mackerel, Spanish Mackerel, Bonito or Tuna—which are among the most important commercially caught fishes of open Barrier Reef waters, as well as ranking among the sporting fishes of the anglers. Or they may be shoals of Kingfish, Trevally, Bream or Swallow-tails. In the early summer months, around October, big game fishermen leave northern ports such as Cairns in search of sharks, Marlin and Sailfish.

Amongst the more important of the edible fishes sought by the fishermen around the reefs, are the so-called Snappers or Sea-perch of the Family Lutjanidae, a widely distributed family of food fishes, with some of its species being found from the east coast of Africa to the Barrier Reef and tropical regions to the north. The Red Emperor, *Lutjanus sebae*, (Text fig. 7), which reaches a length of between three and four feet and a weight of 40 lbs and more, is regarded as one of the highlights of the reef fishing catch.

Other large fish caught close in around the reefs are the Sweetlips of the Family Lethrinidae, and the various members of the Family Epinephelidae. These include the reef or coral cods, the Coral-trout, *Plectropoma leopardus*, which is regarded by many as having the highest qualities among the edible fishes of the reefs, and the giant, so-called Queensland Groper, *Promicrops lanceolatus*, with recorded lengths up to twelve feet and weights of over 600 lbs. Actually this fish is wide-spread throughout the tropical Indo-Pacific, ranging across to the east coast of Africa, and generally is known as a Sea Bass. It is now fully protected in Queensland.

It is possible merely by walking over the reef flats at low water, to see a considerable number of different kinds of fish. On the sandy flats, in shallow water, and in tide pools the small characteristically rounded, snub-nosed Gobies, and the slender, long-finned Blennies may be extremely common, often so well-coloured against their backgrounds that it is only movement which reveals their presence. In deeper coral-lined pools on the outer reef areas one is usually fortunate enough to see many of the small, colourful fishes which are so closely tied to their coral bastions, both for food and shelter. Large pools and crevices filled with drab, dead corals, are conspicuously lacking in fishes.

A large anemone, embedded deep in a cluster of coral colonies, may be seen to house a pair of

The Five-barred Tang, *Acanthurus triostegus*.

The Wedge-tailed Blue Tang, *Paracanthus hepatus*, one of the most brilliantly coloured Surgeon fishes.

The Butterfly Cod, *Pterois volitans*, and its elaborately frilled fins. ▶

A shoal of large Black-spot Sea Perch, *Lutjanus fulvifla*

Characteristic large mouth and sharp teeth of the Family Epinephelidae are shown in the Coral trout, regarded as one of the finest edible fish of the Barrier Reef.

colourful little Clown- or Anemone fish of the Family Amphiprionidae, a unique relationship and apparently of mutual benefit and of widespread occurrence. Shoals of exquisite little blue-green Demoiselles or Damsel fish of the Family Pomacentridae, hover above the plate-like species of *Acropora*—and disappear when disturbed. Amongst the most colourful of all are the Butterfly fishes or Coral fishes of the Family Chaetodontidae. Their relatively deep and very slender bodies, arrayed with stout, protective dorsal spines, are ideally suited for darting in among the branching corals. And their dainty mouths, on small, sharp-pointed heads, are beautifully adapted for nibbling the tiny polyps from the coral branches.

The colourful Wrasses of the Family Labridae are as typical of coral reefs as the corals themselves, and are amongst the most striking and numerous of the reef species. The huge Double-headed Maori Wrasse, *Cheilinus undulatus*, may reach a size of six feet and more, and is sometimes captured by spear fisherman in deeper waters of the outer reefs. The Wrasses are found widely distributed in the various types of reef habitat and range in size down to the tiny 'cleaner-fish' such as *Labroides dimidiatus*, the Bridled Beauty, only a few inches in length.

Mention has already been made of the cleaning habits of a number of small fishes and shrimps. This phenomenon has been found to be of such widespread occurrence in the marine environment that it is believed to have considerable survival value to its participants—the usefulness of these smaller animals to their larger predatory neighbours has served to protect them to a certain degree from the menace of their surroundings.

Man will continue to play his role as one of the greatest predators of many of the inhabitants of the sea. Today the ever-increasing numbers of Marine Gardens and Aquaria, Underwater Observatories, and the greatly improved free-diving techniques are presenting him with opportunities to see, and perhaps to appreciate, the activities of some of the weird and wonderful, the large and terrifying, the small and exquisite creatures which live in the seas around him. Hopefully, he may learn to conserve, to take only what he needs and help spare the rest.

There are two extremes among alternatives for the development of the Great Barrier Reef:
—The preservation of a unique national heritage—the conservation of its living natural resources in a manner which best ensures their continued survival—the selection of sites and the planning of tourist facilities to enable the greatest number of visitors to enjoy the reefs without detracting from or destroying their natural beauty.
or
—The utilization of *all* natural resources to their fullest extent in a short-term interest of the national economy of the country—regardless of whether or not this exploitation results in despoilation of the reefs and possible death to the living communities of animals and plants which created them.

The responsibility for the Great Barrier Reef's future development within these extremes lies with all Australians.

An overall plan for the administration of the development of the Great Barrier Reef province as an entity is an objective for which we should all strive.

Planning by a highly qualified authority (under the joint auspices of the State of Queensland and the Commonwealth of Australia—necessary because of the rulings of international law) is the only means by which it will be possible to ensure not only the best exploitation of the reefs for the more immediate benefits to the country, but also their continued preservation for posterity.

Isobel Bennett,
November 1970.

On 20 June 1975, the Commonwealth Government's Great Barrier Reef Marine Park Act became law. This Act was passed in response to widespread concern of uncontrolled use of part of Australia's National Heritage. It is designed to ensure the control, care and development of the Great Barrier Reef as a resource to be enjoyed and utilized by today's generation, and maintained with a minimum of disturbance to its natural state, for the enjoyment and utilization of future generations.

Under the Act, the Great Barrier Reef Marine Park Authority was established in 1976. This Authority is responsible for recommending areas for declaration as parts of the Marine Park, preparing zoning and management plans for these areas, and ensuring that research relevant to the Marine Park is carried out. There is also a Consultative Committee, with wide representation of all relevant scientific, conservation and Government bodies, whose membership was agreed after close consultation between the Commonwealth and Queensland Governments.

The Authority, with headquarters in Townsville, has already been responsible for a considerable amount of scientific research. It is now able to act as a co-ordinating body, directing research projects, and storing accumulated data.

With the Proclamation by the Prime Minister, on 21 October 1979, of the Capricornia Section as a Marine Park (see Map, page 177) the first part of the Authority's planned objective was achieved.

On 21st October, 1981, the Cormorant Pass Section was proclaimed by the Governor General, with the further proclamations on 19th November, 1981, of the Cairns Section and on 31st August, 1983, of the Far Northern Section. Thus, three more important areas have now been added to the Marine Park.

Isobel Bennett,
May, 1984

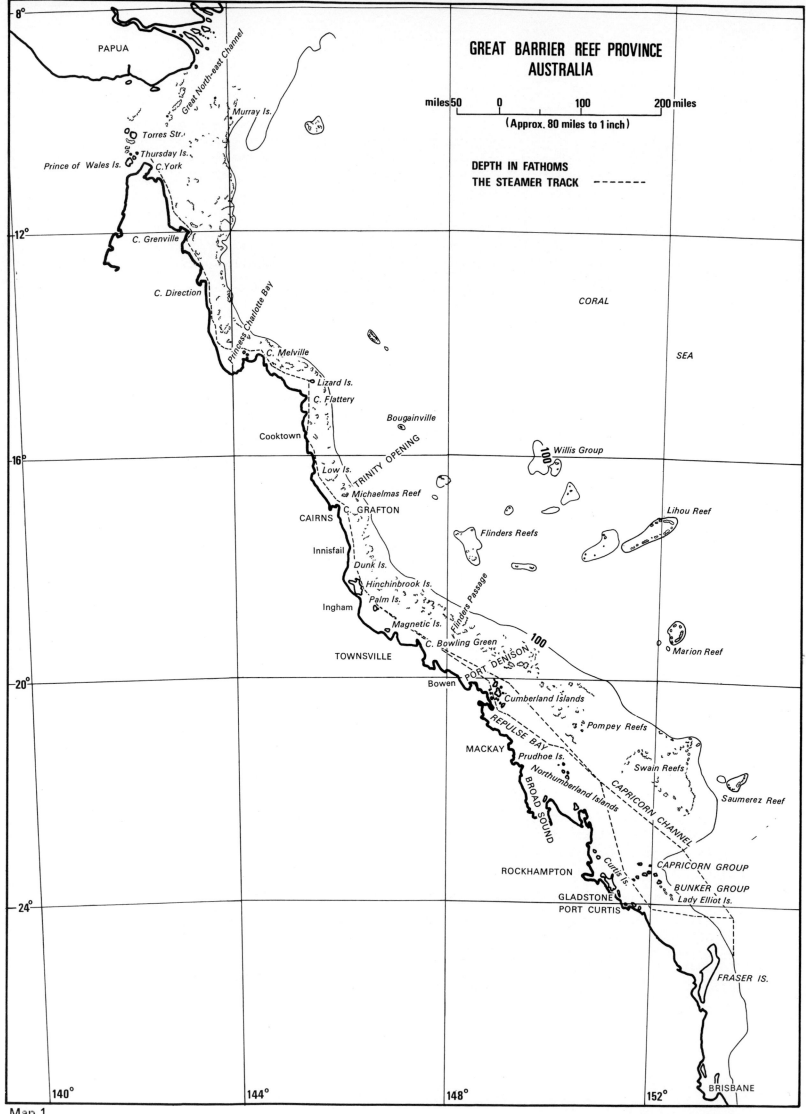

GREAT BARRIER REEF PROVINCE
AUSTRALIA

miles 50   0   100   200 miles

(Approx. 80 miles to 1 inch)

DEPTH IN FATHOMS
THE STEAMER TRACK   - - - - - - -

PAPUA

Great North-east Channel

Murray Is.

Torres Str.

Thursday Is.

Prince of Wales Is.   C. York

C. Grenville

C. Direction

Princess Charlotte Bay

C. Melville

Lizard Is.

C. Flattery

Bougainville

Cooktown

Low Is.

TRINITY OPENING

Michaelmas Reef

CAIRNS   C. GRAFTON

Innisfail

Dunk Is.

Hinchinbrook Is.

Ingham   Palm Is.

Magnetic Is.

Flinders Passage

C. Bowling Green

TOWNSVILLE

PORT DENISON

Bowen

Cumberland Islands

REPULSE BAY

MACKAY   Prudhoe Is.

Pompey Reefs

Northumberland Islands

BROAD SOUND

Swain Reefs

CAPRICORN CHANNEL

ROCKHAMPTON

Curtis Is.

CAPRICORN GROUP

BUNKER GROUP

GLADSTONE

PORT CURTIS   Lady Elliot Is.

FRASER IS.

BRISBANE

CORAL

SEA

100   Willis Group

Lihou Reef

Flinders Reefs

Marion Reef

100

Saumerez Reef

8°

12°

16°

20°

24°

140°   144°   148°   152°

Map 1

174

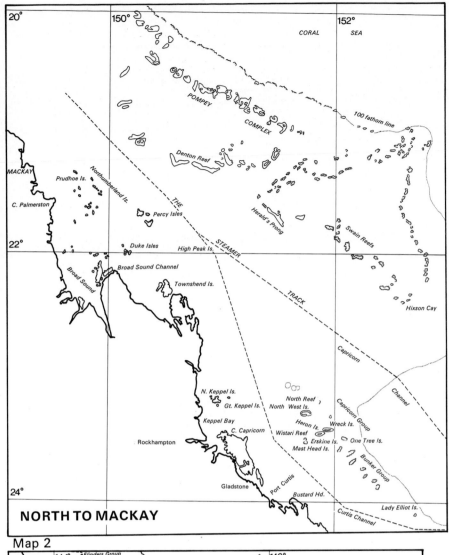

Map 2 — NORTH TO MACKAY

20° · 150° · CORAL · SEA · 152° · POMPEY COMPLEX · 100 fathom line · Denton Reef · MACKAY · Prudhoe Is. · Northumberland Is. · C. Palmerston · Percy Isles · Herald's Prong · THE STEAMER · Duke Isles · High Peak Is. · 22° · Swain Reefs · Broad Sound · Broad Sound Channel · Townshend Is. · TRACK · Hixson Cay · Capricorn · Channel · N. Keppel Is. · Gt. Keppel Is. · North Reef · North West Is. · Capricorn Group · Keppel Bay · Heron Is. · Wreck Is. · C. Capricorn · Wistari Reef · Erskine Is. · One Tree Is. · Rockhampton · Mast Head Is. · Bunker Group · 24° · Gladstone · Port Curtis · Bustard Hd. · Lady Elliot Is. · Curtis Channel

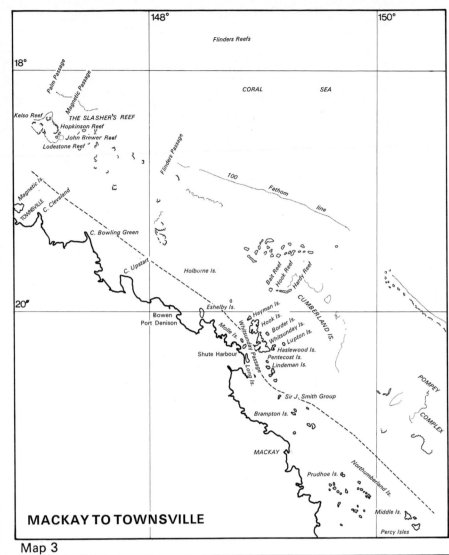

Map 3 — MACKAY TO TOWNSVILLE

148° · 150° · Flinders Reefs · 18° · Palm Passage · Magnetic Passage · CORAL · SEA · Kelso Reef · THE SLASHER'S REEF · Hopkinson Reef · John Brewer Reef · Lodestone Reef · Flinders Passage · 100 Fathom line · Magnetic Is. · TOWNSVILLE · C. Cleveland · C. Bowling Green · Bait Reef · Hook Reef · Hardy Reef · C. Upstart · Holborne Is. · CUMBERLAND IS. · 20° · Eshelby Is. · Hayman Is. · Hook Is. · Border Is. · Bowen · Molle Is. · Whitsunday Is. · Lupton Is. · Port Denison · Whitsunday Passage · Haslewood Is. · Shute Harbour · Long Is. · Pentecost Is. · Lindeman Is. · POMPEY COMPLEX · Sir J. Smith Group · Brampton Is. · MACKAY · Prudhoe Is. · Northumberland Is. · Middle Is. · Percy Isles

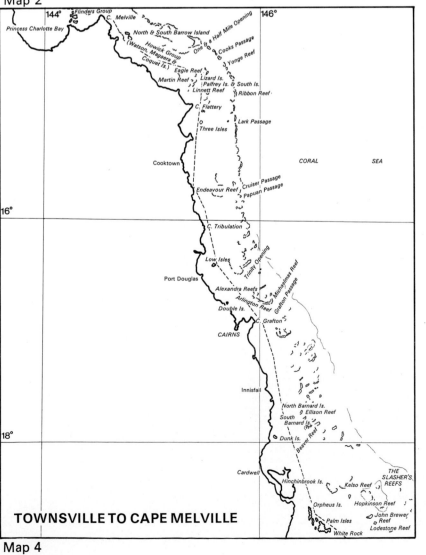

Map 4 — TOWNSVILLE TO CAPE MELVILLE

144° · 146° · Flinders Group · C. Melville · North & South Barrow Island · One & a Half Mile Opening · Princess Charlotte Bay · Howick Group · Cooks Passage · (Watson, Megaera & Coquet Is.) · Yonge Reef · Eagle Reef · Lizard Is. · Martin Reef · Palfrey Is. & South Is. · Linnett Reef · Ribbon Reef · C. Flattery · Lark Passage · Three Isles · Cooktown · CORAL · SEA · Endeavour Reef · Cruiser Passage · Papuan Passage · 16° · C. Tribulation · Low Isles · Trinity Opening · Port Douglas · Michaelmas Reef · Alexandra Reefs · Arlington Reef · Grafton Passage · Double Is. · C. Grafton · CAIRNS · Innisfail · North Barnard Is. · Ellison Reef · South Barnard Is. · Dunk Is. · Beaver Reef · 18° · Cardwell · THE SLASHER'S REEFS · Hinchinbrook Is. · Kelso Reef · Hopkinson Reef · Orpheus Is. · John Brewer Reef · Palm Isles · Lodestone Reef · White Rock

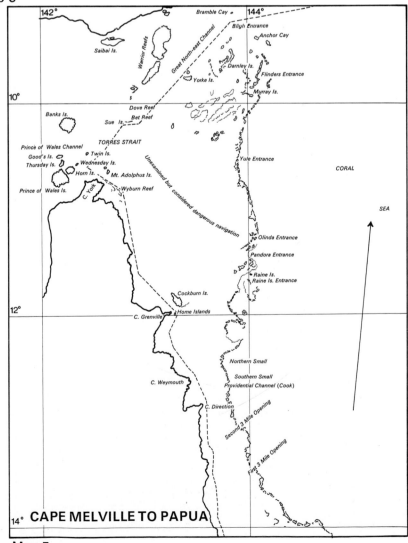

Map 5 — CAPE MELVILLE TO PAPUA

142° · 144° · Bramble Cay · Bligh Entrance · Anchor Cay · Saibai Is. · Warrior Reefs · Great North-east Channel · Darnley Is. · Flinders Entrance · Yorke Is. · Murray Is. · 10° · Dove Reef · Banks Is. · Sue Is. · Bet Reef · Prince of Wales Channel · TORRES STRAIT · Yule Entrance · Good's Is. · Twin Is. · CORAL · Thursday Is. · Wednesday Is. · Unexamined but considered dangerous navigation · Horn Is. · Mt. Adolphus Is. · Prince of Wales Is. · C. York · Wyburn Reef · SEA · Olinda Entrance · Pandora's Entrance · Raine Is. · Cockburn Is. · Raine Is. Entrance · 12° · C. Grenville · Home Islands · Northern Small · C. Weymouth · Southern Small · Providential Channel (Cook) · C. Direction · Second 3 Mile Opening · 14° · First 3 Mile Opening

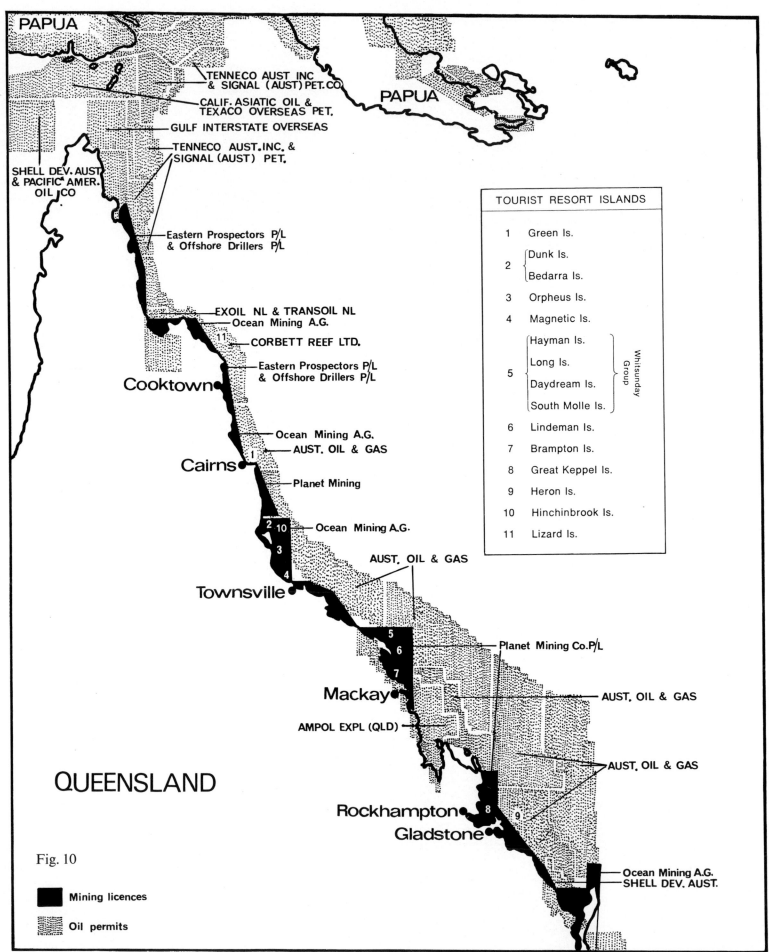

PAPUA

TENNECO AUST INC & SIGNAL (AUST) PET.CO.

PAPUA

CALIF. ASIATIC OIL & TEXACO OVERSEAS PET.

GULF INTERSTATE OVERSEAS

TENNECO AUST.INC. & SIGNAL (AUST) PET.

SHELL DEV. AUST & PACIFIC AMER. OIL CO

Eastern Prospectors P/L & Offshore Drillers P/L

EXOIL NL & TRANSOIL NL
Ocean Mining A.G.

11 CORBETT REEF LTD.

Eastern Prospectors P/L & Offshore Drillers P/L

Cooktown

Ocean Mining A.G.
AUST. OIL & GAS

1

Cairns

Planet Mining

2 10 Ocean Mining A.G.

3

4 AUST. OIL & GAS

Townsville

5 Planet Mining Co.P/L

6

7 AUST. OIL & GAS

Mackay

AMPOL EXPL (QLD)

AUST. OIL & GAS

QUEENSLAND

Rockhampton 8 9 AUST. OIL & GAS

Gladstone

Ocean Mining A.G.
SHELL DEV. AUST.

Fig. 10

■ **Mining licences**

░ **Oil permits**

	TOURIST RESORT ISLANDS
1	Green Is.
2	Dunk Is. / Bedarra Is.
3	Orpheus Is.
4	Magnetic Is.
5	Hayman Is. / Long Is. / Daydream Is. / South Molle Is. (Whitsunday Group)
6	Lindeman Is.
7	Brampton Is.
8	Great Keppel Is.
9	Heron Is.
10	Hinchinbrook Is.
11	Lizard Is.

Map of the Great Barrier Reef Province showing: (1) the position of tourist resorts on the various islands (as at December 1980); (2) the locations for which licences have been granted to explore the Continental Shelf for minerals (from G. A. Brown (1968) 'Australia . . . the potential', *Hydrospace*, London, Vol. I No. 2); and (3) the locations of offshore oil permits to prospect (from: Petroleum Search in Australia—Map, 31 March 1970, issued by the Petroleum Information Bureau (Australia), Sydney). On 4 June 1979, the Prime Minister issued a statement reiterating the Government's decision that there should be no renewal of petroleum exploration permits in the Province until the results of both short and long term research are known.

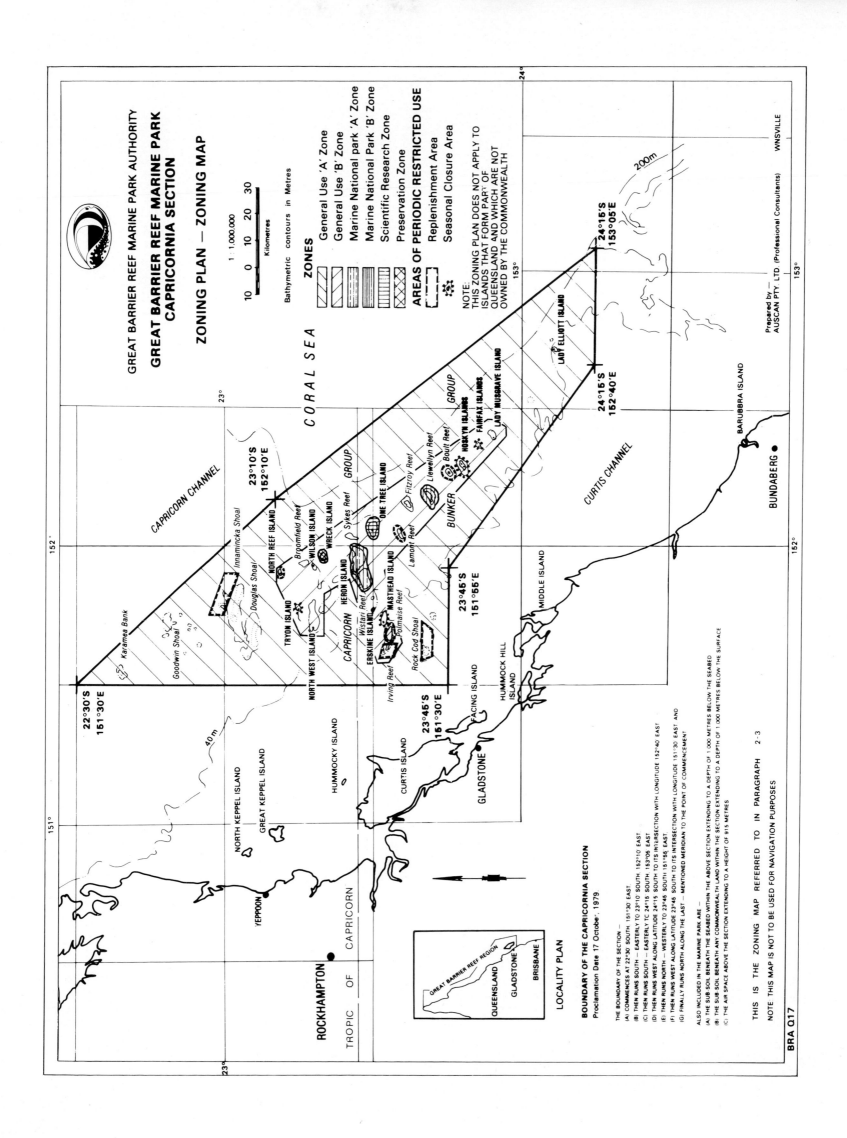

GREAT BARRIER REEF MARINE PARK AUTHORITY

GREAT BARRIER REEF MARINE PARK
CAPRICORNIA SECTION

ZONING PLAN — ZONING MAP

1 : 1,000,000

10   0   10   20   30
Kilometres

Bathymetric contours in Metres

ZONES

General Use 'A' Zone
General Use 'B' Zone
Marine National park 'A' Zone
Marine National Park 'B' Zone
Scientific Research Zone
Preservation Zone

AREAS OF PERIODIC RESTRICTED USE

Replenishment Area
Seasonal Closure Area

NOTE:
THIS ZONING PLAN DOES NOT APPLY TO
ISLANDS THAT FORM PART OF
QUEENSLAND AND WHICH ARE NOT
OWNED BY THE COMMONWEALTH

CORAL SEA

22°30'S
151°30'E

23°10'S
152°10'E

24°15'S
153°05'E

24°15'S
152°40'E

23°45'S
151°55'E

23°45'S
151°30'E

CAPRICORN CHANNEL

Karamea Bank

Douglas Shoal

Imamincka Shoal

Goodwin Shoal

North Reef Island

Broomfield Reef

Tryon Island

Wilson Island

Wreck Island

Sykes Reef

One Tree Island

North West Island

CAPRICORN   GROUP

Heron Island

Wistari Reef

Masthead Island

Erskine Island

Polmaise Reef

Irving Reef

Rock Cod Shoal

Lamont Reef

Fitzroy Reef

Llewellyn Reef

Boult Reef

BUNKER   GROUP

Hoskyn Islands

Fairfax Islands

Lady Musgrave Island

Lady Elliott Island

CURTIS CHANNEL

Middle Island

Hummock Hill Island

Facing Island

Gladstone

Curtis Island

Hummocky Island

North Keppel Island

Great Keppel Island

Yeppoon

ROCKHAMPTON

TROPIC   OF   CAPRICORN

Barubbra Island

BUNDABERG

TNSVILLE

200m

40 m

Prepared by
AUSCAN PTY. LTD. (Professional Consultants)

LOCALITY PLAN

GREAT BARRIER REEF REGION

Queensland
Gladstone
Brisbane

BOUNDARY OF THE CAPRICORNIA SECTION
Proclamation Date 17 October: 1979

THE BOUNDARY OF THE SECTION —

(A) COMMENCES AT 22°30 SOUTH 151°30 EAST
(B) THEN RUNS SOUTH — EASTERLY TO 23°10 SOUTH, 152°10 EAST
(C) THEN RUNS SOUTH — EASTERLY TO 24°15 SOUTH, 153°05 EAST
(D) THEN RUNS WEST ALONG LATITUDE 24°15 SOUTH TO ITS INTERSECTION WITH LONGITUDE 152°40 EAST
(E) THEN RUNS NORTH — WESTERLY TO 23°45 SOUTH 151°55 EAST
(F) THEN RUNS WEST ALONG LATITUDE 23°45 SOUTH TO ITS INTERSECTION WITH LONGITUDE 151°30 EAST AND
(G) FINALLY RUNS NORTH ALONG THE LAST — MENTIONED MERIDIAN TO THE POINT OF COMMENCEMENT

ALSO INCLUDED IN THE MARINE PARK ARE —

(A) THE SUB SOIL BENEATH THE SEABED WITHIN THE ABOVE SECTION EXTENDING TO A DEPTH OF 1,000 METRES BELOW THE SEABED
(B) THE SUB SOIL BENEATH ANY COMMONWEALTH LAND WITHIN THE SECTION EXTENDING TO A DEPTH OF 1,000 METRES BELOW THE SURFACE
(C) THE AIR SPACE ABOVE THE SECTION EXTENDING TO A HEIGHT OF 915 METRES

THIS IS THE ZONING MAP REFERRED TO IN PARAGRAPH 2·3

NOTE THIS MAP IS NOT TO BE USED FOR NAVIGATION PURPOSES

BRA Q17

Selected Bibliography

Atoll Research Bulletins. Vol. 1, 1951 +. Pacific Science Board, Nat. Acad. Sci. Washington, D.C.

Australia Pilot. Vol. III, 5th ed. 1960. Vol. IV, 5th ed. 1962+ Supplt. to 1966. Hydrographic Dept., London.

Australian Academy of Science (1970) *Acanthaster planci*, (Crown of Thorns Starfish) and the Great Barrier Reef. *Reports*, No. 11.

Australian Conservation Foundation (1969) *The Future of the Great Barrier Reef*. Spec. pubn. No. 3.

Bakus, G. J. (1966) Some relationships of fishes to benthic organisms on coral reefs. *Nature, Lond.* **210**: 280-4.

Barnes, J. H. (1966) The Crown of Thorns Starfish as a Destroyer of Corals. *Aust. Nat. Hist.* 15: 257-261.

Barnes, J. H. (1966) Studies on Three Venomous Cubomedusae. In: *The Cnidaria and Their Evolution*. Symp. Zool. Soc. Lond. 16: 307-332.

Beaglehole, J. C. (Ed.) (1955) *The Journals of Captain James Cook on his Voyages of Discovery*. Vol. I. The voyage of the *Endeavour*, 1786-71. Hakluyt Society and Cambridge University Press.

Beaglehole, J. C. (Ed.) 1962) *The Endeavour Journal of Joseph Banks, 1768-71*. Vols. I and II. Trustees, Public Library and Angus and Robertson, Sydney.

Bennett, Isobel (1966) *The Fringe of the Sea*, Rigby Ltd. Adelaide.

Bergqueist, Patricia R. (1969) Shallow Water Demospongiae from Heron Island. *Great Barrier Reef Comm. Univ. Q'land.* I (4): 63-72.

Bruce, A. J. (1976) Coral Reef Caridea and 'commensalism'. *Micronesia*, 12 (1): 83-98.

Bruce, A. J. *Shrimp: The Complex Life Relationships of Shrimps on the Great Barrier Reef*, GEO, Vol. 2 No. 3, 1980, pp 39-53.

Bustard, H. R. (1972) *Australian Sea Turtles*. Their natural history and conservation. Collins, London and Sydney.

Carcasson, R. H. (1977) *A Field Guide to the Reef Fishes of Tropical Australia and the Indo-Pacific Region*. Collins, London and Sydney.

Carr, A. and Ogren, L. H. (1960) The ecology and migrations of Sea Turtles. *Bull. Amer. Mus. Nat. Hist.* **121**: 1-48.

Chesher, R. H. (1969) Destruction of Pacific Corals by the Sea Star, *Acanthaster planci*. *Science*, 165: 280-2.

Choat, H. (1966) Parrot Fish. *Aust. Nat. Hist.* **15** (8): 265-8.

Clark, Ailsa M. and Rowe, F.W.E. (1971) *Monograph of the shallow-water Indo-west Pacific Echinoderms*. British museum, London.

Clark, H. L. (1921) The Echinoderm Fauna of Torres Strait. Carneg. Inst. Wash. *Dept. of Marine Biol. X.*

Clark, H. Lyman. (1946) *The Echinoderm Fauna of Australia*. Its Composition and Origin. Carnegie Inst. Wash. Pubn. 566. 567 pp.

Cleland, J. B. and Southcott, R. V. (1965) *Injuries to Man from Marine Invertebrates in the Australian Region*. Nat. Health & Med. Res. Cl. Report 12. Canberra.

Coleman, N. (1975) *What Shell Is That?* Paul Hamlyn, Sydney.

Coral Reef Symposia: *Proc. 2nd Int. Coral Reef Symp*. Vols. I and II, 1974 G.B.R.C. Brisbane. *Proc. 3rd Int. Coral Reef Symp*. Vols. I and II, 1977 Miami.

Cribb, A. B. (1966) The Algae of Heron Island, Great Barrier Reef, Australia. *Great Barrier Reef Comm. Univ. Q'land.* I (1): 1-23.

Cribb, A. B. (1969) The Vegetation of North West Island. *Qld. Nat.* 19 (4-6): 85-93.

Cribb, A. B. (1973) The Algae of the Great Barrier Reefs. *In:* Jones, O. A. and Endean, R. (eds) *The Biology and Geology of Coral Reefs. 2, Biol.* 1; 47-75.

Daly, R. A. (1910) Pleistocene Glaciation and the Coral Reef Problem. *Amer. J. of Sci.* 30: 297-308.

Daly, R. A. (1915) The glacial control theory of coral reefs. *Proc. Am. Acad. Arts Sci.* **51**: 155-251.

Daly, R. A. (1948) Coral Reefs — a review. *Am. J. Sci.* **246**: 193-207.

Dana, J. D. (1846-49) Zoophytes. U.S. Expl. Exped. 1836-42.

Dana, J. D. (1872) *Corals and Coral Islands*. Dodd, Mead & Co. N.Y., 440 pp.

Darwin, C. (1842) *The Structure and Distribution of Coral Reefs*. Smith, Elder & Co. London. 214 pp (Reprinted 1962 by Univ. Calif. Press, Berkeley — Los Angeles, California.)

Davies, P. J. and Marshall, J. F. (1979) Aspects of Holocene Reef Growth — Substrate Age and Accretion Rate. *Search 10* (7-8): 276-279.

Davis, W. M. (1928) The Coral Reef Problem. *Amer. Geogr. Soc. Spec. Publ.* 9.

Dawson, E. Y. (1961) The Rim of the Reef. (Calcareous algae occupy a major role in the growth of atolls.) *Nat. Hist.,* 70 (6): 8-17.

Deas, W. and Domm, S. (1976) *Corals of the Great Barrier Reef*. Ure Smith, Sydney.

Dunson, W. A. (ed.) (1975) *The Biology of Sea Snakes*. University Park Press, Baltimore.

Edmonds, C. (1975) *Dangerous Marine Animals of the Indo Pacific Region*. Melbourne, Wedneil Publications.

Edwards, H. Milne, and Haime, J. (1848) Observations sur les polypes de la famille des astreides. *Acad. Sci. Paris,* C.R. 27:446-469; 490-497.

Eguchi, M. (1938) Reef-building corals of the Palao Islands. *Palao Trop. Sta.* Studies 3.

Endean, R. (1957) The Biogeography of Queensland's Shallow-water Echinoderm Fauna (excluding Crinoidea), with a Rearrangement of the Faunistic Provinces of Tropical Australia. *Aust. J. Mar. Freshw. Res.* **8** (3): 233-273.

Endean, R. (1961) A study of the distribution, habitat, behaviour, venom apparatus, and venom of the stone-fish. *Aust. J. Mar. Freshw. Res.* 12: 177-190.

Endean, R. (1966) Marine Toxins. *Science Journal*. September.

Endean, R. (1969) 'Report on Investigations made into aspects of the current *Acanthaster planci* (Crown of Thorns) Infestation of certain Reefs of the Great Barrier Reef.' (Fisheries Branch, Dept. of Primary Industries, Brisbane).

Endean, R., Kenny, R. and Stephenson, W. (1956) The Ecology and distribution of Inter-

178

tidal Organisms on the Rocky Shores of the Queensland Mainland. *Aust. J. Mar. Freshw. Res.* **7** (1): 88-146.

Endean, R. and Rudkin, Clare (1965) Further Studies on the Venoms of Conidae. *Toxicon,* **2**: 225-249.

Endean, R., Stephenson, W. and Kenny, R. (1956) The Ecology and Distribution of Intertidal Organisms on Certain Islands off the Queensland Coast. *Aust. J. Mar. Freshw. Res.* **7** ((3): 317-342.

Fairbridge, R. W. (1950) Recent and Pleistocene Coral Reefs of Australia. *J. Geol.* **58** (4): 330-401.

Fairbridge, R. W. (1967) Coral Reefs of the Australian Region, pp. 386-417 in: Jennings, J. N. O. & Mabbutt, J. A. (eds) *Landforms from Australia and New Guinea.* Aust. Nat. Univ. Press, Canberra.

Flood, P. G. (1977) Coral Cays of the Capricorn and Bunker Groups, Great Barrier Reef. *Atoll Res. Bull.* **195**: 1-7.

Fosberg, F. R., Thorne, R. F. and Moulton, J. M. (1961) Heron Island, Capricorn Group, Australia *Atoll Res. Bull.* **82**: 1-16.

Frankel, E. (1977) Previous *Acanthaster* aggregations in the Great Barrier Reef. *Proc. 3rd Int. Coral Reef Sym.* pp. 201-8.

Frankel, Edgar (1978) *Bibliography of the Great Barrier Reef Province.* Great Barrier Reef Marine Park Authority. Aust. Govt. Publ. Service. Canberra.

Gardiner, J. S. (1931) *Coral Reefs and Atolls.* MacMillan, London-New York, N.Y. 181 pp.

George, J. D. and George, Jennifer (1979) *Marine Life.* An illustrated Encyclopedia of Invertebrates in the Sea. (Rigby, Australia)

Gibson, R. (1979) Nemerteams of the Great Barrier Reef. 1 Anopla Palaeonemertea. *Zool. J. Linn Soc.* **65**, 4: 305-337.2 Anopla Heteronemertea (Baseodiscidae). *Zool. J. Linn Soc.* **66**, 2: 137-160.

Gillett, K. and McNeill, F. (1962) *The Great Barrier Reef and Adjacent Isles.* (Coral Press, Sydney).

Goreau, T. F. (1961) Problems of Growth and Calcium Deposition in Reef Corals. *Endeavour.* **20** (77): 32-39.

Goreau, T. F. (1962) On the predation of coral by the spiny starfish, *Acanthaster planci* (L.) in the Southern Red Sea. *Israel S. Red Sea Exped.* 1962. Red. 2.23-26.

Goreau, T. F. (1963) Calcium carbonate deposition by coralline algae and corals in relation to their roles as reef-builders. *Ann. N.Y. Acad. Sci.* **109**: 127-167.

Goreau, T. F. and Hartman, W. D. (1963) Boring sponges as controlling factors in the formation and maintenance of coral reefs. In: *Mechanism of Hard Tissue Destruction. Amer. Assoc. Adv. Sci. Pubn.* **75**: 25-54.

Grant, E. (1978) *Guide to Fishes.* Dept. of Primary Industry, Brisbane.

Great Barrier Reef Committee. *Reports,* Vol. 1+.

Great Barrier Reef Committee (1977) *Conservation and Use of the Capricorn and Bunker Groups of Islands and reefs.* G.B.R.C. Brisbane.

Great Barrier Reef Expedition (1930)+ Scientific Reports. British Museum (Natural History) London.

Great Barrier Reef Marine Park Authority (1978) *Workshop on the Northern Sector of the Great Barrier Reef.* G.B.R.M.P.A. Workshop Series 1.

Hand, C. (1956) Are corals really herbivorous? *Ecology,* **37**: 384-85.

Harry, R. R. (1953) Ichthyological field data of Raroia Atoll, Tuamota Archipelago. *Atoll Res. Bull.* **18**: 1-190.

Harvey, N., Davies, P. J., and Marshall, J. F. (1979) Seismic refraction — a tool for studying coral reef growth *BMR J. Aust.* Geol. Geophys. **4**, 141-47.

Heatwole, Harold (1976) The ecology and biogeography of coral cays. in: Jones, O. A. and Endean, R. eds. *The Biology and Geology of Coral Reefs.* 3 Biol. 2: 369-387. Academic Press. N.Y.

Hedley, C. (1925) The natural destruction of a coral reef. *Rep. Gt. Barrier Reef Comm.* **1** 35-40.

Hedley, C. and Taylor, T. G. (1908) Coral Reefs of the Great Barrier, Queensland. *Rep. Aust. Assn. Adv. Sci.,* 11th Meeting Adelaide. 397-416.

Henry, S. M. (Ed.) (1966) *Symbiosis* Vol. I. Academic Press, N.Y., London.

Hiatt, R. W. and Strasburg, D. W. (1960) Ecological relationships of the fish fauna on coral reefs of the Marshall Islands. *Ecol. Monog.* **30** (1): 65-127.

Hindwood, K. A. (1964) Birds of the Coral Sea Isles. *Aust. Nat. Hist.* **15** (10): 305-311.

Hiro, F. (1937-1938) Studies on the animals inhabiting reef corals. *Palao trop. biol. Stn. Stud.* **1**: 137-54, and 391-416.

Hopley, D., McLean, R. F., Marshall, J., and Smith, A. S. (1978) Holocene-Pleistocene boundary in a fringing reef: Hayman Island, north Queensland. *Search,* **9**, 323-25.

Hopley, D. (1977) The age of the outer ribbon reef surface, Great Barrier Reef, Australia; implications for hydro-isostatic models. *Proc. 3rd Intern. Symp. Coral Reefs,* Miami, **2**, 23-28.

Jamieson, B. G. M. (1977) Marine meiobenthic Oligochaeta from Heron and Wistari Reefs (Great Barrier Reef) of the genera *Clitellio, Limnodriloides* and *Phallodrilus* (Tubificidae) and Grania (Enchytraeidae). *Zool. J. Linn Soc.* **61**: 329-349.

Jeffrey, S. W. (1968) Pigment composition of Siphonales Algae in the Brian Coral *Favia. Biol. Bull.* **135**: 141-8.

Jeffrey, S. W. and Haxo, F. T. (1968) Photosynthetic Pigments of Symbiotic Dinoflagellates (Zooxanthellae) from corals and clams. *Biol. Bull.* **135**: 149-165.

Jell, J. S. and Flood, P. G. (1978) Guide to the Geology of the reefs of the Capricorn and Bunker Groups, Great Barrier Reef Province, with special reference to Heron Island. *Pap. Dep. Geol. Univ. Qld.* **8** (3): 1-85.

Jones, O. A. and Endean, R. (eds) (1973)+ *Biology and Geology of Coral Reefs.* 4 vols. Academic Press, N.Y.

Jukes, J. B. (1847) *Narrative of the Surveying Voyage of H.M.S. Fly.* Boone, London. I: 424 pp. II: 362 pp.

Kawaguti, S. (1937-44) On the physiology of Reef Corals. Nos. 1-7. *Palao Trop. Biol. Sta. Stud.* **2**: 199-679.

Kawaguti, S. (1964) An electron microscope proof for a path of nutritive substances from Zooxanthellae to the reef coral tissue. *Proc. Jap. Acad.* **40**: 832-35.

Kawaguti, S. (1966) Electron microscopy on the mantle of the giant clam with special reference to zooxanthellae and iridophores. *Biol. J. Okayama Univ.* **12**: 81-92.

Kenchington, R. A. (1978) The Crown-of-Thorns Crisis in Australia. A retrospective analysis *Environmental Conservation* **5** (1): 11-20.

Kikkawa, J. (1976) The Birds of the Great Barrier Reef. in: *Biology and Geology of Coral Reefs* (O. A. Jones and R. Endean eds.) *III*: 279-341. Academic Press, N.Y.

Kinsman, D. J. J. (1964) Reef coral tolerance of high temperature and salinities, *Nature,* **202** (4939): 1280-82.

Knox, G. A. (1963) The Biogeography and intertidal ecology of the Australasian coasts. *Oceanogr. Mar. Biol. Ann. Rev.* **1**. 341-404.

Knudson, J. W. (1967) *Trapezia* and *Tetralia* (Decapoda, Brachyura, Xanthidae) as obligate ecto-parasites of procilloporid and acroporid corals. *Pacif. Sci.* **21**: 51-7

Kott, Patricia (1974) Evolution and Distribution of Australian tropical Ascidiacea. *Proc. 2nd Int. Coral Reef Symp.* **1**: 405-423. G.B.R.C. Brisbane.

Ladd, H. S. (1961) Reef Building. *Science.* **134** (3481): 703-715.

Ladd, H. S. (1968) Preliminary Report on Conservation and Controlled Exploitation of The Great Barrier Reef. Dept. of Mines, Queensland.

Limbaugh, C. (1961) Cleaning Symbiosis. *Scient. Amer.* **205** (2): 42-49.

Limpus, C. J. (1978) The reef. (pp. 187-222) in: *Exploration North: Australia's Wildlife from desert to reef.* (Ed. H. J. Lavery.) Richmond Hill Press, Richmond.

Manton, S. M. (1977) *The Arthropoda.* Habits, functional morphology, and evolution. 527 pp. Oxford: Clarendon.

Manton, S. M. and Stephenson, T. A. (1935) Ecological Surveys of Coral Reefs. *Sci. Rept. Great Barrier Reef Expedition,* **3**: 273-312.

Marine Biological Association U.K. (1968) *"Torrey Canyon" Pollution and Marine Life.* (Ed. J. E. Smith, Cambridge Univ. Press, Cambridge.)

Mariscal, R. N. (1966) The Symbiosis between Tropical Sea Anemones and Fishes: A Review. In: *The Galapagos.* Univ. of Calif. Press. Berkeley.

Marshall, T. C. (1964) *Fishes of the Great Barrier Reef and coastal waters of Queensland.* Angus and Robertson, Sydney. 566 pp. 72 colour plates 64 B/W.

Mather, Patricia and Bennett, Isobel (1978) eds. *A Coral Reef Handbook.* G.B.R.C. Brisbane.

Maxwell, W. G. H. (1968) *Atlas of the Great Barrier Reef.* Elsevier Publishing Company, London. 166 figs. 258 pp.

Mayer, A. G. (1918) Ecology of the Murray Island coral reef. *Carn. Inst. Wash. Publ.* **213**: 1-48.

Moorhouse, F. W. (1933) Notes on the Green Turtle (*Chelonia mydas*). *Rept. Gt. Br. R. Comm.* **4**: 1-22.

179

Mortensen, Th. (1931) Contributions to the study of the development and larval forms of Echinoderms. *D. Kgl. Danske Vidensk. Selsk. Skrifter. Naturvidensk, og Matemat. Aft. del.* 9th Ser. V. **4** (1): 1-39.

Munro, I. S. R. (1967) *The Fishes of New Guinea.* Dept. of Agriculture, Stock and Fisheries, Port Moresby, N.G.

Murray, J. (1880) On the structure and origin of coral reefs and islands. *Proc. Roy. Soc. Edin.* **10**: 505-518.

Muscatine, L. (1967) Glycerol excretion by symbiotic algae from corals and *Tridacna* and its control by the host. *Science, N.Y.* **156**: 516-9.

Muscatine, L. and Hand, C. (1958) Direct evidence for the transfer of materials from symbiotic algae to the tissues of a coelenterate. *Proc. Nat. Acad. Sci.* **44** (12): 1259-1263.

Odum, H. T. and Odum, E. P. (1955) Trophic structure and productivity of a windward coral reef community on Eniwetok Atoll. *Ecol. Monog.* **25** (3): 291-320.

Orme, G. R. and Flood, P. G. (1977) The Geological history of the Great Barrier Reef. A reappraisal of some aspects in the light of new evidence. *Proc. 3rd Int. Coral Reef Symp.* (2): 37-43.

Otter, G. W. (1937) Rock-destroying organisms in relation to coral reefs. *Sci. Rept. Great Barrier Reef Expedition.* **1** (12): 323-352.

Patton, W. K. (1966) Decapod Crustacea commensal with Queensland branching Corals. *Crustaceana*, **10** (3): 271-295.

Pearson, R. G. and Endean, R. (1969) A Preliminary Study of the Coral Predator *Acanthaster planci* (L.) (Asteroidea) on The Great Barrier Reef. *Fisheries Notes*, Dept. Harbours and Marine, Q. **3** (1): 27-55.

Pickard, G. L., Donguy, J. R., Henin, C., Rougerie, F. (1977) *A Review of the Physical Oceanography of the Great Barrier Reef and Western Coral Sea. Aust. Inst. Mar. Sci. Monogr.* **2**.

Rippingale, O. H. and McMichael, D. F. (1961) *Queensland and Great Barrier Reef Shells.* Jacaranda Press, Brisbane. 210 pp.

Rosewater, J. (1965) The Family Tridacnidae in the Indo-Pacific. *Indo-Pacific Mollusca*, **1**, 6: 347-408.

Rowe, F. W. E. and Doty, J. E. (1977) The shallow water Holothurians of Guam. *Micronesia*, **13** (2): 217-250.

Russell, R. J. and McIntire, W. G. (1965) Southern Hemisphere Beach Rock. Geog. Rev. **LV** (1): 17-45.

Saenger, P. (ed.) (1977) *The Great Barrier Reef. A Diver's Guide.* Aust. Underwater Federation, Brisbane.

Sale, P. F., Potts, D. C. and Frankel, E. (1976) Recent studies on *Acanthaster planci. Search* **7** (8): 334-338.

Saville-Kent, W. (1893) *The Great Barrier Reef of Australia.* Allen, London. 387 pp.

Smith, D., Muscatine, L. and Lewis, D. (1969) Carbohydrate movement from autotrophs to heterotrophs in parasitic and mutualistic symbiosis. *Biol. Rev.* **44**: 17-90.

Spender, M. A. (1930) Island Reefs of the Queensland coast. *Geog. J.* **76**: 194-214. 273-297.

Stark, Lillian M., Almodovar, L. and Krauss, R. W. (1969) Factors affecting the rate of Calcification in *Halimeda opuntia* (L) Lam. and *Halimeda discoidea* Dec. *J. Phycol.* **5**: 305-312.

Steers, J. A. (1929) The Queensland coast and the Great Barrier Reefs. *Geogr. J.* **74**: 232-257, 341-370.

Steers, J. A. (1938) Detailed notes on the islands surveyed and examined by the geographical expedition to the Great Barrier Reef in 1936. *Rept. Great Barrier Reef Comm.* 4 (3): 51-96.

Stephenson, T. A. and Marshall, S. M. (1933) The breeding of reef animals, 1. The corals. *Sci. Rept. Great Barrier Reef Expedition.* **3** (8): 219-245.

Stephenson, T. A. and Stephenson, Anne (1933) Growth and asexual reproduction in corals. *Sci. Rept. Great Barrier Reef Expedition.* **3** (7): 167-217.

Stephenson, T. A., Stephenson, A., Tandy, G. and Spender, M. (1931) The structure and ecology of Low Isles and other reefs. *Sci. Rept. Great Barrier Reef Expedition.* **3** (2): 17-112.

Stephenson, W. (1961) Experimental studies on the ecology of intertidal environments at Heron Island. II The effect of substratum. *Aust. J. Mar. Freshw. Res.* **12** (2): 164-176.

Stephenson, W., Endean, R. and Bennett, Isobel. (1958) An ecological survey of the marine fauna of Low Isles, Queensland. *Aust. J. Mar. Freshw. Res.* **9** (2): 261-318.

Stephenson, W. and Searles, R. B. (1960) Experimental studies on the ecology of intertidal environments at Heron Island. 1. Exclusion of fish from beach rock. *Aust. J. Mar. Freshw. Res.* **11** (2): 241-267.

Stephenson W. and Wells, J. W. (1956) The corals of Low Isles, Queensland. August 1954. *Zool. Pap. Univ. Qld.* **1** (4): 1-59.

Stoddart, D. R. (1969) Ecology and Morphology of Recent Coral Reefs. *Biol. Rev.* **44**: 433-498.

Stoddart, D. R. and Yonge, C. M. (Intro.) (1978) *The Northern Great Barrier Reef.* A Royal Society Discussion. London: The Royal Society.

Talbot, F. H. (1965) A description of the coral structure of Tutia Reef (Tanganyika Territory, East Africa) and its fish fauna. *Proc. Zool. Soc. Lond.* **145**: 431-470.

Taylor, D. L. (1969) Identity of Zooxanthellae isolated from some Pacific Tridacnidae. *J. Phycol.* **5**: 336-40.

Vaughan, T. W. (1918) Some shoal-water corals from Murray I., Cocos-Keeling Is., and Fanning I. *Carneg. Inst. Wash. Pubn.* **213**: 51-234.

Vaughan, T. W. (1919) Corals and the formation of coral reefs. *Smithson. Inst. Ann. Pept. for* **1917**. 189-276.

Vaughan, T. W. and Wells, J. W. (1943) Revision of the sub-orders families and genera of the Scleractinia. *Geol. Soc. Am. Spec. Pap.* **44**: 1-363.

Veron, J. E. N. and Pichon, M. (1976) *Scleractinia of eastern Australia.* Part I *Aust. Inst. Mar. Sci. Monogr.* **1**.

Veron, J. E. N. and Pichon, M. (1979) *Scleractinia of eastern Australia.* Part III *Aust. Inst. Mar. Sci. Monogr.* **4**.

Veron, J. E. N. and Pichon, M. (1982) *Scleractinia of eastern Australia*, Part IV, *Aust. Inst. Mar. Sci. Monogr.* **5**.

Veron, J. E. N., Pichon, M. and Wijsman-Best, Maya (1977) *Scleractinia of eastern Australia*, Part II. *Aust. Inst. Mar. Sci. Monogr.* **3**.

Veron, J. E. N. and Wallace, Carden (1983) *Scleractinia of eastern Australia*, Part V. *Aust. Inst. Mar. Sci. Monogr.* **6**.

Von Holt, C & M. (1968) Transfer of Photosynthetic Products from Zooxanthellae to Coelenterate Hosts. *Comp. Biochem. & Physiol.* **24**: 73-81.

Wallace, Carden, C. (1978) The Coral Genus *Acropora* (Scleractinia, Astroncoeniina, Acroporidae) in the Central and Southern Great Barrier Reef Province. *Mem. Qd. Mus.* **18** (2): 273-319.

Walsh, R. J., Harris, C. L., Harvey, J. M., Maxwell, W. G. H., Thomson, J. M. and Tranter, D. J. (1971) *Report of the Committee on the Problem of the Crown-of-thorns Starfish (Acanthaster planci).* Melbourne: C.S.I.R. 45 pp.

Walsh, J. R., Harvey, J. M., Maxwell, W. G. H. and Thomson, J. M. (1976) *Report on the Research sponsored by the Advisory Committee on Research into the Crown-of-thorns Starfish.* Aust. Govt. Publ. Service. Canberra.

Wells, J. W. (1955) A survey of the distribution of reef coral genera in the Great Barrier Reef region. *Rept. Great Barrier Reef Comm.* VI (2): 1-9.

Wells, J. W. (1957) Coral reefs. (pp. 609-631). Corals (Bibliog.) (pp. 1087-1104). In: *Treatise on Marine Ecology and Paleoecology.* Vol. 1. (Ed. J. W. Hedgpeth) *Geol. Soc. Amer. Mem.* **67**.

Wiens, H. J. (1962) *Atoll environment and ecology.* Yale University Press, New Haven. 532 pp.

Willey, A. (1902) Contributions to the Natural History of the Pearly Nautilus. *Zoological Results*, Cambridge University Press. Pt. VI: 736-826.

Wood-Jones, F. (1912) *Corals and Atolls.* Lovell-Reeve, London. 392 pp.

Yonge, C. M. (1930) *A Year on the Great Barrier Reef.* Putnam, London and N.Y. 245 pp.

Yonge, C. M. (1930-1932) Studies on the physiology of corals. Nos. 1-6. *Sci. Rept. Great Barrier Reef Expedition.* **1**: 13-91. 135-251.

Yonge, C. M. (1936) Mode of life, feeding, digestion and symbiosis with Zooxanthellae in the Tridacnidae. *Sci. Rept. Gt. Barrier Reef Exped.* **1**: 283-321.

Yonge, C. M. (1944) Experimental analysis of the Association between Invertebrates and Unicellular Algae. *Biol. Rev.* **19**: 68-80.

Yonge, C. M. (1957) Symbiosis. In: *Treatise on Marine Ecology and Paleoecology*, 1. (Ed. J. H. Hedgpeth.) *Geol. Soc. Amer. Mem.* **67** (1): 429-442.

Yonge, C. M. (1958) Ecology and physiology of reef-building corals. In: *Perspectives in Marine Biology.* (Ed. Buzzati-Traverso) Univ. Calif. Press, Berkeley. pp. 117-135.

Yonge, C. M. (1963) The biology of coral reefs. In: *Advances in Marine Biology.* (Ed. Russell) Academic Press, London. pp. 209-260.

Yonge, C. M. (1968) Living Corals. *Proc. Roy. Soc. B.* **169**: 329-344.

Index

Scientific Index

183

All photographs, other than those acknowledged below, are by the author.
The copyright © of the photographs used in this book is vested in the Institutions listed and the individual photographers.

AQUAVISUALS, Box 5590, M.S.O. Townsville
86; 112; 120/8
AUSTRALIAN INSTITUTE OF MARINE SCIENCE (J. Barnett)
92/2; 92/6; 99/8
AUSTRALIAN INSTITUTE OF MARINE SCIENCE (Len Zell)
87/4; 92/5; 93/3; 93/7; 97/2; 97/3; 97/4; 97/5; 97/6; 97/7; 99/4; 99/7; 99/10; 99/11; 100/3; 101/1; 101/2; 101/4
BENNETT, Phyll
18
BIDDLE, Geoff
10/2; 138/1
BROWN, Theo
146/5; 160/1; 160/2

BRUCE, A. J.
105/3
CHESTERMAN, Harold
68/2
CROLL, Ian
166/5; 168/5; 170/1
GREAT BARRIER REEF MARINE PARK AUTHORITY (Len Zell)
Jacket (back); 10/8; 21/2; 36/2; 45; 50/3; 51; 53/1; 57/4; 58/2; 62/3; 63/1; 64/4; 79; 91/3; 91/7; 91/8; 92/4; 93/5; 97/1; 99/2; 101/5; 101/6; 103/2; 105/2; 106/4; 114/5; 115/2; 123/4; 138/1; 135/5; 140/3; 150/2; 152/2; 155/1; 157/2; 157/3; 157/4; 164/2
GRIGG, Lloyd
58-59; 84-85; 113/5; 119; 125/1; 139/6; 139/7; 156/1; 167/5; 167/7; 168/2; 168/3; 168/4; 170/2; 170-171; 172/1; 172/2
HARBISON, Richard
108/2
HEMSLEY, Flo
136/4

LITTLER, Rob
91/2; 106/2; 113/7; 115/1; 116/3; 125/3; 139/1; 139/3; 145/2; 145/3; 164/3; 166/4
MARSH, Loisette
123/1
McMILLAN, R. B.
81
MORRISON, Reg
Jacket (front)
POWER, Allan
12; 165
STEENE, Roger
135/5
WILSON, D.
61/1
WOOD, Bill
104/2; 115/3; 121/2; 121/4; 137/2; 138/4; 146/4; 149/3; 159; 161/4; 164/4; 164/5; 164/6; 168/1; 168-169